Wilders, Geert.

Marked for death

27.95

DATE DUE

sand in back cover

MARKED FOR
DEATH

MARKED FOR DEATH

Islam's War Against the West and Me

GEERT WILDERS

Since 1947
**REGNERY
PUBLISHING, INC.**
An Eagle Publishing Company • Washington, DC

Cataloging-in-Publication data on file with the Library of Congress
ISBN 978-1-59698-796-8

Published in the United States by
Regnery Publishing, Inc.
One Massachusetts Avenue NW
Washington, DC 20001
www.Regnery.com

Manufactured in the United States of America
10 9 8 7 6 5 4 3 2 1
Books are available in quantity for promotional or premium use. Write to
Director of Special Sales, Regnery Publishing, Inc., One Massachusetts Avenue
NW, Washington, DC 20001, for information on discounts and terms or call
(202) 216-0600.

Distributed to the trade by
Perseus Distribution
387 Park Avenue South
New York, NY 10016

To freedom

Contents

FOREWORD

by

Mark Steyn

When I was asked to write a foreword to Geert Wilders' new book, my first reaction, to be honest, was to pass. Mr. Wilders lives under 24/7 armed guard because significant numbers of motivated people wish to kill him, and it seemed to me, as someone who's attracted more than enough homicidal attention over the years, that sharing space in these pages was likely to lead to an uptick in my own death threats. Who needs it? Why not just plead too crowded a schedule and suggest the author try elsewhere? I would imagine Geert Wilders gets quite a lot of this.

And then I took a stroll in the woods, and felt vaguely ashamed at the ease with which I was willing to hand a small victory to his enemies. After I saw off the Islamic enforcers in my own country, their frontman crowed to the Canadian Arab News that, even though the Canadian Islamic Congress had struck out in three different jurisdictions in their attempt to criminalize my writing about Islam, the lawsuits had cost my magazine (he boasted) two million bucks, and thereby "attained our strategic objective—to increase the cost of publishing anti-Islamic material." In the Netherlands, Mr. Wilders' foes, whether murderous jihadists or the multicultural establishment, share the same "strategic objective"— to increase the cost of associating with him beyond that which most people are willing to bear. It is not easy to be Geert Wilders. He has spent almost a decade in a strange, claustrophobic, transient, and tenuous existence little different from kidnap victims or, in his words, a political prisoner. He is under round-the-clock guard because of explicit threats to murder him by Muslim extremists.

Yet he's the one who gets put on trial for incitement.

In twenty-first-century Amsterdam, you're free to smoke marijuana and pick out a half-naked sex partner from the front window of her shop. But you can be put on trial for holding the wrong opinion about a bloke who died in the seventh century.

And, although Mr. Wilders was eventually acquitted by his kangaroo court, the determination to place him beyond the pale is unceasing: "The far-right anti-immigration party of Geert Wilders" (the *Financial Times*)..."Far-right leader Geert Wilders" (the *Guardian*)..."Extreme right anti-Islam politician Geert Wilders" (AFP) is "at the fringes of mainstream politics" (*Time*). Mr. Wilders is so far out on the far-right extreme fringe that his party is the third biggest in parliament. Indeed, the present Dutch government governs only through the support of Wilders' Party for Freedom. So he's "extreme" and "far-right" and out on the "fringe," but the seven parties that got far fewer votes than him are "mainstream"? That right there is a lot of what's wrong with European political discourse and its media coverage: maybe he only seems so "extreme" and "far-right" to them because *they're* the ones out on the fringe.

And so a Dutch parliamentarian lands at Heathrow to fulfill a public appearance and is immediately deported by the government of a nation that was once the crucible of liberty. The British Home Office banned Mr. Wilders as a threat to "public security"—not because he was threatening any member of the public, but because prominent Muslims were threatening him: the Labour Party peer Lord Ahmed pledged to bring a

10,000-strong mob to lay siege to the House of Lords if Wilders went ahead with his speaking engagement there.

Yet it's not enough to denormalize the man himself, you also have to make an example of those who decide to find out what he's like for themselves. The South Australian Senator Cory Bernardi met Mr. Wilders on a trip to the Netherlands and came home to headlines like "Senator Under Fire For Ties to Wilders" (the *Sydney Morning Herald*) and "Calls for Cory Bernardi's Scalp over Geert Wilders" (the *Australian*). Members not only of the opposing party but even of his own called for Senator Bernardi to be fired from his post as parliamentary secretary to the Leader of Her Majesty's Loyal Opposition. And why stop there? A government spokesman "declined to say if he believed Mr Abbott should have Senator Bernardi expelled from the Liberal Party." If only Bernardi had shot the breeze with more respectable figures—Hugo Chavez, say, or a spokesperson for Hamas. I'm pleased to report that, while sharing a platform with me in Adelaide some months later, Bernardi declared that, as a freeborn citizen, he wasn't going to be told who he's allowed to meet with.

For every independent-minded soul like Senator Bernardi, or Lord Pearson of Rannoch and Baroness Cox (who arranged a screening of Wilders' film *Fitna* at the House of Lords), there are a thousand other public figures who get the message: steer clear of Islam unless you want your life consumed—and steer clear of Wilders if you want to be left in peace.

But in the end the quiet life isn't an option. It's not necessary to agree with everything Mr. Wilders says in this book—or, in fact, *anything* he says—to recognize that, when the leader of the third biggest party in one of the oldest democratic legislatures on earth has to live under constant threat of murder and be forced to live in "safe houses" for almost a decade, something is badly wrong in "the most tolerant country in Europe"—and that we have a responsibility to address it honestly, before it gets worse.

A decade ago, in the run-up to the toppling of Saddam, many media pundits had a standard line on Iraq: it's an artificial entity cobbled together from parties who don't belong in the same state. And I used to joke that anyone who thinks Iraq's various components are incompatible ought to take a look at the Netherlands. If Sunni and Shia, Kurds and Arabs can't be expected to have enough in common to make a functioning state, what do you call a jurisdiction split between post-Christian bi-swinging stoners and anti-whoring anti-sodomite anti-everything-you-dig Muslims? If Kurdistan's an awkward fit in Iraq, how well does Pornostan fit in the Islamic Republic of the Netherlands?

The years roll on, and the gag gets a little sadder. "The most tolerant country in Europe" is an increasingly incoherent polity where gays are bashed, uncovered women get jeered in the street, and you can't do *The Diary of Anne Frank* as your school play lest the Gestapo walk-ons are greeted by audience cries of "She's in the attic!"

According to one survey, 20 percent of history teachers have abandoned certain, ah, problematic aspects of the Second World War because, in classes of a particular, ahem, demographic disposition, pupils don't believe the Holocaust happened, and, if it did, the Germans should have finished the job and we wouldn't have all these problems today. More inventive instructors artfully woo their Jew-despising students by comparing the Holocaust to "Islamophobia"—we all remember those Jewish terrorists hijacking Fokkers and flying them into the Reichstag, right? What about gangs of young Jews preying on the elderly, as Muslim youth do in Wilders' old neighborhood of Kanaleneiland?

As for "Islamophobia," it's so bad that it's, er, the Jews who are leaving. "Sixty per cent of Amsterdam's orthodox community intends to emigrate from Holland," says Benzion Evers, the son of the city's chief rabbi, five of whose children had already left by 2010. Frommer's best-selling travel guide to "Europe's most tolerant city" acknowledges that "Jewish visitors who dress in a way that clearly identifies them as Jewish" are at risk of attack, but discreetly attributes it to "the Israeli-Palestinian conflict." "Jews with a conscience should leave Holland, where they and their children have no future," advised Frits Bolkestein, former Dutch Liberal leader. "Anti-Semitism will continue to exist, because the Moroccan and Turkish youngsters don't care about efforts for reconciliation."

If you're wondering what else those "youngsters" don't care for, ask Chris Crain, editor of the *Washington Blade*, the gay newspaper of America's capital. Seeking a break from the Christian fundamentalist redneck theocrats of the Republican Party, he and his boyfriend decided to treat themselves to a vacation in Amsterdam, "arguably the 'gay-friendliest' place on the planet." Strolling through the streets of the city center, they were set upon by a gang of seven "youngsters," punched, beaten, and kicked to the ground. Perplexed by the increasing violence, Amsterdam officials commissioned a study to determine, as *Der Spiegel* put it, "why Moroccan men are targeting the city's gays."

Gee, that's a toughie. Beats me. The geniuses at the University of Amsterdam concluded that the attackers felt "stigmatized by society" and "may be struggling with their own sexual identity."

Bingo! Telling Moroccan youths they're closeted gays seems just the ticket to reduce tensions in the city! While you're at it, a lot of those Turks seem a bit light on their loafers, don't you think?

But not to worry. In the "most tolerant nation in Europe," there's still plenty of tolerance. What *won't* the Dutch tolerate? In 2006, the Justice Minister, Piet Hein Donner, suggested there would be nothing wrong with Sharia if a majority of Dutch people voted in favor of it—as, indeed, they're doing very enthusiastically in Egypt and other polities blessed by the Arab Spring. Mr. Donner's previous response to "Islamic radicalism" was (as the author recalls in the pages ahead) to propose a new blasphemy law for the Netherlands.

In this back-to-front world, Piet Hein Donner and the University of Amsterdam researchers and the prosecutors of the Openbaar Ministerie who staged his show trial are "mainstream"—and Geert Wilders is the "far" "extreme" "fringe." How wide is that fringe? Mr. Wilders cites a poll in which 57 percent of people say that mass immigration was the biggest single mistake in Dutch history. If the importation of large Muslim populations into the West was indeed a mistake, it was also an entirely unnecessary one. Some nations (the Dutch, French, and British) might be considered to owe a certain post-colonial debt to their former subject peoples, but Sweden? Germany? From Malmo to

Mannheim, Islam transformed societies that had hitherto had virtually no connection with the Muslim world. Even if you disagree with that 57 percent of Dutch poll respondents, the experience of Amsterdam's chief rabbi and the gay-bashed editor and the elderly residents of Kanaleneiland suggests at the very minimum that the Islamization of Continental cities poses something of a challenge to Eutopia's famous "tolerance." Yet the same political class responsible for this unprecedented "demographic substitution" (in the words of French demographer Michèle Tribalat) insists the subject remain beyond discussion. The British novelist Martin Amis asked Tony Blair if, at meetings with his fellow prime ministers, the Continental demographic picture was part of the "European conversation." Mr. Blair replied, with disarming honesty, "It's a subterranean conversation"—i.e., the fellows who got us into this mess can't figure out a way to talk about it in public, other than in the smiley-face banalities of an ever more shopworn cultural relativism.

That's not enough for Geert Wilders. Unlike most of his critics, he has traveled widely in the Muslim world. Unlike them, he has read the Koran—and re-read it, on all those interminable nights holed up in some dreary safe house denied the consolations of family and friends. One way to think about what is happening is to imagine it the other way round. Rotterdam has a Muslim mayor, a Moroccan passport holder born the son of a Berber imam. How would the Saudis feel about an Italian Catholic mayor in Riyadh? The Jordanians about an American Jewish mayor in Zarqa? Would the citizens of Cairo and Kabul agree to become minorities in their own hometowns simply because broaching the subject would be too impolite?

To pose the question is to expose its absurdity. From Nigeria to Pakistan, the Muslim world is intolerant even of ancient established minorities. In Iraq half the Christian population has fled, in 2010 the last church in Afghanistan was razed to the ground, and in both cases this confessional version of ethnic cleansing occurred on America's watch. Multiculturalism is a unicultural phenomenon; as my *National Review* colleague John Derbyshire put it, "No Muslim country would allow

Christians—let alone Jews!—to settle in huge numbers in their territory; and in that respect, they are wiser than we are."

But Europe's political establishment insists that unprecedented transformative immigration can only be discussed within the conventional pieties—or what Derbyshire calls "romantic fantasies of human universalism"; we tell ourselves that, in a multicultural society, the nice gay couple at Number 27 and the polygamous Muslim with four child-brides in identical niqabs at Number 29 Elm Street can live side by side, each contributing to the rich, vibrant tapestry of diversity. And anyone who says otherwise has to be cast into outer darkness.

Geert Wilders thinks we ought to be able to talk about this—and indeed, as citizens of the oldest, freest societies on earth, have a duty to do so. Without him and a few other brave souls, the views of 57 percent of the Dutch electorate would be unrepresented in parliament. Which is a pretty odd thing in a democratic society, when you think about it. Most of the problems confronting the Western world today arise from policies on which the political class is in complete agreement; at election time in Europe, the average voter has a choice between a left-of-center party and an ever so mildly right-of-left-of-center party and, whichever he votes for, they're generally in complete agreement on everything from mass immigration to unsustainable welfare programs to climate change. And they're ruthless about delegitimizing anyone who wants a broader debate. In that Cory Bernardi flap Down Under, for example, I'm struck by how much of the Aussie coverage relied on the same lazy shorthand about Geert Wilders. From the *Sydney Morning Herald*:

> Geert Wilders, who holds the balance of power in the Dutch parliament, likened the Koran to *Mein Kampf* and called the Prophet Muhammad a paedophile...

The *Australian*:

> He provoked outrage among the Netherlands' Muslim community after branding Islam a violent religion, likening the

Koran to Hitler's *Mein Kampf* and calling the Prophet
Mohammed a pedophile.

Tony Eastley on ABC Radio:

> Geert Wilders, who controls the balance of power in the Neth-
> erlands' parliament, has outraged Dutch Muslims by compar-
> ing the Koran to Hitler's work *Mein Kampf* and calling the
> Prophet Muhammad a pedophile...

Golly, you'd almost think all these hardworking investigative reporters
were just cutting-and-pasting the same lazy précis rather than looking up
what the guy actually says. The man who emerges in the following pages
is not the grunting thug of media demonology but a well-read, well-
traveled, elegant and perceptive analyst who quotes such "extreme"
"fringe" figures as Churchill and Jefferson. As to those endlessly reprised
Oz media talking points, *Mein Kampf* is banned in much of Europe; and
Holocaust denial is also criminalized; and, when a French law on Arme-
nian genocide denial was struck down, President Sarkozy announced he
would immediately draw up another genocide denial law to replace it. In
Canada, the Court of Queen's Bench upheld a lower-court conviction of
"hate speech" for a man who merely listed the chapter and verse of
various Biblical injunctions on homosexuality. Yet, in a Western world
ever more comfortable with regulating, policing, and criminalizing books,
speech, and ideas, the state's deference to Islam grows ever more fawning.
"The Prophet Muhammed" (as otherwise impeccably secular Westerners
now reflexively refer to him) is an ever greater beneficiary of our willingness to torture logic and law and liberty in ever more inane ways in the
cause of accommodating Islam. Consider the case of Elisabeth Sabaditsch-Wolff, a Viennese housewife who has lived in several Muslim countries. She was hauled into an Austrian court for calling Muhammed a
pedophile on the grounds that he consummated his marriage when his
bride, Aisha, was nine years old. Mrs. Sabaditsch-Wolff was found guilty
and fined 480 euros. The judge's reasoning was fascinating:

> Pedophilia is factually incorrect, since pedophilia is a sexual
> preference which solely or mainly is directed towards chil-
> dren. Nevertheless, it does not apply to Mohammad. He was
> still married to Aisha when she was 18.

So you're not a pedophile if you deflower the kid in fourth grade but keep her around till high school? There's a useful tip if you're planning a hiking holiday in the Alps. Or is this another of those dispensations that is not of universal application?

A man who confronts such nonsense head on will not want for enemies. Still, it's remarkable how the establishment barely bothers to disguise its wish for Wilders to meet the same swift and definitive end as Pim Fortuyn and Theo van Gogh. The judge at his show trial opted to deny the defendant the level of courtroom security afforded to Moham-med Bouyeri, van Gogh's murderer. Henk Hofland, voted the Nether-lands' "Journalist of the century" (as the author wryly notes), asked the authorities to remove Wilders' police protection so that he could know what it's like to live in permanent fear for his life. While Wilders' film *Fitna* is deemed to be "inflammatory," the movie *De moord op Geert Wilders* (The Assassination of Geert Wilders) is so non-inflammatory and respectable that it was produced and promoted by a government-funded radio station. You'd almost get the impression that, as the website Gates of Vienna suggested, the Dutch state is channeling Henry II: "Who will rid me of this turbulent blond?"

There's no shortage of volunteers. In the Low Countries, a disturbing pattern has emerged: those who seek to analyze Islam outside the very narrow bounds of Eutopian political discourse wind up either banned (Belgium's Vlaams Blok), forced into exile (Ayaan Hirsi Ali), or killed (Fortuyn, van Gogh). How speedily "the most tolerant country in Europe" has adopted "shoot the messenger" as an all-purpose cure-all for "Islamophobia."

It's not ironic that the most liberal country in western Europe should be the most advanced in its descent into a profoundly illiberal hell. It was entirely foreseeable, and all Geert Wilders is doing is stating the obvious:

a society that becomes more Muslim will have less of everything else, including individual liberty.

I have no desire to end up living like Geert Wilders or Kurt Wester-gaard, never mind dead as Fortuyn and van Gogh. But I also wish to live in truth, as a free man, and I do not like the shriveled vision of freedom offered by the Dutch Openbaar Ministerie, the British immigration authorities, the Austrian courts, Canada's "human rights" tribunals, and the other useful idiots of Islamic imperialism. So it is necessary for more of us to do what Ayaan Hirsi Ali recommends: share the risk. So that the next time a novel or a cartoon provokes a *fatwa*, it will be republished worldwide and send the Islamic enforcers a message: killing one of us won't do it. You'd better have a great credit line at the Bank of Jihad because you'll have to kill us all.

As Geert Wilders says of the Muslim world's general stagnation, "It's the culture, stupid." And our culture is already retreating into preemptive capitulation, and into a crimped, furtive, (Blair again) subterranean future. As John Milton wrote in his *Areopagitica* of 1644, "Give me the liberty to know, to utter, and to argue freely according to conscience." It is a tragedy that Milton's battles have to be re-fought three-and-a-half centuries on, but the Western world is shuffling into a psychological bondage of its own making. Geert Wilders is not ready to surrender without exercising his right to know, to utter, and to argue freely—in print, on screen, and at the ballot box. We should cherish that spirit, while we can.

CHAPTER ONE

The Axe Versus the Pen

The future doesn't belong to the fainthearted.

—Ronald Reagan

On January 1, 2010, at 10:00 p.m., a 74-year-old man fled from his living room. As fast as he could move with his cane, he made for the bathroom and locked himself inside. Then there was a terrible banging on the bathroom door, the clang of steel on steel. Screams for "Blood!" and "Revenge!" rang out as someone hacked at the door with an axe, trying to force himself in, seeking to chop the old man to pieces.

The scene took place in a modest bungalow in Viby, a middle-class suburb of Aarhus, Denmark's second largest city. One observer compared the attack to the famous scene from Stanley Kubrick's 1980 horror movie *The Shining* in which Jack Torrance, played by Jack Nicholson, maniacally chops his way through a bathroom door with an axe in an attempt to murder his wife.[1]

The old man is Kurt Westergaard. I met him once. He is a tall, soft-spoken grandfather with a grey beard, invariably dressed in bright red pants, a black shirt, and a flowing red scarf. When he goes out, he wears a black Stetson hat. "Black and red are the colors of anarchism," he says. He is an artist who prefers to paint landscapes, but prior to his retirement he made a living by drawing cartoons for *Jyllands-Posten* (the *Jutland Post*), a local newspaper in Aarhus.

In September 2005, Westergaard's paper asked him, among other artists, to draw a cartoon of the Islamic prophet Muhammad. His editors planned to publish the drawings to address a growing trend of self-censorship in Europe on the topic of Islam. They were particularly bothered by an incident in which several artists refused to illustrate a children's book on Muhammad, and the artist who finally agreed to do it insisted on anonymity.[2] Westergaard accepted the paper's request and recycled an idea he had drawn up twenty years earlier—an image of a fierce-looking terrorist with a bomb tucked in his turban.

Westergaard's cartoon has become an iconic image of our age, turning the kindhearted artist into "the most hated man in Mecca."[3] His simple drawing, published in an obscure Danish newspaper, sparked riots and attacks on Danish embassies and properties throughout the Islamic world, resulting in over 130 deaths. The reverberations reached Britain and America, where many media outlets refused to show the cartoons even as they reported on the controversy; this included the esteemed Yale University Press, which banned a book on the cartoon riots from reproducing the cartoons themselves or any other images of Muhammad.[4]

And the cartoon led to the nightmare in Viby, where Muhudiin M. Geele, a 28-year-old Somali Muslim immigrant, turned up at Westergaard's house with an axe and a butcher's knife on New Year's Day 2010. Luckily, due to the many death threats Westergaard had already received from Islamic extremists, along with a previous plot to murder him that resulted in three arrests, the Danish authorities had fortified the Westergaard home, installing bulletproof glass and surveillance cameras, reinforcing the front door, and crucially, transforming the family bathroom into a panic room with a steel door and an emergency button to contact the Viby police station.

Westergaard was sitting in his living room when Geele, who had broken into the garden, began to smash his way through the glass door to the living room. The door, made of reinforced bulletproof glass, eventually gave way, but Westergaard had time to lock himself in the bathroom. From there he alerted the police, who arrived three minutes later. Meanwhile, the young Somali, screaming with rage, was smashing at the steel bathroom door with his axe. When the police arrived, Geele attacked an officer with his axe before other policemen shot him in the knee and shoulder. If the attack on Westergaard had happened later in the evening when the cartoonist was asleep, he might not have managed his narrow escape. "It was close, really close," he told a journalist.[5]

Since he drew his Muhammad cartoon, Westergaard has endured what he calls "an existence full of angst."[6] In September 2011, he had to cut short a visit to Norway after police arrested yet another person suspected of plotting to assassinate him.[7] Time has clearly not healed the "wounds" felt by fanatical Muslims, who want Westergaard dead for offending them with a cartoon that tells a truth they do not want to hear. His drawing, the artist explained at Princeton University in October 2009, "was an attempt to expose those fanatics who have justified a great number of bombings, murders and other atrocities with references to the sayings of their prophet. If many Muslims thought that their religion did not condone such acts, they might have stood up and declared that the men of violence had misrepresented the true meaning of Islam. Very few of them did so."[8]

The Islamic reaction to Geele's attempt to kill Westergaard proved his point. So-called "radical" Muslims such as the aptly named Ali Mohamud Rage, spokesman of al-Shabab, the Somali Islamic group with which Viby's axe-wielding zealot sympathized, congratulated the would-be assassin. Though Rage denied that Geele belonged to the group, he declared, "We welcome the brave action he did. It was a good and brave step taken by that Somali man against the criminal cartoonist—we liked it."[9]

Equally worrisome was the response from so-called "moderate" Muslims, such as the editorial staff of *Gulf News*, an English-language newspaper based in the United Arab Emirates. In a short editorial, the paper blamed the assassination attempt on Westergaard himself, morally equating Westergaard's actions with Geele's. "There is no doubt that the cartoon was deeply offensive to all Muslims," the paper wrote. "For his work Westergaard is regarded with the greatest possible contempt by all who believe in the true faith of Islam. Targeting him, however, is descending to the level of a contemptuous and despicable man. This revenge attack merely again serves to highlight the insult wrought by Danish newspapers, stoking the embers of insult with the oxygen of hatred. Westergaard and his ilk are better forgotten."[10]

Thus, the *Gulf News*, widely hailed for its supposed "moderation," criticized the would-be assassin not for attempting to kill Westergaard, but for having "descended to the level" of this "contemptuous and despicable man." Obviously, even some so-called "moderate" Muslims fail to see there is a world of difference between drawing a cartoon and trying to hack a human being to pieces.

There is no better metaphor to illustrate the difference between Western values and the "true faith of Islam" than the difference between a pen and an axe. We settle our arguments with the former; Islam uses the latter. It is a frightening metaphor in some ways, indicating that when we are attacked with axes, we only have pens with which to defend ourselves.

Unlike Kurt Westergaard, I was never chased around my home by an axe-wielding Islamic fanatic. However, I do live with this kind of threat every day, which is why, like Westergaard, I have a panic room in my house, where I am supposed to take refuge if one of the adherents of the "religion of peace" makes it past my permanent security detail and into my home.

In fact, it's not really my home at all—I live in a government safe house, heavily protected and bulletproof. Since November 2004, when a Muslim murdered Dutch filmmaker Theo van Gogh for the crime of offending Islam, I have been surrounded by police guards and stripped of nearly all personal privacy. I am driven every day from the safe house to my office in the Dutch Parliament building in armored police cars with sirens and flashing blue lights.

I wear a bulletproof jacket when I speak in public. Always surrounded by plainclothes police officers, I have not walked the streets on my own in more than seven years. When I occasionally go to a restaurant, security has to thoroughly check the place in advance. When I go to a movie theater, the last rows of seats are cleared for me and my guards. We come in after the movie has begun and leave before it ends—the last time I saw the beginning or the end of a movie in a Dutch theater, George W. Bush was still serving his first term as U.S. president.

Why do I need this protection? I am not a president or a king; I am a mere member of the Dutch Parliament, one of 150 elected parliamentarians in the *Tweede Kamer*, the House of Representatives of the Netherlands, a small country of 16.5 million in Western Europe.

However, I have joined Westergaard in a rapidly growing group of individuals throughout the world who have been marked for death for criticizing Islam. For asserting our rights to say what we really think about this political ideology that disguises itself as a religion, we have been hounded by Muslims seeking to make an example of us. *Offend us*, they are saying to the world, *and you will end up in hiding like Wilders, attacked like Westergaard, or dead like van Gogh.*

Free men and women everywhere must resist this violent intimidation at all costs. Armed only with our pens, we must defy Islam's axes and knives. We must continue to speak our minds, knowing there is nothing more powerful than the truth. This is why we write our books and speeches, draw our cartoons, and make our movies and documentaries. The truth will set us free. That is what we really believe.

There is an old Biblical expression, "An eye for an eye."[11] The acceptance of this archaic law, dating back to the days of Abraham, was the first step that lifted mankind out of its barbarian state, because it restricted the extent of revenge and retribution to an equitable punishment. Though some pretend that Islam is an Abrahamic faith like Judaism and Christianity, Islam does not restrict revenge and retribution. It does not retaliate against a cartoon with another cartoon; it demands a head for a cartoon—a head for every drawing, book, speech, or movie that it deems to be "insulting."[12]

In many countries—in Islamic nations, of course, but increasingly in the West as well—cartoonists, writers, bloggers, and elected officials such as myself have been prosecuted for the crime of insulting Muslims or Islam. In court, our only defense once again is the pen—expressing the truth as we honestly see it. Yet we are constantly confronted by those who want to rob us even of that weapon. They want to break our pens and force us into silence. Some say that critics of Islam like myself should keep quiet because we are just as bad and just as dangerous as the axe-wielding barbarians who invade our homes.

We will not be picking up axes and breaking into people's homes. But we will not remain silent either. Moderation in the face of evil is not what our age needs. As Ronald Reagan declared, "The future doesn't belong to the fainthearted."[13]

We must uncap our pens; we must speak words of truth. We are facing a determined enemy who is striving through all means to destroy the West and snuff out our traditions of free thought, free speech, and freedom of religion. Make no mistake: if we fail, we will be enslaved.

We must not let the violent fanatics dictate what we draw, what we say, and what we read. We must rebel against their suffocating rules and thuggish demands at every turn. You can help the fight just by reading this book, which explains the many ways in which Islam has marked for death not just me, but all of Western civilization.

We must, in the words of Revolutionary War veteran General John Stark, "Live free or die."

CHAPTER TWO

On Freedom

The precept of the Koran is, perpetual war against all who deny, that Mahomet is the prophet of God.

—John Quincy Adams

In 2008, I made a short movie called *Fitna*, which is the Arabic word for "ordeal," or more specifically, "a test of faith in times of trial." *Fitna* is a documentary meant to warn people about the Koran's violent commandments and about the dangerous ideology of Islam.[1] Some people think that it is because fanatical Muslims feel "insulted" by *Fitna* that now, in 2012, I still have to live in a government safe house and travel in an armored car, that I have lost all privacy, that I sometimes have to wear a bulletproof vest, and that I have to leave theaters before the movies end. They are wrong

Fitna was released in March 2008, more than three years after my ordeal began. Long before I made *Fitna*, I had lost my freedom because of death threats related to my political activities. I lost my freedom because I am a politician, not because I am a filmmaker.

I received my first death threats in September 2003 after I asked the Dutch government to investigate, and if necessary close down, the al-Furqan mosque in Eindhoven, a city about eighty miles southeast of

Amsterdam. Its main mosque was suspected of being a hotbed of Islamic extremism.[2] A second wave of threats followed a year later when I left my political party, the *Volkspartij voor Vrijheid en Democratie* (People's Party for Freedom and Democracy, or VVD) because, among other things, I disagreed with its support for Turkey's entry into the European Union. When I decided to leave the VVD and sit as an independent parliamentarian, extremists swamped me with threatening emails. "Wilders, you are a dead man," one wrote. "We are going to cut your head off." In October 2004, a video appeared on the internet demanding that I be decapitated. The message was accompanied by wailing in Arabic along with pictures of me and my colleague Ayaan Hirsi Ali.

Ayaan, at the time also a VVD parliamentarian, is a former Muslim originally from Somalia. Having experienced female genital mutilation and other cruel Islamic customs, she fled in the early 1990s to the Netherlands, where she became a successful politician. She was one of my closest political allies, having cooperated with me in 2003 in asking the Dutch government to crack down on radical mosques. She, too, had been receiving death threats for many months. In fact, she was subject to far more threats than I was. By renouncing her Islamic faith, she had committed apostasy, the ultimate crime in Islam, for which the Koran prescribes the death penalty; once you are Islamic, you are never allowed to leave.

Due to the video decapitation threat, I received my first personal security detail. Bodyguards followed me when I went out, but I was allowed to continue living in Venlo, my hometown in the eastern Netherlands, and keep up my normal activities.

A few weeks later, however, everything changed. On November 2, 2004, Dutch filmmaker Theo van Gogh was assassinated by a young Muslim; two days later, just after America re-elected George W. Bush as president, I lost my freedom and became a political prisoner in my own country.

I never met Theo van Gogh, who was a talented but very provocative filmmaker and columnist. Van Gogh used language that I would never use. He called Muslims "goat f***ers," their prophet Muhammad a "f***er of little girls," their imams "scum from Allah's sewers," and their god "a pig called Allah."[3]

He was equally aggressive toward Christianity and Judaism; he referred to Jesus as "that rotting fish of Nazareth,"[4] and he ridiculed the Holocaust, joking that "cremated Jewish diabetics smelled of caramel."[5] It's not widely known that van Gogh attacked Christianity and Judaism alongside Islam, because Christians and Jews didn't react to his diatribes by murdering him.

Van Gogh, the great-great-grandnephew of the painter Vincent van Gogh, liked to shock people. His movies were cynical, nihilistic, and morbid, often depicting orgies of blood and sadism—many of his countrymen were particularly offended by one film in which he ran kittens through a washing machine. Theo van Gogh was, in the words of the Dutch novelist Leon de Winter, "an artiste provocateur—troublesome, offensive and hyperbolic but, it should be said, accepted within the wide boundaries of Dutch culture."[6]

From the late 1990s, van Gogh was concerned by the spread of Islam in the Netherlands, a trend he believed threatened Holland's legendary liberalism. He used his usual acid, mocking style while speaking out against Islam, leading to numerous death threats. But he refused to take the threats seriously or accept police protection. "Who would want to kill the village idiot?" he asked. He was either courageous, naïve, or both.

But he underestimated the violent wrath of his Islamic enemies. In 2004, Theo van Gogh was slaughtered on a busy Amsterdam street, Linnaeusstraat, on a Tuesday morning during Ramadan. The killer was Mohammed Bouyeri, a 26-year-old Dutchman of Moroccan descent who had just finished his morning prayers in Amsterdam's El-Tawheed mosque, another radical Dutch mosque that Ayaan and I had asked the authorities to investigate.

Like the 2010 murder attempt on Kurt Westergaard, the scene in Linnaeusstraat on the fateful morning of November 2, 2004, could have come straight from a horror film—one set in a typically Dutch locale, since both the murderer and his victim were riding bikes. At around 9:00 a.m., as van Gogh was biking to work, Bouyeri overtook him, pulled a gun, and shot and wounded the filmmaker, knocking him off his bike. The assassin, who was dressed in an Arabian *djellaba*, jumped on the 47-year-old man, pulled out a butcher's knife, and slit van Gogh's throat according to the Islamic slaughtering ritual. Then he planted the knife in the filmmaker's chest and used a second knife to pin a five-page letter into van Gogh's stomach.

Three months before his assassination, van Gogh had finished a ten-minute documentary entitled *Submission*, the English translation of the Arabic word for "Islam." Discussing the abuse of women in Islam, the film had been broadcast on Dutch television in late August 2004. The documentary showed a woman whose naked body was visible through her transparent chador and gown. On her body were calligraphed verses describing the physical punishments prescribed by the Koran for "disobedient" women.

It was a powerful, almost poetic film with a shocking message. Van Gogh had made a subtle and subdued movie, refraining from his usual vulgar language. In fact, the script for *Submission* had been written by my colleague, Ayaan Hirsi Ali, who as a child and young woman had herself experienced the terrifying plight of Islamic women.

After the release of *Submission*, both Ayaan and Theo van Gogh received death threats from Islamic fanatics. Van Gogh insisted that he feared more for Ayaan's safety than his own, noting that "she is the apostate."[7] Some people believe van Gogh was murdered because of *Submission*; friends of the killer, however, claim that the filmmaker had to die because he had once called Allah a pig.[8] Perhaps Bouyeri simply picked van Gogh because, having refused police protection, he was an easier target than Ayaan or myself.

On the morning of van Gogh's murder, my guards accompanied me to my office at the *Tweede Kamer*. A few minutes later, they came back and told me Theo van Gogh had been assassinated. Journalists soon began calling and visiting me to get my reaction. I remember my legs were shaking with shock and indignation. I do not pretend to be a man who knows no fear, but when I heard about van Gogh's murder I can honestly say I felt anger, not fear. I defiantly proclaimed to the journalists that I would not allow anyone to intimidate me into silence.

I was angry at the assassin and his accomplices, I was angry at Islam—this doctrine that has people murdered for their opinions—and I was angry at the naïve politicians, journalists, and so-called intellectuals in the West who refuse to admit how dangerous Islam is and how fundamentally incompatible it is with our Western values and ideals. I was also mystified why Theo van Gogh had been so careless—he had told everyone that Islam was dangerous, but he refused to take precautions.

I was angry because, whatever one may think about Theo van Gogh, he was slaughtered like an animal simply for criticizing Islam. Nevertheless, on the very day of his assassination, academics, politicians, imams, and Islamic spokesmen—even those of Amsterdam's El-Tawheed mosque, where the murderer had prayed just before he killed van Gogh—were already on the radio and television spouting their usual apologetics: that Islam is a "religion of peace," that the murderer did not represent "real Islam," and even that the assassination had been, according to Mohamed Ousalah, Deputy Chairman of the Association of Dutch Imams, an "anti-Islamic act"[9]—as if a Muslim were the victim instead of the assassin.

Stunningly, a few years later, the Dutch government would adopt the same language. Since April 2007 the website of the official Dutch counterterrorism agency has stated that the Dutch authorities avoid using the terms "Islamic terrorism," "Muslim terrorism," "Islamist terrorism" or "religiously inspired terrorism" because "the large majority of Muslims sees terrorism as un-Islamic."[10] Most European governments have now adopted this misguided policy. In January 2008, the British government officially adopted new language for declarations about Islamic terrorism. Islamic terrorists were henceforth to be referred to as people pursuing "anti-Islamic activity"—because, they say, "linking terrorism to Islam is inflammatory, and risks alienating mainstream Muslim opinion."[11]

Of all the upsetting things about van Gogh's killing, the cowardice of the Dutch government angered me the most. One would think the government, if it were really concerned about the safety and security of its citizens, would react to van Gogh's murder by launching a sustained crackdown on Islamic extremism in the Netherlands—shutting down radical mosques, investigating suspected extremists, and stopping the spread of this ideology by reducing Islamic immigration. Instead, the government took a much different approach—on November 10, 2004, barely a week after van Gogh's assassination, Justice Minister Piet Hein Donner, a Christian Democrat, and Interior Minister Johan Remkes, VVD, wrote a letter to the Speaker of the *Tweede Kamer* suggesting that the Netherlands "prevent and counter Islamic radicalization" by penalizing "insults and blasphemy."[12]

In the hours and days that followed the murder, the media revealed many disturbing details, including the fact that van Gogh had been ritually slaughtered. The police also revealed the content of the five-page letter impaled on his body. It was an open letter in Dutch and Arabic to Ayaan Hirsi Ali in which Bouyeri complained that the Netherlands was "controlled by the Jews" and called for *jihad*—Islamic holy war—against non-Muslims. He threatened Ayaan's life and boasted that she, the Netherlands, Europe, and America would soon perish. The police also discovered a similar open letter that Bouyeri had addressed to me, "the filthy thing Wilders." It warned that I, and people of my ilk, would soon be "destroyed."[13]

The killing of van Gogh was a shock, but I could not foresee that in just two days' time, it would dramatically impact nearly every aspect of my everyday life.

On the evening of November 4, 2004, my guards accompanied me home to Venlo, wished me good night, and left. It was around 7:00 p.m. Fifteen minutes later they were back, wearing bulletproof vests and carrying machine guns. "You will have to leave at once," they announced. After giving me ten minutes to pack, they pushed me into an armored car and drove me off into the night. That was the last time I was in my house.

The guards told me they had to bring me to a safe place because the authorities had discovered imminent threats to assassinate me. They would not tell me where we were going, and they refused my demand to call the Minister of the Interior to find out exactly what was happening. Later, I learned that even the guards themselves initially had not known where they had to take me. They drove me around for several hours and changed cars a couple times before delivering me to an army barracks in the woods near the Belgian border.

Shortly before midnight I arrived at the barracks, where I met my fellow parliamentarian Ayaan Hirsi Ali and my wife, both of whom had been taken there separately. We were not allowed to go out, call anyone, or meet anyone, and we had no radio or television. Even the soldiers at the barracks were not allowed to know we were there. My wife and I were brought to a small, ice-cold room that had only a table, two chairs, and two single beds. We had no warm water or central heating.

The next morning, Ayaan managed to contact a friend and tell her where she was. When the friend tried to reach her by calling the barracks, our cover was blown. The angry guards moved us to another place, a nearby school for police officers that was empty for the weekend. The following morning we were driven to yet another location.

Meanwhile, the international media reported that Ayaan and I, two "anti-Muslim politicians," had "gone into hiding after death threats."[14] They portrayed us as having run away like cowards, shunning responsibility for our alleged hatred of Muslims. In reality, we found ourselves practically imprisoned in our own country for the mere fact that we had spoken out against enemies of the West.

On June 4, 2009, I watched President Barack Obama on television give his famous speech at al-Azhar University in Cairo. I heard Obama proclaim that he "consider[ed] it part of [his] responsibility as President of the United States to fight against negative stereotypes of Islam wherever they appear."[15] I remember thinking, *But what if these so-called "negative stereotypes of Islam" are the truth—will you denounce people for telling the truth? And if violent Islam is really just a "negative stereotype," then*

why have I had to live like a virtual prisoner for more than four years due to death threats from Muslims?

Normally, as a Dutch politician, I would refrain from judging the U.S. president. I admire the American people, I respect their political choices, and they chose Barack Obama as their leader. However, the U.S. president is also seen as the leader of the free world. As such, President Obama's Cairo speech affected not only America, but also Europe and the entire world. As someone who has experienced a different side of Islam than Obama has, I feel entitled to speak frankly about his remarks.

First, we must understand the significance of the location of Obama's speech. Cairo's al-Azhar University is the chief center of Sunni Islamic learning in the world. It is sometimes called "the nearest thing to a Sunni Vatican,"[16] as its Islamic scholars pronounce *fatwas* (Islamic edicts) regarding proper conduct for Muslims. In typical Islamic fashion, al-Azhar practices institutional apartheid. Non-Muslims such as Copts— members of Egypt's indigenous Christian minority—are banned from studying there. The ban covers not just the faculty of Islamic theology, but also non-religious faculties such as medicine, economics, agriculture, and all others.[17]

Ignoring this blatant discrimination, President Obama praised al-Azhar as "a beacon of Islamic learning." He also declined to mention the fate of Abdelkareem Soliman Amer, a 22-year-old al-Azhar student who was expelled from the university in 2006 for writing a blog that supported freedom of religion, freedom of speech, and women's rights. In February 2007, the young Muslim was given a four-year jail sentence for, among other things, calling al-Azhar a "university of terror" and accusing the school of suppressing free thought.[18] Amer was still in prison while Obama spoke, but the president wasn't moved to mention the plight of a young man whose own father has called for his execution under Islamic law.[19]

Previous American presidents, of course, have given their own historic speeches, such as John F. Kennedy's famous "*Ich bin ein Berliner*" speech and Ronald Reagan's legendary address demanding that Gorbachev "tear down this wall." We are compelled to add President Obama's Cairo speech to this list, for it is just as important as Kennedy's and Reagan's remarks, though in a much different way.

In Obama's address to "Muslims around the world," for the first time in America's 233-year history, a U.S. president offered a pact to the followers of one particular religion. By announcing a "partnership between America and Islam" and by explicitly stating that "I consider it part of my responsibility as President of the United States to fight against negative stereotypes about Islam," Obama bestowed upon Islam a privileged position above all other religions and ideologies. Neither he nor any of his predecessors have taken a pilgrimage to the Vatican to offer a "partnership between America and Christianity" and to pledge to use the power of their office "to fight against negative stereotypes" about Christians. Such a move would rightly be seen as an act of American submission to a faith system. And that's exactly the way the Islamic world interpreted Obama's naïve declarations in Cairo—that henceforward, America's president would be subservient to Islam's political agenda. Islam has a word for such a pact of subservience. It is called a *dhimma*, and non-Muslims who accept subservience to Islam are called *dhimmis*. In Cairo, simply put, Obama indicated to the Islamic world that he was a dhimmi.

This is how his speech was understood by, among many others, Wafa Sultan, a courageous Arab ex-Muslim. She was a psychiatrist in Syria before she was forced to emigrate to the United States, where she became an American citizen. Wafa is a voice of moderation and a beacon of light, widely known in the Arab world through her participation in political debates on al Jazeera.

President Obama's Cairo speech, Wafa wrote, "makes my work and that of others who speak up against intolerant Islamic doctrines more challenging. He undermines this mission by placating abusive, xenophobic policies and enabling those within the Islamic world to subjugate others, to coerce others to its beliefs, and to continue these pursuits with his blessing." She continued, "The president failed to join freedom-loving individuals, liberated Arabs like myself. He failed to lead the Muslim world into modernization and vital reform."[20]

By pandering to Islam, Obama let down Wafa and other Arabs who yearn for freedom. He also let down America. Not once did the president mention the words "terrorism," "terrorist," or "terror," let alone the need to fight this scourge. Ten times, however, he used the word "respect," soaking his speech in professions of reverence for Islam.

Obama further proclaimed that "Islam is a part of America," arguing that America and Islam "overlap and share common principles." He asserted there are "nearly 7 million American Muslims in our country today" and stressed that "Islam has always been a part of America's story." To prove the latter, he referred to Thomas Jefferson keeping the "Holy Koran...in his personal library"; to Morocco "being the first nation to recognize my country"; and to "our second President, John Adams," who "in signing the Treaty of Tripoli in 1796, wrote, 'The United States has in itself no character of enmity against the laws, religion or tranquility of Muslims.'"

While Obama undeniably has deep personal links to Islam stemming from his upbringing in Indonesia and his Islamic ancestry through his father's lineage in Kenya, his arguments supposedly proving that America is indebted to Islam, and has been so from the beginning of the Republic, are thoroughly flawed.

It is simply not true, at least not yet, that there are 7 million American Muslims—that is a wild exaggeration put forward by U.S.-based Islamic interest groups. According to the nonpartisan Pew Forum on Religion & Public Life, a mere 0.8 percent of the American population was Muslim in 2010, yielding a figure of 2.6 million American Muslims.[21]

It is also untrue that Morocco was "the first nation to recognize" the United States. Morocco signed a treaty with the U.S. in 1786, after major European countries such as France (1778), the Netherlands (1782), Britain (1783), Sweden (1783), Prussia (1785), and Spain (1786) had already done so.[22]

While it is true that Thomas Jefferson possessed a Koran, in no way did he regard it as "holy," as Obama implied. In 1801 Jefferson waged war against the Islamic Barbary states of north Africa in order to stop the pillaging of ships and the enslavement of more than a million Christians.

The ambassador of these Islamic nations had told Jefferson and John Adams that Muslims justify their slaughter and enslavement of non-Muslims through the "Laws of the Prophet" and the Koran. Jefferson kept a copy of the book to understand the hostile nature of Islam, not because he admired it.[23]

There is also no proof that John Adams, America's second president, was convinced of the "tranquility of Muslims," since Adams did not write the lines Obama attributed to him.[24] But John Adams' son, John Quincy Adams, America's sixth president, wrote several essays on the threat that Islam posed throughout world history. He used words such as "fanatic" and "imposter" to describe Muhammad, calling him a "false prophet" who "spread desolation and delusion over an extensive portion of the earth." Adams said Muhammad had perverted faith in God "by adapting all the rewards and sanctions of his religion to the gratification of the sexual passion." Muhammad, Adams argued, "poisoned the sources of human felicity at the fountain, by degrading the condition of the female sex, and the allowance of polygamy; and he declared undistinguishing and exterminating war, as a part of his religion, against all the rest of mankind. THE ESSENCE OF HIS DOCTRINE WAS VIOLENCE AND LUST: TO EXALT THE BRUTAL OVER THE SPIRITUAL PART OF HUMAN NATURE"[25] [emphasis in original].

Further contradicting Obama's innocent view of Islamic history, John Quincy Adams wrote that war had been raging between Islam and Christianity for twelve hundred years. This conflict, he argued, cannot "cease but by the extinction of that imposture [Islam], which has been permitted by Providence to prolong the degeneracy of man." He posited that as long as "the merciless and dissolute dogmas of the false prophet shall furnish motives to human action, there can never be peace upon earth."[26]

President Obama, like his immediate predecessor George W. Bush, refuses to admit that Adams was right. Contrary to the entire history of Islam—from the caravan raiding, warfare, and slave-trading that was condoned by Muhammad himself, to Islam's bloody spread throughout the Middle East and beyond, to the honor killings, suicide bombings, wanton violence against non-Muslims, and countless other outrages that characterize Islamic countries today—President Bush parroted the mantra that "Islam is peace."[27] Echoing this ahistorical falsehood, Obama told his audience in Cairo, "Throughout history, Islam has demonstrated through words and deeds the possibilities of religious tolerance.... Islam is not part of the problem in combating violent extremism—it is an important part of promoting peace."[28]

It is ironic that Obama's Cairo address mentioned the 1796 Treaty of Tripoli. While his speechwriters invoked it to prove that Islam has been part of America's history from the very beginning, the treaty in fact proves something else—that from the earliest days of the Republic, Islam was trying to enslave American citizens.

The Tripoli Treaty was signed between the young, weak United States and the Bey of Tripoli, a leader of the ruthless Barbary pirates who were raiding American ships and enslaving American sailors. In this treaty, America agreed to pay tribute to the Bey so that he would stop attacking its ships. A quote often cited by Islamic apologists—that "the United States has in itself no character of enmity against the laws, religion or tranquility of Musselmen"—is from article 11 of this treaty.[29]

By 1800, the annual tribute and ransom payments to the Barbary pirates reached about $1 million, comprising 20 percent of the U.S. federal budget.[30] Seeking to end this blackmail, Thomas Jefferson waged war on the pirates shortly after he became president in 1801. Captain Stephen Decatur Jr. bombarded their harbors and the U.S. Marines brought the war to the shores of Tripoli.

John Quincy Adams explains in his writings that the pirates' conduct was in line with the coercive, violent nature of Islam as well as their religious duty to lie and deceive in order to advance Islam. "The precept of the Koran," Adams wrote, "is, perpetual war against all who deny, that Mahomet is the prophet of God. The vanquished may purchase their lives, by the payment of tribute; the victorious may be appeased by a false and delusive promise of peace; and the faithful follower of the prophet, may submit to the imperious necessities of defeat: but the command to propagate the Moslem creed by the sword is always obligatory, when it can be made effective. The commands of the prophet may be performed alike, by fraud, or by force."[31]

He subsequently referred to an episode during the Barbary War when the Dey of Algiers (a colleague of the Bey of Tripoli)[32] tried to deceive American diplomats:

> Of Mahometan good faith, we have had memorable examples ourselves. When our gallant Decatur had chastised the pirate of Algiers, till he was ready to renounce his claim of tribute from the United States, he signed a treaty to that effect: but the treaty was drawn up in the Arabic language, as well as in our own; and our negotiators, unacquainted with the language of the Koran, signed the copies of the treaty, in both languages, not imagining that there was any difference between them. Within a year the Dey demands...an indemnity in money.... Our Consul demands the foundation of this pretension; and the Arabic copy of the treaty, signed by himself is produced, with an article stipulating the indemnity, foisted into it, in direct opposition to the treaty as it had been concluded. The arrival of Chauncey, with a squadron before Algiers, silenced the fraudulent claim of the Dey, and he signed a new treaty in which it was abandoned; but he disdained to conceal his intentions; my power, said he, has been wrested from my hands; draw ye the treaty at your pleasure, and I will sign it; but beware of the moment, when I shall recover my power, for with that moment, your treaty shall be waste paper.... Such is the spirit, which governs the hearts of men, to whom treachery and violence are taught as principles of religion.[33]

Most people today, even most Christians, will acknowledge that many Christians throughout history committed terrible crimes in the name of Christ. Adams, however, rightly observed that such actions actually violate Christian doctrine. This is not the case with Islam, since the Koran plainly sanctions violence in the name of Allah. A Christian who pro-claims hatred to any group of people violates Christian principles. Not so with the Muslims, said Adams:

> This appeal to the natural *hatred* of the Mussulmen towards the infidels, is in just accordance with the precepts of the Koran. The document does not attempt to disguise it, nor even pretend that the enmity of those whom it styles the infidels, is any other than the necessary consequence of the hatred borne by the Mussulmen to them.... No state paper from a Christian hand, could, without trampling the precepts of its Lord and Master, have commenced by an open proclamation of hatred to any portion of the human race. The Ottoman lays it down as the foundation of his discourse.[34]

Adams concluded, "As the essential principle of his faith is the subjuga-tion of others by the sword; it is only by force, that his false doctrines can be dispelled, and his power annihilated."[35]

President John Quincy Adams appears to have been an avid reader of the Koran, which has many chapters that call for violence and hatred against non-Muslims, or infidels (called *kafirs*).[36] I myself am a fervent reader of the Koran, a book that must be taken seriously, considering that hundreds of millions of people believe it is the literal word of Allah. It is simply impossible to study the Koran and the *Hadith* (stories from Muhammad's life), and their calls for limitless warfare against non-Muslims throughout the entire world, without noticing how fundamen-tally different Islam is from all other religions.

I have read the Koran several times, including readings in some of the safe houses where my guards took me to protect me against the book's followers. For a few weeks in late 2004 and early 2005, my wife and I were constantly moved from one place to another. At a moment's notice, we had to pack the few belongings we had with us and leave. It eventually became a routine, though an unsettling one. Sometimes we stayed in prisons, sometimes in army barracks, sometimes in a house or apartment in some city, town, or village. I was not allowed to leave the car without disguising myself in a brown wig, a hat, and an ill-fitting fake mustache. I thought everyone would see through the ridiculous costume, but it apparently worked.

One Sunday morning in December, we had again been brought to an army barracks. Suddenly the siren went off. The guards grabbed their machine guns and ran to their positions. One of the guards—a real professional—ran straight out of the shower, grabbed his gun, and dashed, stark naked and dripping wet, to take his position on the roof. It was freezing cold, and I don't know how he avoided catching pneumonia. Other guards positioned themselves in front of our door, yelling at us to stay inside. It was a frightening experience, but it was a false alarm; apparently the steam from the guard's shower had triggered a fire alarm. The military fire fighters arrived, but the guards kept them out of our room—even the firemen were not allowed to know that Geert Wilders was in the barracks.

During this period, my wife and I were not allowed to have any visitors—no family, no friends, no colleagues. When the cleaners came, we had to move out so they would not see us. For a few weeks, we lived in a small wooden house near the runway on the Soesterberg military airbase. From there we were taken to a jail in Camp Zeist, having been informed that a prison was one of the safest places for us to stay. The guards drove me to Parliament every morning and back again every evening. Every morning at 7:00, including the weekends, the lights automatically switched on in our cell, as they did in all other cells. After I complained several times that we should not be treated like common prisoners, they finally put our cell on a different circuit than the rest of the prison so we could control our own lights.

Camp Zeist is a former U.S. Air Force base near the town of Zeist, not far from Utrecht in the central Netherlands. In 1999 a high-security prison was installed there. This is where, in 1999–2001, two Libyans stood trial for blowing up Pan Am Flight 103 over the Scottish village of Lockerbie in 1988, killing 270 people. In fact, we spent our days in the very cell that held Abdelbaset Ali Mohmed al-Megrahi, the Libyan terrorist sentenced to life imprisonment for the Flight 103 bombing. There was some bitter irony in the jail cell serving as home both to Islamic terrorists and their intended victims. Incidentally, in August 2009 the Scottish government released Megrahi and sent him back to Libya, where he was welcomed as a returning hero. Amid pressure for his release by the Libyan government, the Scots had let him go for "humanitarian reasons," claiming he was expected to die from prostate cancer within three months. More than two years later, at the time of this writing, Megrahi is still alive and living in freedom, while Kurt Westergaard, Ayaan Hirsi Ali, Wafa Sultan, myself, and other critics of Islam have yet to be "released" for "humanitarian reasons" by the hounds of Islam. When will we be able to resume a normal life without the fear of an assassin showing up at our door?

The cells at Camp Zeist were more comfortable than the places where we had previously stayed. We had a bedroom with two single beds, which we put next to each other, and some closets for our clothes. We also had a bathroom with a shower (but no heating), a living room with a couch and a television set, and a red carpet. Red curtains adorned barred windows that looked out at a six-foot-high wall. We could even see a little slice of the sky.

Despite the improvement in our situation, we still lived like prisoners. Whenever we left our premises, bells started ringing and guards came running. We had no privacy and were hardly ever alone.

Leading a life like that got me thinking about some big questions. It is sometimes said that Americans and Europeans differ a lot and that they are growing further apart. I disagree—we share the same fundamentals, and that binds us together. Western societies guarantee their citizens something that no other civilizations grant them: privacy. It's one of those things you tend to take for granted unless you lose it.

The importance of privacy is unique to Western society with its notion of the sovereign individual. In stark contrast to Western norms, Islam robs people of their privacy and dignity. Islamic societies—including Islamic enclaves in the West—exert tight social control that is indicative of the totalitarian character of Islam.

The Koran teaches, "Believers, do not enter the dwellings of other men until you have asked their owners' permission and wished them peace."[37] This verse always makes me laugh. One only needs to think of axe-wielding Muhudiin Geele invading Kurt Westergaard's house to understand that this small dose of privacy does not apply to non-Muslims. Infidels have no rights in Islam. Their "dwellings" are not protected, as Muhammad himself made clear—he had five of his followers break into the house of Abu Rafi, a chief of the Jewish-Arab Banu Nadir tribe, and murder him.[38]

The Koran tells all sorts of similar stories and issues myriad instructions indicating a total lack of respect for the privacy and even the lives of non-Muslims. Referring to apostates, the Koran says, "If they desert you, seize them and put them to death wherever you find them."[39] The death penalty is to be taken literally, as is the phrase "wherever you find them." Clearly, no permission is needed to enter the dwellings of these renegades.

How can there be privacy in a system that does not allow people to change their minds? The American Constitution and the Bill of Rights are based on the belief that people "are endowed by their Creator with certain unalienable Rights" including "Life, Liberty and the pursuit of Happiness." Connected to their recognition of man as a sovereign being, these documents also imply a basic right to privacy—that people will be left alone in their homes, entitled to freedom of conscience and the right to live freely regardless of their religious affiliation. In Islam, by contrast, man is not sovereign; Allah is sovereign, and man must submit to Allah.

Jews and Christians believe their God is a loving God; He longs for human beings to love Him. Since love by definition must be freely given, man must by definition be free and sovereign. Allah, however, does not ask for love; he demands *islam*—"submission." As Ali Sina and other founding members of Islam Watch, an organization of ex-Muslims, write on their website, "The only way to escape from the tyranny of Islam is to leave it altogether."[40] There is no privacy in a theocracy, just as there is no freedom in Islam.

In recent decades, Islamic immigration to the West has rapidly accelerated, resulting in the appearance of large Muslim minorities for the first time in many countries' history. Meanwhile, Islamic extremists throughout the world have become increasingly successful at intimidating—either through the threat of legal action or the threat of violence—anyone, anywhere, from criticizing or satirizing Islam. These days, cartoons published in Denmark are enough to stoke deadly riots in Islamic countries. Or consider the fate of Molly Norris, a Seattle cartoonist who proposed an "Everybody Draw Muhammad Day" on Facebook as a protest against Islamic censorship and threats. As a result of this simple protest, Norris ended up on an Islamic terrorist hit list and, at the FBI's advice, changed her name and went into hiding.[41]

Due to these two trends—increasing Islamic emigration to the West and rising Islamic intimidation of the non-Muslim world—the West is confronted by Islam in a way it has never been confronted before, with our most fundamental rights hanging in the balance.

Many Western countries, including my own, have sought to appease Islam by restricting freedom of speech. The Dutch Penal Code decrees that anyone who either "publicly, verbally or in writing or image, deliberately expresses himself in any way that incites hatred against a group of people" or "in any way that insults a group of people because of their race, their religion or belief, their hetero- or homosexual inclination or their physical, psychological or mental handicap, will be punished...."[42] I know this part of the penal code well—at the behest of various Islamic groups, I was prosecuted on these charges merely for criticizing Islam, and I could have faced more than a year in jail if convicted.

America—unlike the Netherlands, Canada, and most European countries—does not have hate speech laws, thanks to its First Amendment. Nevertheless, even in America, criticism of Islam and its basic tenets is often equated with religious intolerance. Thus, in America, too, there seems to be a growing conflict between freedom of religion and freedom of speech. Indeed, as President Obama indicated in Cairo, he considers the "fight against negative stereotypes of Islam wherever they appear" to be a major obligation of the U.S. president.

At first sight, this deference to Islam may seem to be consistent with the views of America's Founding Fathers, who posited that the state should not interfere in religious matters. In America, freedom of religion is as sacrosanct as freedom of speech. That is only logical; freedom is indivisible. Europeans such as myself admire America precisely because it is the freest nation in the world.

And yet, freedom of speech is being undone in the West by allowing too much freedom for Islam. How is this possible? The explanation is that Islam is not just a religion, as many Americans believe, but primarily a political ideology in the guise of a religion.

In an op-ed piece commenting on my 2010–11 trial for allegedly insulting Muslims and inciting hatred and discrimination, Ayaan Hirsi Ali demonstrated how Islamic organizations abuse our liberties in order to curtail our freedoms. "There are," she wrote, "the efforts of countries in the Organization of the Islamic Conference to silence the European debate about Islam. One strategy used by the 57 OIC countries is to treat Muslim immigrants to Europe as satellite communities by establishing Muslim cultural organizations, mosques and Islamic centers, and by insisting on dual citizenship. Their other strategy is to pressure international organizations and the European Union to adopt resolutions to punish anyone who engages in 'hate speech' against religion. The bill used to prosecute Mr. Wilders is the national version of what OIC diplomats peddle at the U.N. and EU."[43]

It is important that the West recognize the nature of the enemy it faces. America's eighteenth-century Founding Fathers had few dealings with Islam. Their own philosophy of freedom, however, indicates how we should deal with Islam today. "The legitimate powers of government extend to such acts only as are injurious to others. It does me no injury for my neighbor to say that there are twenty gods or no God. It neither picks my pocket nor breaks my leg," Thomas Jefferson said in one of his paeans to religious freedom.[44] But he made this statement in 1781, five years before he and John Adams met a representative of the Barbary pirates and discovered that the Koran *does* in fact command its followers to inflict violence on non-Muslims.

To avoid any misunderstandings, I wish to emphasize—as I always do—that I am talking about the ideology of Islam, not about individual Muslim people. There are many moderate Muslims, but that does not change the fact that the political ideology of Islam is not moderate—it is a totalitarian cult with global ambitions.

We should not treat Islam more leniently than other political ideologies like communism and fascism just because it claims to be a religion. We must treat Islam as we do every other despotic creed that calls for the submission of those who do not adhere to it. "If anything pass in a religious meeting seditiously and contrary to the public peace, let it be punished in the same manner and no otherwise than as if it had happened in a fair or market," Jefferson wrote in 1776, the year of America's independence.[45] I agree.

We are fortunate that the majority of the world's 1.5 billion Muslims do not act according to the Koran, although a significant and growing minority does. Given Islam's dangerous and seditious political message, we must ask ourselves whether it is wise to allow its unhindered propagation. We extend freedom of speech at our own peril to those who incite violence against us. As Abraham Lincoln declared in connection with slavery, "Those who deny freedom to others, deserve it not for themselves; and under a just God, can not long retain it."[46]

Under the guise of freedom of religion, Islam is exploiting our laws to erode everyone else's freedom of speech. We should not allow total freedom to an ideology that intends to force upon us the grim choice of death, enslavement, or conversion to Islam—which is the fate of all non-Muslims as prescribed by Muhammad himself.[47] Using methods described later in this book, we must stop the Islamization of Western civilization. This should not even be a political issue—it has become a simple matter of self-preservation.

CHAPTER THREE

Islamofascism

*Wherever the Christians have been unable to resist
[the Mohammedans] by the sword, Christianity
has ultimately disappeared.*

—Teddy Roosevelt

My bodyguards are always there. They rule my life, even on days of death and sorrow. I was at my parents' house when my dad passed away in August 2005—and so were my bodyguards, who are under orders from the Dutch government to go everywhere I go.

After Dad died, the guards drove me back to my hiding place. In the car, I wanted to be strong, but I couldn't do it. The tears welled up and I broke down, sobbing my heart out. It was like a dam that suddenly caved in. The bodyguards felt uneasy and embarrassed, not knowing what to do. "Shall we stop for a moment, *mijnheer?*" one of them asked. They are good, decent guys, but they are still strangers—awkward, unwilling witnesses of my grief at a moment when I most needed to be alone or with my nearest and dearest. "No, it's all right," I told them, but the tears kept coming.

The bodyguards were there during Dad's funeral, too, discrete but alert. To this day, they accompany me whenever I visit my father's grave.

I'm not complaining about their presence, though. I only need to think of Teddy Roosevelt, America's twenty-sixth president—of Dutch stock and one of my favorite historical figures—who, as vice president, was unexpectedly called to the highest office when President William McKinley was murdered in 1901. Roosevelt himself survived an assassination attempt in 1912—he was shot in the chest as he was about to give a speech, though the bullet was slowed by his eyeglass case and by a copy of his speech he carried in his jacket. Despite his wound, Roosevelt insisted on delivering his full 90-minute address before being rushed to a hospital. Knowing that McKinley had died after an operation to dislodge the bullet, Roosevelt refused to have the bullet removed. It remained in his body until his death in 1919.

"Only those are fit to live who do not fear to die," Roosevelt wrote in 1918, after his 20-year-old son had been killed in World War I. "Both life and death are parts of the same Great Adventure.... All of us who give service, and stand ready for sacrifice, are torch-bearers. We run with the torches until we fall, content if we can pass them to the hands of some other runners."[1]

I was born on September 6, 1963, in Venlo, a town along the banks of the river Maas in Limburg, the southernmost of the Netherlands' twelve provinces. Limburg forms the long, narrow panhandle part of the Netherlands. Belgium—or rather the Belgian half of Limburg—is to its west, Germany to its east.

Our house was less than three miles from the German border, yet Dad never visited our eastern neighbor after World War II. Hearing German brought back too many terrible memories of the war, when he had assisted the resistance and had been forced into hiding from the Nazis. He was so averse to everything German that there were no congratulations when I came home from school with good marks for German—a sharp contrast from his delight when I'd show him good grades for French.

Populating one of the most Catholic parts of the Netherlands, Limburgians have a strong sense of identity stemming from their attachment to their land, their traditions, and their faith. The province holds slightly over 1 million people, who according to the 2003 census are 78 percent Roman Catholic, 2 percent Protestant, 5 percent non-Christian religious, and 15 percent non-religious.

Growing up in Venlo, I was a rebellious, difficult kid, especially between the ages of ten and eighteen; I must have driven my parents crazy. I was one of the 15 percent of Limburgians classified as non-religious, having declared myself an atheist in the fervor of my youth. As I have grown older and wiser, my atheist radicalism has mellowed into agnosticism. I no longer categorically declare that there is no God; I simply acknowledge that I do not know whether God exists. Moreover, I realize now how important religion is for the vibrancy and the very survival of a culture. I have come to agree with Friedrich Hayek, who wrote, "I long hesitated whether to insert this personal note here, but ultimately decided to do so because support by a professed agnostic may help religious people more unhesitatingly to pursue those conclusions that we do share. Perhaps what many people mean in speaking of God is just a personification of that tradition of morals or values that keeps their community alive."[2]

Defenders of Western civilization, whether religious or not, should unite in protecting our way of life. The criticism of our traditional culture that permeates Western society today is disproportionate and self-destructive. No doubt Judeo-Christian civilization is imperfect, but it's unfair to denounce its faults in a historical vacuum. When you compare the West to any other culture that exists today, it becomes clear that we are the most pluralistic, humane, democratic, and charitable culture on earth. I realized that fact while talking to my former colleague, Ayaan Hirsi Ali, who grew up as a Muslim and was the victim of genital mutilation performed by her own grandmother. This relative, no doubt, was convinced that subjecting her granddaughter to this barbaric procedure was the right thing to do. "She was doing it out of love," says Ayaan.[3]

Nevertheless, you don't see Christian parents in Europe or America inflicting this loving act on their daughters.

I do not come from a political family. We did know, however, that Dad was pro-American, grateful for America's contribution in liberating Europe from the Nazis. We also knew why he abhorred Nazi Germany—because of its unspeakable atrocities.

Usurping the powers of religion, Nazi rulers substituted a political ideology for the conscience of the free individual. Ideocratic states like Nazi Germany are ruled by governments whose legitimacy is grounded in claims to be the guardian of morality and truth. Anyone who opposes such a state is considered to be an enemy of the truth, a vessel of immorality and falsehood who deserves to be silenced. This explains why such states—whether revolutionary France, the Soviet Union, or Nazi Germany—exterminated their perceived enemies with guillotines, gulags, and gas chambers.

There is no fundamental difference between ideocratic states and theocratic states, because the totalitarian impulse erases the difference between state and religion. A state can use religion to enforce draconian social control, such as in Iran or Saudi Arabia today, or it can be totalitarian absent a religious framework, such as the Soviet Union and Nazi Germany. A state can also be rooted in religious principles without being theocratic, such as the United States—a strongly religious country that proudly proclaims itself "one nation under God," as the U.S. Pledge of Allegiance says.[4] This God is the Judeo-Christian God.

"Our Saviour...has taught us to judge the tree by its fruit," Thomas Jefferson, America's third president, wrote to Martin Van Buren, America's eighth president.[5] That is precisely what we should do with regard to Islam, which constitutes the greatest political threat facing the West today. Many people underestimate this threat. Some do not see it at all, believing Islam is merely a religion like any other. The threat, however, is political, because Islam seeks to exert totalitarian control over every aspect of life. Islam claims it all: God's part, but also Caesar's.

Some are driven to despair by the threat; the new totalitarian enemy is so huge, representing the faith of 1.5 billion people, that they do not see how we can ever defeat it. We should not lose heart, however. The Polish philosopher Leszek Kolakowski, a former Stalinist and a deep thinker about the totalitarian impulse, was fundamentally optimistic. Why? Because, Kolakowski argued, totalitarianism is incompatible with human nature.

"People need mental security, and this leaves them open to the devilish temptation of an ideocratic order," Kolakowski wrote. "But they need to be human as well, and thus to use their freedom in questioning orders, in suspecting every truth, in venturing into uncharted realms of the spirit. The need for security is not specifically human; the need to take risks in exploring the unknown is."[6] Kolakowski is right. If the Dutch had valued the security of the known over the exploration of the unknown, they would never have settled New York.

Kolakowski also emphasized that the outcome of the struggle between totalitarianism and freedom, between evil and good, or as Kolakowski puts it, "between the devil and God," depends on every one of us: "We are not passive observers or victims of this contest, but participants as well, and therefore our destiny is decided on the field on which we run and play. To say this is trivial, and, like many trivial truths, is well worth repeating."[7] As Ronald Reagan said, "Freedom is...never more than one generation away from extinction. It is not ours by inheritance; it must be fought for and defended constantly by each generation."[8]

That is why every free man and woman is a torchbearer for liberty.

People who reflexively insist that Islam is a religion of peace apparently are unfamiliar with the religion's history and how it spread. Islam began in 610 AD, 1,400 years ago,[9] when the 40-year-old Muhammad, husband of the rich Meccan trader and caravan agent Khadija, climbed a mountain near Mecca, in the countryside of Hejaz, to meditate in the cave of Hira, as he was wont to do. There, during what Muslims[10] call the Night of Qadr, the archangel Jibreel (Gabriel) came to Muhammad with an order from Allah. "Recite," Jibreel said, and he began to dictate to Muhammad the content of the Koran:[11] "Recite in the name of your Lord who created, created man from clots of blood! Recite! Your Lord is the Most Bountiful One, who by the pen taught man what he did not know."[12]

Muhammad returned home and told Khadija that when the angel, in the guise of a man, first came to him, he feared he had gone mad. Allah reassured him, "By the Pen, and what they write, you are not mad."[13] But Muhammad still wondered whether he was possessed by the devil. The man, whom only he could see, continued to visit him with verses, not only during moments of meditation in the cave, but also at other places. Muhammad wanted to know whether the man was truly the archangel Jibreel. Fortunately, Khadija knew how to determine this. During Jibreel's next visit, she told Muhammad to have sex with her. Lo and behold, as soon as Muhammad penetrated his wife, the visitor disappeared. Surely he must have been an angel, Khadija concluded,[14] since the devil would have stayed to watch their sexual escapades.

In Muhammad's day Arabia was inhabited by Jewish, Christian, and pagan tribes. There is evidence of a Jewish presence in the Hejaz as early as the sixth century BC,[15] 1,200 years before Muhammad's birth. Mecca was a trading hub, with contacts to Ethiopia, India, Persia, Egypt, and the Levant. It was also an important religious locale where worship centered on the *Kaaba*, a black stone that is possibly the remnant of a meteorite. The pre-Islamic *Kaaba* was a shrine housing a pantheon of gods. It contained up to 360 idols, with three female deities—Al-Lat, Al-Uzzah, and Manat—as the most prominent, but also with statues of Hindu gods and icons of Jesus and the Virgin Mary.[16] The Meccans were multiculturalists *avant la lettre*. They were pluralistic and tolerant, willing to accommodate new religious groups.

Consequently, when Muhammad began to gather a group of followers, including his rich and influential wife and her cousin, who was a Christian Nazarene priest,[17] the pagan establishment in Mecca was prepared to accommodate the new godly revelation Muhammad preached.

The Meccans were convinced that Muhammad's Koranic revelations were "but a medley of dreams" and "inventions."[18] Some even thought Muhammad was "possessed" and had become a "madman,"[19] but they had a tradition of tolerance toward novelties, including the bizarre. Moreover, they all knew Muhammad, who had led many successful trading caravans to Damascus. He came from a respected family that was part of the Banu Hashim or Hashemites, a clan of the Quraish tribe, the dominant tribe in Mecca.

Since Muhammad was not powerful enough to impose his will on everyone, the Islamic prophet initially agreed to a *modus vivendi* with the Meccan Quraishi establishment. He thus produced Koranic verses allowing Muslims to pray to Mecca's female deities as intercessors before Allah. Later Muhammad revoked these verses, claiming they had been inspired by the devil. These so-called "Satanic Verses" were replaced by new ones that denounced the non-Islamic deities, declaring, "Have you thought on Al-Lat and Al-Uzzah, and, thirdly, on Manat? Is He to have daughters and you sons? This is indeed an unfair distinction! They are but names which you and your fathers have invented: Allah has vested no authority in them."[20]

As Muhammad's following grew, he became intolerant and demanding, and the controversy between Mecca's pluralist polytheists and Muhammad became ever more virulent. One day, Muhammad entered the *Kaaba* shrine and addressed the Meccans with a menacing threat: "By Him who holds my life in His hand: I bring you slaughter."[21]

Muhammad initially hoped the Jewish and Christian tribes would support him in his conflict with the Meccan establishment. This explains why some of the Koran's early verses are friendly toward Jews and Christians. When it became clear, however, that the Jewish tribes distrusted him and that Jewish poets even mocked him in verse and song, the Koran became extremely hostile toward Jews.[22] Later still, when Muhammad realized that many Christians would not support him either, the Koran began to predict hell and damnation for Christians as well.[23]

Muslims later became embarrassed by these contradictions between earlier and later Koranic verses. Islamic theologians solved this problem

with the concept of *al-nasih wal mansuh* ("the abrogating and the abro-
gated"). According to this concept, whenever there are contradictions
in the Koran, later verses overrule earlier ones; in other words, Allah
revoked what he had earlier revealed. This means, in effect, that the
earlier verses speaking favorably of Jews and Christians are overruled
by later, hostile verses, and that tolerant verses are overruled by intolerant ones. Speaking about the often-quoted, tolerant verse, "There shall
be no compulsion in religion,"[24] Pope Benedict XVI observed, "According to some of the experts, this is probably one of the suras of the early
period, when Muhammad was still powerless and under threat." It is
contradicted, as the Pope pointed out, by "the instructions, developed
later and recorded in the Koran, concerning holy war."[25]

Muhammad showed in word and deed his rejection of the Meccans'
pluralism. In 619, Abu Talib, the highly respected clan leader of the
Hashemites and Muhammad's uncle and foster father, lay on his death-
bed. The other Quraishi leaders used the occasion to try to reconcile with
Muhammad and establish peaceful coexistence between Muslims and
non-Muslims. The prophet, however, rejected all their proposals and
demanded that Mecca unconditionally submit to Allah—in other words,
submit to him.

By 622, after the deaths of both Abu Talib and Khadija, Muhammad
realized he had lost his most influential protectors. Consequently, the
Muslims slipped out of Mecca and began their *hijra*, or "emigration," to
the oasis of Yathrib, 210 miles to the north. Yathrib was a predominantly
Jewish area[26] that was just as tolerant as Mecca. The *Muhajirun*, or
"immigrants," as the Yathribians called Muhammad and his gang, were
welcome to stay, and the Jewish tribes even asked Muhammad to medi-
ate their quarrels. It was a foolish request with devastating consequences,
for Muhammad used the opportunity to establish a political dictatorship
based on his Koranic revelations.

Yathrib was soon renamed Medina an-Nabi, "the City of the
Prophet," later shortened to Medina, or "the City"—the name the town
still has today. The day Muhammad's group left Mecca for Yathrib,
September 9, 622, became the first day of the Islamic calendar. This

indicates that in Islam, the establishment in Medina of Islamic political rule is a far more important event than the Night of Qadr, when Jibreel first brought Allah's religious message to Muhammad. Yathrib also became the site of the Muslims' first mosque, a symbol of their political domination over the town.

Muhammad presented his personal tyranny as a theocracy, exploiting his ability to abrogate Koranic verses and fabricate new ones on the spot according to whatever the situation demanded. After Khadija's death, Muhammad decided to take more than one wife. Conveniently, Jibreel suddenly announced that Muslims were allowed to take several wives, thus permitting the prophet, then in his fifties, to marry the 6-year-old Aisha. Soon afterward, when Muhammad fell in love with the wife of his adopted son, the latter offered to divorce her. Arab incest taboos, however, did not allow a man to marry the ex-wife of an adopted son. Hence, Allah *ordered* Muhammad to marry the woman so that, says the Koran, "it should become legitimate for true believers to wed the wives of their adopted sons if they divorced them. Allah's will must be done. No blame shall be attached to the Prophet for doing what is sanctioned for him by Allah."[27] Before long, Muhammad had eleven wives, including the child Aisha.

The Arabs were not stupid, and many realized how opportunistic Muhammad's "revelations" were. Even Muhammad's scribe, who had to write down the prophet's revelations, renounced Islam and returned to Mecca. Others, however, were terrorized into submission. "I shall cast terror into the hearts of the infidels. Strike off their heads, maim them in every limb!" declares the Koran.[28]

From Medina, Muhammad began raiding the camel caravans of Arab traders traveling between Mecca and other Arab towns and oases. These plundering raids are called *ghazi* in Arabic, from which the word *razzia* is derived. Muhammad organized eighty-two *razzias*, twenty-six of which he personally led. "Fighting is obligatory for you, much as you dislike it," says the Koran.[29]

The pre-Islamic Arabs had a chivalrous war code. Muhammad, however, frequently violated it, allowing him to defeat his opponents who obeyed the rules and who simply could not imagine that their enemy would not do the same. This is an early example of a trend that Kolakowski identifies—that ideological and theocratic regimes fundamentally changed the character of war. Because these regimes have made "the universal truth" (as they see it) into a political ideology, they do not obey rules of warfare. Prisoners are slaughtered and the concept of betrayal applies only to those who renounce the side that pretends to be the vehicle of truth.[30]

To protect their caravans, the Meccans gave them armed escorts. In the Battle of Badr, in March 624, about 300 Muslims led by Muhammad defeated a Meccan escort three times their number and captured several important Quraishi leaders. The spoils of the battle went to Muhammad in accordance with a Koranic revelation that came to Muhammad immediately after the battle. It ordered, "They ask you about the spoils. Say: 'The spoils belong to Allah and the Apostle.'"[31] Not content with mere robbery, Muhammad had the captured Quraishi leaders massacred because, according to the Koran, "a prophet may not take captives until he has fought and triumphed in his land."[32] A Jewish poet from Medina was so indignant about this atrocity that he wrote a eulogy commemorating the slain leaders. Islam's prophet had the poet murdered for it. When a woman spoke out against Muhammad for killing the poet, the prophet beseeched his followers to murder her as well. "Who will rid me of Marwan's daughter?" he asked. One of his followers obediently killed her in her house.[33]

The next year, in March 625, at the Battle of Mount Uhud, the Meccans defeated an army led by Muhammad. A Koranic verse that was revealed immediately after the battle attributed the outcome to the Muslims' disobedience to Muhammad and their desire for loot.[34] In a fateful decision, the peace-loving Meccans, satisfied they had taught Muhammad a lesson, chose not to march on Medina, destroy the Muslim powerbase, and liberate Yathrib from Muhammad's tyranny.

During the following years, the Muslims continued raiding Arab caravans and wantonly murdering innocent people. "A prophet must slaughter before collecting captives," declared Muhammad. "Allah desires killing them to manifest the religion."[35] Muhammad also ordered people to be tortured, such as Kinana al-Rabi, the man who had custody of the treasure of the Banu Nadir, a Jewish tribe from Yathrib. When al-Rabi refused to reveal the location of the treasure despite a fire being lit over his chest, he was decapitated.[36] As the Koran states, "Lay hold of him and bind him. Burn him in the fire of Hell, then fasten him with a chain seventy cubits long. For he did not believe in Allah, the Most High, nor did he care to feed the poor."[37]

Tortured to death were also eight men from 'Ukil who had joined the Muslim state in Medina but had apostatized and run away. Muhammad had them apprehended, had their hands and feet cut off, and had them left to die in the desert. This was all in accordance with the Koran, which says that "those that make war against Allah and His apostle and spread disorders in the land shall be put to death or crucified or have their hands and feet cut off on alternate sides."[38]

In order to stop this reign of terror, in March 627 a confederate army of Meccans, Jews, and other Arab tribes marched on Medina. The skirmish that followed, the so-called Battle of the Trench, was undecided. The anti-Muslim alliance then fell apart because of internal disagreements, ending the siege of Medina. Muhammad used the opportunity to exterminate his opponents in Yathrib. The Banu Qurayza, one of the oasis's largest Jewish tribes, was annihilated and all its men were decapitated on the order of Allah's prophet. Some 700 boys and men were butchered, with Muhammad himself actively participating in the massacre. The women and children were sold as slaves.[39]

In March 628, Muhammad signed a 10-year truce with the Meccans, giving him time to rebuild and strengthen his army. In January 630, sooner than expected, he was able to march on Mecca with 10,000 men. Outnumbered by a merciless enemy, Abu Sufyan, the 70-year-old leader of the largest Quraish clan and the commander of the Meccan forces, surrendered the city to Muhammad without a fight. Abu Sufyan soon accepted Allah, proclaiming that the Meccan gods had not been able to defeat the Muslims. (His conversion served him well, for Abu Sufyan's son became the founder of the Umayyad dynasty, which ruled the Islamic

world from 661 until 750.) After his victory, Muhammad brought his
theocracy from Medina to Mecca. He eliminated all the idols from the
Kaaba and declared it a holy shrine of Islam, claiming it had originally
been built for Allah by Ibrahim (Abraham). He also cleansed Mecca of
all the polytheist pagans, Jews, and Christians. In the following two years
he subjugated the whole of Arabia.

Muhammad died on June 8, 632, in Medina. Within a century his
followers conquered most of the civilized world, from the Pyrenees in
the West to the Indus in the East. The Persian Empire fell quickly and
was completely eliminated. The whole southern half of the Byzantine
Empire, from Syria downward, was lost; the entire Middle East and the
whole of north Africa—previously Christian—were lopped off by the
Muslims.

By then, Christianity had been weakened by 300 years of theological
disputes that had led to the emergence of strong heretical churches rejecting the divine nature of Christ and the existence of the Holy Trinity. The
heresies of Arianism, Nestorianism, Monophysitism, Ebionism, and the
Nazarene sect became the dominant forms of Christianity in many
regions—though not in Rome, Constantinople, or the Greek heartland
of the Byzantine Empire.

Many of these heretical movements felt attracted to the simplicity of
Islam, which adhered to similar beliefs that there was no Trinity and that
Jesus was not divine but merely a prophet of God. Consequently, Mono-
physite Syria and Arian North Africa and Spain could not muster the
resistance to oppose Islam. By 700, Christianity had lost more than half
its territory. In contrast, Trinitarian Christianity—whether Greek Orthodox or Roman Catholic—resisted Islamic encroachments. Constantinople,
the Byzantine capital, was besieged twice by the Arabs, in 674–78 and in
717. The Byzantines held Islam at bay for 800 years, twenty-five generations long, before finally succumbing to the Turks in 1453. The valiance
of the Greeks, the tenacity of Byzantine culture, and the strength of

Constantinople's walls saved the rest of Europe from an Islamic invasion from the East. In 1683, the Turks pressed into the heartland of Europe but were defeated at Vienna by John III Sobieski, the King of Poland.

Islam's western assault on Europe had already been stopped at Tours 950 years earlier, in 732, by Charles Martel and his ferocious Franks. The Franks had converted from Germanic paganism to Trinitarian Christianity around 500 AD. If they had become Arians like the Goths and the Vandals, history might have taken a far different course.

I have no idea what Charles Martel told his army before confronting the Muslims at Tours. It may have been something Rooseveltian like, "We stand at Armageddon, and we battle for the Lord,"[40] or it may have been a simple appeal to self-preservation. It certainly was not an Obama-style speech about them and us sharing the same values and believing in the same god.

Teddy Roosevelt understood the importance of the victories at Tours and Vienna for the survival of Western civilization. "Christianity is not the creed of Asia and Africa at this moment solely because the seventh century Christians of Asia and Africa had trained themselves not to fight, whereas the Moslems were trained to fight. Christianity was saved in Europe solely because the peoples of Europe fought," Roosevelt wrote in his 1916 book *Fear God and Take Your Own Part*. He continued, "Wherever the Mohammedans have had a complete sway, wherever the Christians have been unable to resist them by the sword, Christianity has ultimately disappeared. From the hammer of Charles Martel to the sword of Sobieski, Christianity owed its safety in Europe to the fact that it was able to show that it could and would fight as well as the Mohammedan aggressor."[41]

Then Roosevelt added something worth pondering for those who believe all religions share the Golden Rule—that is, that we should do unto others as they would do unto us:

> To make a statement that all religions are the same is as naive as saying that all political parties are the same. Some religions and belief systems give a higher value to each human life and

some religions and belief systems give a lower value. As generations of Americans past, our time has come to defend the beliefs and values that made this nation great, such as equality before the law.... There are such "social values" today in Europe, America, and Australia only because during those thousand years the Christians of Europe possessed the warlike power to do what the Christians of Asia and Africa had failed to do—that is, to beat back the Moslem invader.[42]

Islam is not a religion preaching that we must do unto others as we would have them do unto us. Instead, it is a totalitarian system aiming for political domination of the world. The Nazis understood this too, recognizing in Islam a kindred evil soul. Adolf Hitler deplored the fact that the Germanic Franks had won in Tours in 732. "Had Charles Martel not been victorious," Hitler told his inner circle, "then we should in all probability have been converted to Mohammedanism, that cult which glorifies the heroism and opens up the seventh Heaven to the bold warrior alone. Then the Germanic races would have conquered the world. Christianity alone prevented them from doing so."[43]

Albert Speer, Nazi Germany's Minister of Armaments, wrote in his diary that Hitler regretted that Muhammad had not come to the Germans instead of the Arabs. "It's been our misfortune to have the wrong religion," he told Speer. "Why did it have to be Christianity with its meekness and flabbiness?"[44]

Similarly, Heinrich Himmler, the leader of the SS, told Felix Kersten, his masseur and confidant, he was aghast that King Sobieski had halted the Turks at the gates of Vienna in 1683.[45] Referring to Muhammad's vow that Muslims who die while waging jihad, Islam's holy war, go straight to heaven and have sex with beautiful women for eternity,[46] Himmler declared, "This is the kind of language a soldier understands. When he believes that he will be welcomed in this manner in the afterlife, he will be willing to give his life, he will be enthusiastic about going to battle and not fear death. You may call this primitive and you may laugh about it, but it is based on deeper wisdom. A religion must speak a man's language."[47]

Documents in the German Federal Archives in Berlin confirm that the SS leadership considered Islam to be "a practical and sympathetic religion for soldiers" because "it promises heaven for those who fall in battle."[48]

Polygyny was appealing to the Nazis for the same reason it appeals to Islam. "Women are your fields: go, then, into your fields as you please," says the Koran.[49] In his 1993 book *Some to Mecca Turn to Pray*, British professor Mervyn Hiskett, who spoke of Muslims with much sympathy, referred to a colleague of his, a "senior Muslim academic of the highest personal integrity, who holds an Honours Degree and PhD of a British university. He is far from being a militant of the stamp of the ayatollahs but is simply a strict and principled Muslim." This man had four wives. "He argues that the future of Islam, and the fulfillment of the Islamic imperative to make Islam the religion of all mankind, largely depend on maintaining the Islamic rule of polygyny."[50] In a similar vein, Himmler encouraged his SS men to have as many "Aryan" children as possible.[51]

It should come as no surprise that the Nazis also admired Islam's zeal for dehumanizing and slaughtering Jews. "We changed [the Jews] into detested apes," says the Koran.[52] "We said to them: 'You shall be changed into detested apes,'"[53] "transforming them into apes and swine."[54]

The admiration between Nazism and Islam is mutual. In 1941, Mohammad Amin al-Husseini, the Grand Mufti of Jerusalem, who led several anti-Jewish pogroms in the Middle East in the 1920s and '30s, visited Hitler and Himmler in Berlin. Adolf Eichmann, the overseer of the Holocaust, gave him a private tour of Auschwitz and showed him the gas chambers. At the post-war Nuremberg Trials, Dieter Wisliceny, Eichmann's deputy, revealed, "The mufti was one of the initiators of the systematic extermination of European Jewry and had been a collaborator and adviser of Eichmann and Himmler in the execution of this plan. He was one of Eichmann's best friends and had constantly incited him to accelerate the extermination measures."[55]

German scholar Johann von Leers, a favorite of Hitler's who wrote the Fuhrer's official biography, also repeatedly expressed his great admiration for Islam. "Mohammed's hostility to the Jews had one result:

Oriental Jewry's backbone was broken.... If the rest of the world had adopted a similar policy, we would not have a Jewish Problem," Leers wrote. "As a religion, Islam indeed performed an eternal service to the world: it prevented the threatened conquest of Arabia by the Jews and vanquished the horrible teaching of Jehovah by a pure religion, which...opened the way to a higher culture for numerous people."[56] After the war Leers settled in Egypt, where he worked for the Egyptian Information Department until he died in 1965. He converted to Islam and changed his name to Omar Amin "in honor of my friend Hadj Amin el Husseini, the Grand Mufti."[57]

It is ironic that some of my critics accuse me and other patriots—who defend our national identity against Islamization and who honor Charles Martel and John III Sobieski as heroes of Western civilization—of fascism and Nazism. It is Islam that lays claim to that charge.

"There's one rule that lies at the heart of every religion—that we do unto others as we would have them do unto us." So proclaimed President Barack Obama during his Cairo address on June 4, 2009.

Obama's Muslim audience applauded. But they knew full well, just as Teddy Roosevelt did, that there is no Golden Rule in Islam. In fact, the Koran states explicitly that non-Muslims are to be treated much worse than Muslims. "Believers, take neither Jews nor Christians for your friends," it says.[58] It further commands, "When the sacred months are over slay the idolaters wherever you find them. Arrest them, besiege them, and lie in ambush everywhere for them."[59] This is consistent with Muhammad's infamous order to his followers, so often repeated throughout the Islamic world today, "You will fight with the Jews till some of them will hide behind stones. The stones will betray them saying, 'O Abdullah [slave of Allah]! There is a Jew behind me; so kill him.'"[60]

"The reason I am against Islam is not because it is a religion," says Ali Sina, an Iranian ex-Muslim who lives in Canada, "but because it is a political ideology of imperialism and domination in the guise of religion.

Because Islam does not follow the Golden Rule, it attracts violent people."[61] While President Obama is apparently unaware that Islam is a cult
of hatred,[62] that fact has been widely known for many centuries in both
the West and the East. Defenders of Western civilization should not
sugarcoat Islam or downplay its violent tendencies out of a misguided
fear of offending its adherents. To the contrary, we must boldly state the
truth about Islam's inherent brutality, as proven time and again throughout history and as shown in Islam's own holy book. Otherwise, we risk
repeating the mistake made by the tolerant inhabitants of Yathrib and
Mecca before their cultures were wiped away by the aggressive ideology
they had once welcomed within their walls.

CHAPTER FOUR

In the Dark Doorways

How dreadful are the curses which
Mohammedanism lays on its votaries!

—Winston Churchill

The smell of burned flesh fills the air, and the charred corpses of schoolgirls blight the landscape. Welcome to Mecca!

On Monday, March 11, 2002, fifteen Saudi girls died as they attempted to flee from their school in Mecca, Islam's holiest city. A fire caused by an electrical short circuit had set the building ablaze. The girls ran to the school gates but found them locked—a typical measure in Saudi Arabia meant to ensure full segregation of the sexes.[1]

The keys were held by a male guard who refused to open the gates because the terrified girls were not wearing the correct Islamic dress including face veils and black robes. As the "indecently" dressed girls frantically tried to escape the fire, Saudi officers beat them back into the burning building. Members of the *Mutaween*,[2] the "Commission for the Promotion of Virtue and Prevention of Vice," as the religious police are known in Saudi Arabia, also beat passers-by and firemen who tried to save the girls. "It is sinful to approach them," the officers warned the girls' would-be saviors.[3]

It is not only sinful, it is also a criminal offence. The Mutaween roam the Saudi streets to enforce dress codes, gender segregation, and the proper performance of Islamic prayers. In Saudi Arabia, even Westerners who do not dress properly or wear non-Islamic religious symbols are beaten and imprisoned by the religious police.

The tragic fate of the fifteen Saudi schoolgirls is indicative of the low status of women in Islam, a "religion" that deems prayers to be nullified if a dog, a donkey, or a woman pass in front of praying men.[4] Nevertheless, the Mecca incident drew angry reactions from many Muslims whose basic sense of humanity was violated by the barbarity shown toward the schoolgirls. Despite the hate-filled, misogynistic tenets of Islam, humanity prevailed in the Meccan fathers who were incensed over their daughters' deaths, in the firemen who confronted the Mutaween and attempted to save the girls, and in the Saudi journalists whose coverage of the fire featured rare criticism of the powerful and much-feared religious police.

The fact that many Muslims refuse to act according to Islamic scripture is an amazing testament to the resilience of human nature. People have withstood 1,400 years—a staggering fifty generations—of relentless indoctrination in the Islamic world, yet the human instinct for love and kindness endures. If the findings of a 2006 Gallup poll run by Dalia Mogahed are correct, and only 7 percent of Muslims can be considered "radical,"[5] this means human nature is so strong that almost a millennium and a half of brainwashing could not eradicate it.

The outrage over the schoolgirls' deaths, however, was unusual—in Islamic societies, protests against Islamic inhumanity are rare. Even in Western countries, most mosque-attending Muslims listen without objection as imams recite repulsive sermons that invoke Koranic verses meant to stir up hatred and paranoia.

In October 2006, Sheik Taj Din al-Hilali, the Grand Mufti of Australia and New Zealand, held a sermon in Sydney's Lakemba Mosque, Australia's largest. Hilali argued that gang rapes can't be blamed entirely on their perpetrators, since there are women who wear makeup and dress immodestly. Moreover, some women "sway suggestively...and then you get a judge without mercy and [he] gives you 65 years," the Grand Mufti proclaimed in defense of Bilal Skaf, an Australian Muslim who had been involved in multiple gang rapes. "But the problem," Hilali shouted furiously, "but the problem all began with who?" He answered his own question by comparing women to meat: "If you take out uncovered meat and place it outside on the street, or in the garden or in the park, or in the backyard without a cover, and the cats come and eat it…whose fault is it, the cats or the uncovered meat? The uncovered meat is the problem." He added, "If she was in her room, in her home, in her hijab [Islamic head covering], no problem would have occured."[6]

Hilali told his congregation that women are "weapons" used by Satan to control men. The responsibility for adultery, he said, "falls 90 per cent of the time on the woman. Why? Because she possesses the weapon of enticement."[7] Although Hilali's remarks later provoked anger and ridicule throughout Australia, not one member of his congregation raised his voice to object on behalf of his own wife (or wives), daughter, or sister. None of them felt the need to declare that women should not be compared to meat and cannot be blamed for being raped.

Why do so few Muslims speak out against the inhuman aspects of Islam? The radicals, obviously, agree with these strictures. As for the moderates, I believe they remain mostly silent for three reasons. First, in light of the radicals' penchant for intimidation and violence, many moderates are afraid of the consequences of speaking out. They are simply cowed into silence, even though they are well aware that these inhuman aspects form the core of Islam, and that there is no such thing as "Islam with a human face," just as there was no real "socialism with a human face" or "national-socialism with a human face." Second, invoking Islamic fatalism, some believe it is useless to speak out because things are the way Allah desires them to be, and no one can do anything about it. And third, many Muslims, even if they themselves are moderate, have been indoctrinated by Islam into *islam*—"submission." They mostly do not notice the inhumanity anymore because they have grown accustomed to it.

"How dreadful are the curses which Mohammedanism lays on its votaries!" Winston Churchill wrote.[8] Indeed, one cannot but pity Muslims, having been subjected to 1,400 years of horrific brainwashing.

Imagine if Adolf Hitler had established his thousand-year Reich—how would this have affected Europeans? What would they be like after 1,400 years of that kind of malevolent indoctrination?

It was Muhammad himself who turned Arabia into a misogynist society. In pre-Islamic Arabia, a woman could run her own business and propose marriage to a man. In fact, Muhammad's first wife, Khadija, was a merchant who had inherited and vastly expanded her father's business. When Khadija was forty years old and had been widowed twice, she proposed to and married Muhammad, one of her employees, who was fifteen years her junior. While they were married, she was Muhammad's sole wife. He only became a polygynist after her death, when he announced to his followers that Allah permits a man to have several wives.[9]

The Koran states that if someone needs witnesses for a legal matter, he has to find two men, "but if two men cannot be found, then one man and two women."[10] This verse establishes the concept that in Islam, a woman has half the worth of a man. Similarly, when it comes to inheritance, "A male shall inherit twice as much as a female."[11] A man can also divorce his wife at will, even if she is blameless, while a woman has no equivalent power toward her husband. In light of the inferior position Islam assigns to women, it should be no surprise that the Koran approves of wife beating. If a man fears disobedience from his wife or wives, the Islamic holy book says, he should "admonish them and send them to beds apart and beat them."[12]

Numerous Koranic verses decree that women must cover themselves. One example is: "Enjoin believing women...to cover their adornments...to draw their veils over their bosoms and not to reveal their finery."[13] This verse immediately follows a verse that says, "Enjoin believing men to turn their eyes away from temptation and to restrain their carnal desires."[14] It is no coincidence that one verse follows the other; according to Islam, women have to cover themselves to spare believing men of carnal temptation. If a woman, however modest, awakens the lust of a Muslim man, then she, not he, is to blame. This is why women in Islamic societies have to dress like mummies. This is also why a Muslim man who sexually assaults a woman, especially if she is not a Muslim, is typically not held responsible in Islam. The woman should not have tempted him. If *he* is tempted, *she* is the whore.

If Muslim women behave "lewdly," their families sometimes kill them in order to save the family's honor. "Confine them in their houses till death overtakes them," says the Koran.[15] Honor killings are a pervasive problem throughout the Islamic world, and as Islamic immigration to the West intensifies, the West too has experienced more and more Islamic honor killings. In December 2007, Aqsa Pervez, a 16-year-old teenager from Mississauga, Canada, was strangled by her father for her refusal to wear a *hijab*, the Islamic headscarf.[16] In January 2008, 18-year-old Amina Said and her 17-year-old sister Sarah were murdered by their father in Lewisville, Texas, because "they had boyfriends."[17] In June 2007, Zeynep Boral, a 24-year-old law student, was killed in Alkmaar, the Netherlands, by her ex-husband, also her cousin, because she was too westernized and had divorced him.[18] In October 2009, 18-year-old Laila Achichi was burned alive by her parents and an "exorcist" in Antwerp, Belgium, because she was a lesbian.[19] In February 2005, 23-year-old Hatun Sürücü was shot dead by her brothers in Berlin, Germany, because she was "a whore who lived and dressed like a German."[20] In October 2002, 16-year-old Heshu Yones was stabbed to death in London, England, by her father because she "was becoming westernized" and did not cover her hair.[21]

In one particularly coldblooded honor killing, on January 29, 2012, a Canadian court convicted three Muslims—Afghan immigrant Mohammad Shafia, one of his wives, and his son—of murdering Mohammad's three teenage daughters and his other wife. The awful details of this case almost defy belief. Longtime victims of domestic abuse in their Islamic household, the three murdered girls, the youngest being thirteen years old, were forcibly drowned for supposedly dishonoring their family by dressing like Westerners and choosing their own boyfriends. (The murdered wife in the polygynous family, according to the *Wall Street Journal*, was killed "because she was a troublesome first wife and lenient stepmother.")[22] Mohammad so hated his daughters that even after their deaths, he called them "filth and whores" and ranted that someone should defecate "on their graves."[23]

Of all the terrible aspects of the Shafia girls' murders, one of the most disturbing is that there were "a dozen school officials, helping professionals and police officers in Montreal who personally either knew the teenage girls in that family were in dire straits or underestimated warning signs."[24] But the authorities, hobbled by political correctness, failed to save the girls from their tormentors. As the *National Post*'s Robert Fulford wrote,

> The Shafia girls were likely the victims, not only of a crime, but of our perverse national habit: We emphasize multicultural propriety more than the welfare of individual human beings. And this goes triple for Muslims.
>
> That's the background that shapes the day-to-day policies of teachers, social workers and even police. It makes them overly anxious to conciliate, to mollify. It disarms their best instincts and prevents them from doing what they would want to do: Get potential victims out of danger.[25]

In a sad testament to the media's enduring determination to whitewash the "religion of peace," both the Associated Press and NBC News reported on the jury's guilty verdict in the Shafia case without mentioning the words "Muslim" or "Islam."[26]

As the Shafia case shows, in Islam, the constant fixation on how women dress is the key to a proper society. "In Islam, women are the slaves of men," says Taslima Nasrin.[27] Like Wafa Sultan, Taslima Nasrin is a physician from an Islamic country who saw firsthand the devastating physical results of the abuse of women by the followers of Muhammad. Like Wafa, she had to flee for her life when she began to speak out against these crimes. And like Wafa, she now lives as an exile in the United States.

I first visited an Islamic country in 1982, when I was eighteen years old. I had traveled with a Dutch friend from Eilat in Israel to the Egyptian Red Sea resort of Sharm-el-Sheikh. We were two almost penniless back-packing students. We slept on the beaches, which was illegal, and found hospitality with Egyptians, who spontaneously invited us to tea. I clearly recall my first impression of Egypt: I was overwhelmed by the kindness, friendliness, and helpfulness of its people.

I also remember my second strong impression of Egypt: the people were afraid. While we were in Sharm-el-Sheikh, fear suddenly engulfed the town when it was announced that President Mubarak was coming to visit. As Mubarak's cavalcade of black cars arrived in the resort, I could feel the overwhelming sense of fear like a cold chill on a hot summer day. The strange fear Egyptians felt for their leader must resemble the fear that the seventh-century Arabs felt around Muhammad, whose presence cast "terror into their hearts."[28]

From Sharm-el-Sheikh, my friend and I took the bus to Cairo. It was illegal for us to go there; in the Egyptian consulate in Eilat we had bought a cheap visa that only allowed us into the Sinai Peninsula. If we were caught in Cairo without a valid visa, we would have been in serious trouble. But when you're eighteen years old, such things don't concern you as much as they should.

Cairo was poor and incredibly dirty. My friend and I were amazed that such a place could be a neighbor of Israel, which was so clean. The Arabs we spoke to explained that they were blameless for their condition, claiming they were victims of a global conspiracy of "imperialists" (meaning America) and "Zionists" (meaning Israel) aimed at oppressing Muslims.

I made a big mistake in Cairo that led to an important revelation. After playing soccer with some local kids, I bought a glass of water from a public water collector. The water gave me terrible diarrhea. Retreating to a hostel where I rented a spot on the floor for two dollars a day, I lay there for several days, a heap of misery in a crowded, stinking room filled with ten other guys. Egypt had once been the most advanced civilization on earth. Why had it failed to progress along with the rest of the world?

It was obvious to me that it wasn't because of any grand conspiracy. The answer was actually pretty simple: *it's the culture, stupid.*

In the late 1890s, Winston Churchill was a young soldier and war correspondent in British India (now Pakistan) and the Sudan. While there, the perceptive Churchill grasped with amazing clarity Islam's fundamental problems:

> Besides the fanatical frenzy...there is this fearful fatalistic apathy. The effects are apparent in many countries. Improvident habits, slovenly systems of agriculture, sluggish methods of commerce, and insecurity of property exist where the followers of the Prophet rule or live.... The fact that in Mohammedan law every woman must belong to a sole man as his absolute property, either as a child, a wife, or a concubine, must delay the final extinction of slavery until the faith of Islam has ceased to be a great power among men.... Individual Moslems may show splendid qualities—but the influence of the religion paralyzes the social development of those who follow it.[29]

Churchill concluded, "No stronger retrograde force exists in the world. Far from being moribund, Mohammedanism is a militant and proselytizing faith. It has already spread throughout Central Africa, raising fearless warriors at every step, and were it not that Christianity is sheltered in the strong arms of science—the science against which it had vainly struggled—the civilization of modern Europe might fall, as fell the civilization of ancient Rome."[30]

Islam tells Muslims that everything they need to know can be found in their holy book, which provides "signs for true believers."[31] As there can be no understanding apart from the Koran, nothing may contradict these "signs" of eternal truth. Hence, Islam is extremely wary of *bida*, or innovation.

In the second half of the seventh century and the first decades of the eighth century, when illiterate and unschooled Arabs conquered the entire Persian Empire and chopped off large chunks of the Byzantine Empire, they gained access to great swathes of the Persians' and Greeks' intellectual property. However, Islam had little consideration for science. In 640, the Arabs sacked the Egyptian metropolis of Alexandria and deliberately burned down its 900-year-old library. Its books were considered dispensable. "They will either contradict the Koran, in which case they are heresy, or they will agree with it, so they are superfluous," the Arab leader, Caliph Omar, said. Books found in Persia were destroyed for the same reason.[32]

Jewish and Christian scholars, however, continued doing scientific and scholarly work after the Islamic conquest of Mesopotamia, Persia, the Levant, north Africa, and Spain. An important Baghdad translator of ancient Greek works into Arabic and Syriac was the Christian physician Hunayn ibn Ishaq, known in the West as Johannitius (809–73). Another famous scholar was the Spanish-born Jewish physician Moses Maimonides (1135–1204). Due to Islamic persecution, Maimonides fled Córdoba for Egypt, where he became the court physician of the Sultan. Maimonides had bitter, firsthand experience of Islamic savagery. In letters to fellow Jews, he expressed "profound contempt for Islam."[33] He observed, "The more we suffer and choose to conciliate [the Muslims], the more they choose to act belligerently towards us."[34]

World leaders today like to flatter Islam by hailing its glorious contributions to science and learning. President Obama sang in this choir, littering his Cairo speech with references to "civilization's debt to Islam" and marveling at how Islam "carried the light of learning through so many centuries, paving the way for Europe's Renaissance and Enlightenment."[35] According to the head of NASA, Obama even injected his Islamic outreach campaign into America's premier space exploration agency, ordering NASA's administrator to "engage much more with dominantly Muslim nations to help them feel good about their historic contribution to science…and math and engineering."[36]

Despite the popularity of these apologetics today, there have been a mere handful of innovative Islamic scholars throughout the entire fourteen centuries of Islamic history. The notable exceptions, such as the Persian Abu Ali Ibn Sina, known in the West as Avicenna (c. 980–1037), and the Spanish-born Ibn Rushd, known as Averroes (1126–98), were looked upon with suspicion in the Islamic world. Ibn Sina often had problems with the authorities due to his membership in an Islamic sect, the Ismaili. Averroes, whose work has been more appreciated outside Islam than within it, was banished from the Sultan's court in Marrakesh on suspicion of heresy.

Islamic apologists claim Greek philosophy came to the West via the "open" and "tolerant" societies of Islamic Spain and Morocco. However, Johannes Scotus Eriugena (John the Irishman) was already translating Greek works into Latin in the mid-800s.[37] In 2008, French professor of medieval history Sylvain Gouguenheim convincingly rejected the thesis that Islam brought Greek thought to Western Europe. Gouguenheim's book, *Aristote au mont Saint-Michel: Les racines grecques de l'Europe Chrétienne* (Aristotle at Mont Saint-Michel: The Greek Roots of Christian Europe),[38] shows that Greek philosophy did not reach the West through intermediary Arabic translations. In fact, comprehensive translations of Aristotle and other ancient Greek philosophers were made at the Mont Saint-Michel monastery in Normandy half a century before Arabic versions of the same texts appeared in Islamic-occupied Moorish Spain. The Greek works were directly translated into Latin by clerics such as Jacobus Veneticus (James of Venice), who had lived and worked for some time in Constantinople in the second quarter of the twelfth century. Europe, says Gouguenheim, "became aware of the Greek texts because it went hunting for them, not because they were brought to them [by the Muslims]."[39]

Gouguenheim explains that his book is a counterpoint to Sigrid Hunke's arguments about Islam's medieval relations to the West. Hunke was a Nazi and a member of an SS think tank, the *Germanistischer Wissenschaftseinsatz* (Germanic Sciences Service), during World War II.[40] She lived in Morocco in the 1940s and was made an honorary member of the Supreme Council for Islamic Affairs at Cairo's al-Azhar University. With that background, it's unsurprising she would claim the West owes its development to "a pioneering, civilizing Islam" that supposedly transmitted Greek philosophy back to Europe.[41] Unfortunately, Hunke's flawed thesis has become widely accepted by Western leaders anxious to pander to Islam's grandiose pretensions.

Western politicians should be expressing their gratitude to the Byzantines, not to Islam. Islam only retained aspects of Greek philosophy that were deemed compatible with the Koran—which were few. Most Greek works, discoveries, and scientific achievements made their way into Western Europe after the conquest of Constantinople by the Islamic Turks in 1453, when Greek refugees found safety in Europe, particularly in Italy.[42] In this sense, Islam did, indeed, "pave the way for Europe's Renaissance and Enlightenment"—by wiping away the great city of Byzantium and enabling Europe to salvage a few pieces. Without Constantinople, major works of Homer and Herodotus, Plato and Aristotle, Sophocles and Aeschylus, would not have survived.

The only field in which Islam made a major contribution to science, at least for a time, was astronomy. This stemmed from the Koran's obligation that Muslims observe the lunar calendar, an unpractical calendar that does not correspond with the seasons. Because the lunar year is eleven days shorter than the solar year (and twelve days shorter during leap years), the two only coincide approximately every thirty-three years. Due to the lunar calendar, Islamic festivals and Islam's holy month of Ramadan always fall on different dates. The lunar calendar obliged Muslims to watch the night skies to observe the moon, causing them to build sophisticated observatories in Baghdad and elsewhere.

Islam also made a contribution to mathematics. Words such as "algebra" and "algorithm" have Arabic origins.[43] Islam for a time was interested in mathematics because it is useful for astronomy and for determining the *Qibla*, the direction toward the *Kaaba* shrine in Mecca, which Muslims must face when they pray. However, its contribution did not include the so-called "Arabic numerals," which are actually of Hindu origin; the eighth-century Persian mathematicians al-Fazari and Ibn Tariq translated Indian astronomical texts into Arabic and adopted the Hindu numerals.

On the whole, the spread of Islam led to ages of stagnation, if not inverted progress, in the occupied territories of Asia and north Africa. If the Franks had not stopped the Arabs at Tours in 732, the progress of

Western civilization would surely have ground to a halt, and the West today would be just another poverty-stricken, underdeveloped colony of Islam.

Although Islam forbids artistic representations of people, beautiful art is found throughout the Islamic world in calligraphy, arabesques, architecture, and other realms. On one of my trips to the Middle East, I became fascinated by the decorative splendor of a copy of the Koran that was for sale. I bought the book, and after I returned home, I found a translation to help me understand the Arabic-language text. I expected to find injunctions to "love thy neighbor" and other commandments similar to those in the Bible, but instead I found the spite of a god who hates.

The Koran consists of 6,360 verses, collected in 114 *suras*, or chapters. The suras are arranged by length, with the longest at the beginning and the shortest at the end. Islam holds that the Koran is eternal. It has existed forever with Allah. The copies on earth are a perfect copy of the *Umm al-Kitab*, the "Mother of the Book" which, written in Arabic by Allah himself, lies on a table in Heaven. Gabriel ordered Muhammad to recite and memorize what the angel dictated from the eternal book. As the Koran was written directly by Allah and not by a human being, it is infallible, inviolate, absolute, and necessarily right. It contains everything man needs to know, and it must be obeyed in all details. Because Allah is the author of the Mother of the Book, any criticism or disrespect expressed toward the Koran is considered blasphemy punishable by death.

Since Allah authored the entire Koran, there is no room to re-interpret its commandments—they simply must be followed, unquestioningly, in their most literal sense. It is fundamentally different from the Bible, whose content is subject to passionate discussion and interpretation. Thus, for example, there is no movement in contemporary Judaism or Christianity seeking to reinstitute the harsh punishments, such as the death penalty for adulterers, laid down in the Jewish Talmud in the fifth century BC.[44]

In fact, these punishments were abandoned long ago. The Gospel relates how an adulterous woman was brought to Jesus with the question of what punishment she deserved. The accusers referred to the old Talmudic law, but Christ told them, "He that is without sin among you, let him cast the first stone."[45] None of them did. Likewise, the Jewish tribes that Muhammad encountered in seventh-century Arabia had renounced the practice of stoning adulterers to death, having reduced the punishment to lashing.

However, when the Jews from Yathrib (Medina) brought an adulterous couple to Muhammad, he scolded them, "Woe to you Jews! What has induced you to abandon the judgment of God which you hold in your hands? I am the first to revive the order of God and His Book and to practice it."[46] Note that Muhammad said he is *the first* to revive the old punishments, indicating they had been abandoned long before the seventh century. Then the prophet ordered the unfortunate couple to be stoned. They must have loved each other; in a moving passage from the Hadith, one of the Muslim witnesses recalled, "I saw the man leaning over the woman to shelter her from the stones."[47]

Adulterers are still being sentenced to death by stoning in Islamic countries such as Afghanistan, Iran, Nigeria, Pakistan, Saudi Arabia, Somalia, Sudan, and the United Arab Emirates.[48] Some provinces in Malaysia and Indonesia have recently introduced stoning.[49] In perhaps an even greater outrage, some Islamic states consider female rape victims to be adulterers liable to be stoned to death.[50] This stems from the Koran's injunction that a female rape victim has to present four male witnesses to support her claim that she has been raped.[51] If she fails to do so, she incriminates herself, and the victim's charge of rape becomes an admission of adultery. At least half the women in prison in Pakistan are behind bars for the crime of being a rape victim.[52]

Indian-born ex-Muslim Ibn Warraq, founder of the Institute for the Secularisation of Islamic Society, calls the Koran "an obscure, incoherent,

bizarre mediaeval text, a curious amalgam of Talmudic Judaism, apoc-
ryphal Christianity and pagan superstitions...full of barbarisms."[53]
Though it covers topics as exotic as how believers should clean themselves
after urinating or defecating when there is no water available—"take
some clean sand and rub your hands and face with it"[54]—the Koran is
brief compared to the Old and even the New Testament.

The Koran claims to be God's final revelation to man. It states that
"Muhammad is the Apostle of Allah and the Seal of the Prophets."[55]
Allah had previously spread his word through other prophets including
Iesa (Jesus), but Islam claims the Jews and Christians deliberately falsified
the scriptures given to them.

The Koran also states that "there is a good example in Allah's apostle
for those who look to Allah and the Last Day."[56] Hence devout Muslims
who want to curry favor with Allah must study Muhammad's life and
follow his example. That is why the Hadith, the collection of Muhammad's acts and sayings, is an authoritative guide to Islamic behavior.

The Hadith teaches the *Sunna*, which explain the model of Muhammad, the ideal man. There is a huge collection of hadith written in the
first two centuries after Muhammad's death, based on the oral tradition
of Muhammad's companions. The most respected is the *Sahih Bukhari*,
compiled by Imam al-Bukhari (810–70). There are five other collections,
all lengthy, that Islam generally regards as trustworthy. Another part of
the *Sunna* is the *Sira*, or biography of Muhammad, written by Ibn Ishaq
(704–73). Its full name is *Sirat Rasul Allah*, the "Biography of the Prophet
of Allah."

Christians and Jews hold that God created man in His image. The
Koran, on the contrary, states that "nothing can be compared with
Allah."[57] Since Allah has absolutely nothing in common with us, he obviously did not create man in his image. The Biblical concept of God as our
father is absent from Islam. The purpose of Islam is the total surrender
of oneself and others to the unknowable Allah, whom we must serve
through total obedience to the teachings of Muhammad.[58]

One thing we *do* know about Allah is that "Allah is One, the Eternal
God. He begot none, nor was He begotten. None is equal to Him."[59]

This concept of "Oneness" is called *tawhid*. Similarly, Muslims have to become one body, the *Umma*, which is the nation of Islam or the Islamic ecumenical world community. Islam is a universal religion that stands for the unity of God and the oneness of mankind. Islam commands the *Umma* to act like an army.

Islam holds that everybody is born a Muslim. Adam, the first man, was created a Muslim. "Mankind were once one nation," says the Koran.[60] According to Islamic theology, human beings are born with *fitra*,[61] an innate knowledge of *tawhid*. Muhammad said, "Every child is born with a true faith of Islam but his parents convert him to Judaism, Christianity or Magainism [Zoroastrianism]."[62] Hence, if some of us today are not Muslims, this is either through our own fault or through the apostasy of our parents. Islam teaches that the unbeliever is doomed; he is always *kafir* ("guilty"), whether by his own or his forefathers' fault.

A Muslim has five religious duties—the so-called "Pillars of Islam." The first is to pronounce the *Shahada*, the Declaration of Faith, and accept its words: "There is no God but Allah: Muhammad is His Messenger." The flag of Saudi Arabia displays the *Shahada* with a sword underneath it, sending an unambiguous message of Islamic conquest. The flags of the Afghan Taliban and the Palestinian terror organization Hamas also display the *Shahada*, while the flag of the Lebanese terror organization Hizbollah (the "Party of God") displays a Kalashnikov assault rifle with the Koranic verse, "The Party of God are sure to triumph."[63]

The second pillar of Islam is *salat*, the obligation to pray five times a day, at fixed times, in the direction of the *Kaaba* in Mecca. *Salat* is becoming a familiar sight in Europe. In September 2011, France even felt compelled to enact a law banning the increasingly common practice of street prayer, whereby huge crowds of Muslims take over the sidewalks and sometimes even the roads, halting all traffic as they worship Allah.[64]

The third pillar is *zakat*, the giving of alms, which is given either on behalf of poor Muslims or "in the cause of Allah" for purposes such as building mosques. Some of these religiously mandated donations are used to finance jihad, or "holy war." As Yusuf al-Qaradawi, head of the European Council for Fatwa and Research and founder of the Islam

Online website, writes, "The meaning of Jihad in our present time particularly refers to striving to liberate Muslim lands from the grip of the disbelievers.... Declaring Jihad to save our land is an Islamic obligation.... It thus needs to be financed from the money of Zakah."[65]

The fourth pillar is the duty to fast during the holy month of Ramadan. This is not a total fast, but an obligation to abstain from food, drink, and sex from dawn to dusk. Some groups are exempted from the requirement, such as old men, whom Muhammad allowed to have sex during Ramadan. The Hadith relates that a man asked Muhammad whether he was allowed to "embrace his wife" during the fast. "[Muhammad] gave him permission; but when another man came to him, and asked him, he forbade him. The one to whom he gave permission was an old man and the one whom he forbade was a youth."[66] The prophet himself did not restrain from all forms of intimacy either; his wife Aisha said that he "used to kiss her and suck her tongue when he was fasting."[67]

The Ramadan fast is broken every evening with a meal after sunset, the so-called *Iftar*. In 1996, President Bill Clinton invited Islamic leaders to the White House for an *Iftar* meal, thus starting an annual tradition continued by George W. Bush and Barack Obama. During the last decade, American embassies across Europe have adopted a similar, annual tradition of inviting local Muslim representatives to an *Iftar* meal at the U.S. Ambassador's residence.

The fifth and final pillar of Islam is the *hajj*, the pilgrimage to the *Kaaba* in Mecca, which a Muslim must make once in his lifetime. The annual pilgrimage was an ancient Arab practice predating the advent of Islam. It occurs during four days in the twelfth month of the Islamic calendar. The pilgrimage ends with the Islamic festival of *Eid al-Adha*, the "Festival of Sacrifice," during which Islamic men all over the world must ritually slaughter a sheep or goat.

While Christian sacraments, such as baptism, the Eucharist, confirmation, confession, matrimony, priestly ordination, and the anointing of the sick, center predominantly on the individual, the pillars of Islam are largely centered on the collective, symbolizing the worldwide solidarity of the *Umma*, the army of Allah.

Since Islam lacks a commitment to individual freedom, it is unsurprising that the ideology downplays the notion that man is responsible for his own fate. To the contrary, Islam teaches Muslims to be fatalistic, because Allah has predestined everyone's future. As such, the Koran is filled with injunctions such as, "Such is the grace of Allah: He bestows it on whom He will"[68]; "Nothing will befall us except what Allah has ordained"[69]; "We have made all things according to a fixed decree," says Allah[70]; "The term of every life is fixed"[71]; and "Allah leaves in error whom He will and guides whom He pleases."[72]

"It was the predestination doctrine that prevailed in Islam," writes Ibn Warraq.[73] Every sura in the Koran begins with the invocation of "Allah, the Compassionate, the Merciful." However, as Mervyn Hiskett observes, "Allah's mercifulness does not require Him to relieve His creatures, whether men or beasts, from the tribulations of life or the pangs of death. It consists solely of demanding less of men by way of worship and service than He otherwise might; and of making Paradise available to those who, inherently, do not deserve it."[74]

The author Aldous Huxley, who lived in north Africa in the 1920s, attributed many of the pathologies plaguing Islamic societies to Islam's deadening fatalism:

> About the immediate causes of things—precisely how they happen—they seem to feel not the slightest interest. Indeed, it is not even admitted that there are such things as immediate causes: God is directly responsible for everything. "Do you think it will rain?" you ask pointing to menacing clouds overhead. "If God wills," is the answer. You pass the native hospital. "Are the doctors good?" "In our country," the Arab gravely replies, in the tone of Solomon, "we say that doctors are of no avail. If Allah wills that a man die, he will die. If not, he will recover." All of which is profoundly true, so true, indeed, that it is not worth saying. To the Arab, however, it seems the last word in human wisdom.... They have relapsed—all except those who are educated according to

Western methods—into pre-scientific fatalism, with its attendant incuriosity and apathy. They are the "dull inquirers who, demanding an account of the phenomena of a watch, shall rest satisfied with being told that it is an engine made by a watchmaker." The result of their satisfaction with this extremely unsatisfactory answer is that their villages look like the ruins of villages, that the blow-flies sit undisturbedly feeding on the eyelids of those whom Allah has predestined to blindness, that half their babies die.[75]

According to Islam, there is only one assurance that a Muslim will go straight to paradise: martyrdom. However, the concept of Islamic martyrdom is fundamentally different from Christian martyrdom, which refers to suffering unto death for the sake of faith. In contrast, the Koran says that Allah promises his garden to those who "fight for His cause, slay, and be slain. Such is the true pledge which He has made them in the Torah, the Gospel and the Koran."[76] Islamic martyrs are not those who suffer and die for the truth, but those who are killed while making others suffer and die. "The hill of the dead grows higher," wrote Salman Rushdie in *The Satanic Verses*, a book that caused the author to spend decades hiding from offended Islamic fanatics seeking to kill him. "In the dark doorways of the city there are mothers with covered heads, pushing their beloved sons into the parade, go, *be a martyr, do the needful, die*."[77]

Throughout history, Islam has brought poverty, social strife, backwardness, intolerance, and tyranny to societies where it is practiced. This trend continues today, as the curse of Islam hampers the quest for freedom and democracy in the Middle East.

The so-called "Arab Spring" of 2011 began when a policewoman in Sidi Bouzid, 190 miles south of the Tunisian capital of Tunis, confiscated a vegetable cart from Mohamed Bouazizi. She reportedly slapped and humiliated the 26-year-old street vendor, who went to a police station to complain. After officers refused to hear Bouazizi's grievance, he poured fuel over himself outside the station and set himself on fire.[78] It was 10:30 a.m. on December 17, 2010—the beginning of the end of numerous despotic Arab dictatorships.

Bouazizi's self-immolation provoked an outburst of pent-up political and social frustration in Tunisia. Young liberal reformers seeking freedom, justice, the rule of law, and democracy took to the streets. Propelled by Facebook, Twitter, and other social media tools, unrest rapidly spread to Tunis and other cities. Bouazizi died in a Tunis hospital on January 4, 2011. Ten days later, President Zine El Abidine Ben Ali resigned after twenty-three years in power and fled to Saudi Arabia. The success of the Tunisian uprising, covered extensively by al Jazeera, broke through barriers of fear that had long possessed Arab populations, triggering a wave of protests across north Africa and the Middle East.

The largest demonstrations were held in Egypt, where in early February over a quarter million demonstrators gathered in Cairo's central Tahrir Square and refused to leave until they succeeded, on February 11, 2011, in ending Hosni Mubarak's 29-year reign as "president."[79] In Libya, a civil war erupted, provoking Western intervention that helped rebels put an end to Moamar Gaddafi's 42-year rule. Uprisings, revolution, and civil war also hit Syria, Yemen, Bahrain, and other countries.

Many Arab people yearn for freedom—this is only natural. However, their hopes of achieving freedom through the Arab Spring will be dashed. Sadly, the freedom-loving youths who triggered the revolts were facing off not only against oppressive autocratic dictatorships—a battle they won in Tunisia and Egypt—but also against "the curses which Mohammedanism lays on its votaries," that is, against the culture and ideology of Islam itself—and that battle they cannot win.

I have travelled many times to the Middle East, visiting Tunisia, Syria, Turkey, Iraq, Iran, Afghanistan, Egypt, and Indonesia. I know the potential these countries and peoples have. If only they could liberate themselves from Islam, they, too, could become prosperous and free nations. Islam is the problem—and we should not be afraid to say so.

A 2010 survey by the Pew Research Center found that 59 percent of Egyptians prefer democracy to any other form of government. While that result may seem promising, it is negated by the people's widespread support for Islamic customs that undermine a democratic society; 54 percent support mandatory gender segregation in the workplace, 82 percent believe adulterers should be stoned, 84 percent want the death penalty for apostates, and 77 percent insist thieves should be flogged or have their hands cut off, as is prescribed in the Koran. Overall, an overwhelming 85 percent say that Islam's influence on politics is good.[80]

Unfortunately for Egypt's youthful revolutionaries, they were immediately outmaneuvered by Islamic activists. On February 18, 2011, the Islamic cleric Yusuf al-Qaradawi led 200,000 people in the first post-Mubarak Friday prayer at Tahrir Square. "The revolution isn't over. It has just started," he told the massive crowd. As the *Christian Science Monitor* commented, the giant rally was "a reminder that political Islam is likely to play a larger role in Egypt than it has for decades."[81] Indeed, Egyptian women soon felt the implications of the resurgence of Islam, which had been somewhat suppressed by Mubarak. On March 8, 2011, International Women's Day, 200 women who were demonstrating for women's rights in Tahrir Square were beat up and dragged away by a group of bearded Islamic zealots.[82] This is the new Egypt: on Monday, people demonstrate for freedom; on Tuesday, the same people assault women because they, too, demand freedom. This is the curse of Islam.

Egypt's Coptic Christians felt the implications as well. As Islam surged with the overthrow of Mubarak, Egypt witnessed escalating Islamic attacks on Coptic communities, including attacks by Egyptian army personnel.[83] According to a September 2011 report by the Egyptian Union of Human Rights Organizations (EUHRO), nearly 100,000 Coptic Christians emigrated since March 2011. "They are coerced into [emigrating] by threats and intimidation by hard line [Islamic radicals] and the lack of protection they are getting from the Egyptian regime," EUHRO director Naguib Gabriel said.[84]

Throughout the Middle East, in the dark doorways of the revolution, major dangers loom. In the wake of the upheavals, the political vacuum in Tunisia, Egypt, Libya, and elsewhere has empowered jihadists.

In February 2011, Italy's Foreign Minister Franco Frattini voiced alarm at reports that anti-Gaddafi rebels had taken control of the Libyan city of Benghazi. "I'm extremely concerned about the self-proclamation of the so-called Islamic Emirate of Benghazi," Frattini told reporters.[85] It was unknown at the time who exactly the Libyan rebels were, but it was clear their ranks included veteran jihadists. Nevertheless, less than a month later, the United Nations and NATO decided to intervene in the conflict on the rebels' side, leading to the extraordinary phenomenon of the United States Air Force fighting alongside Islamic extremists who had earlier battled against U.S. troops in Iraq and Afghanistan.[86] Western intelligence officers also warned that extremist groups had pillaged the Libyan Army's military arsenals and acquired large stocks of sophisticated weapons.[87]

"The wildly spreading instability that has accompanied the Arab Spring is custom-made for the jihadists' needs," warned Christopher Dickey, *Newsweek*'s Middle East regional editor.[88] Israeli counter-terrorism specialist Boaz Ganor fears the Arab Spring might ultimately lead to a biting Arab Winter, just as the Iranian Revolution of 1979 turned the most developed Muslim country into an Islamic theocracy. "Democracy is not only about free elections," says Ganor. "Democracy is a state of mind and a set of values. Democracy is human rights and women's rights."[89] When this state of mind is absent, when a country has hardly any civil institutions, when there is no rule of law and no culture of tolerance, a disciplined movement of ruthless ideologues will easily hijack the democratic process.

The bottom line, unfortunately, is this: there can be no freedom in countries where Islam is dominant.

Islam is primarily a political ideology, not a religion.

"Although we carelessly speak of Islam as a 'religion,' that word carries many overtones of the special history of western Europe," wrote the historian J. M. Roberts in his authoritative book *The Triumph of the West*. "The Muslim is primarily a member of community, the follower of a certain way, an adherent to a system of law, rather than someone holding particular theological views."[90]

"Islam is an ideology. In the Western world, it was not called a 'religion' until the twentieth century," explains Hugh Fitzgerald. "Rather, it was a 'faith' or, to many Western travelers, a 'fanatical faith.' Islam does contain rituals of worship—the so-called Five Pillars of Islam.... These duties are to be performed. They do not require, nor do they promote, moral development."[91]

Egyptian-born ex-Muslim Nonie Darwish, the daughter of an Egyptian Islamic "martyr," writes, "Those who confine their observance to the Five Pillars become what the West calls 'moderate' Muslims.... But what a Muslim says in his prayers and time of prayers is not a choice for a Muslim who must recite what is ordered at specific times."[92] Islam as a whole, says Darwish, is "a political and legal system of totalitarian control.... The most flaring evidence that Islam is hardly a 'religion' is in its apostasy law—the order to kill those who leave it. That immediately moved Islam from the realm of religion to the realm of totalitarian political ideology."[93]

It is crucial for the West to understand why Islam is not a true religion—it is because Islam rejects the principle of voluntarism that is common to all authentic religions. Whereas Christianity and other religions lay obligations only on their own members who have voluntarily joined the faith, Islam levels commands even at non-Muslims and orders them to submit.

Darwish also points to another characteristic of authentic religions that Islam lacks: it does not teach the golden rule—that we should treat others as we would have them treat us. Instead, Islam institutionalizes inequality, sanctioning discrimination against certain groups of people such as women and non-Muslims.

Overall, Islam fails four major tests that religions should fulfill:

1. Adherence to the religion must be a personal choice.
2. No religion should demand that those who leave it be killed.
3. A religion must never mandate the killing and subjugation of those who choose not to belong.
4. A religion must be in accord with basic human rights.[94]

American political scientist Mark Alexander writes that "one of our greatest mistakes is to think of Islam as just another one of the world's great religions." He states that the fundamental nature of Islam differs very little from despicable totalitarian political ideologies such as National Socialism and communism. Alexander lists characteristics that Islam shares with these ideologies: they use political purges to "cleanse" society of what they consider undesirable; they obliterate "the liberal distinction between areas of private judgment and public control"; they subdue people and assign them second-class status; they induce "a frame of mind akin to...fanaticism"; they are anti-Semitic; and they are abusive to their opponents, regarding "any concession on their own part as a temporary expedient and on a rival's part as a sign of weakness."[95]

"In my view" says Flemish Professor Urbain Vermeulen, "Islam is primarily a legal system, a law. The prophet Muhammad has come to indicate the difference (*al-furqan*) between what is allowed (*al-halal*) and what is forbidden (*al-haram*). Islam is not concerned primarily with the detailed content of the faith...but with what the believer must and/or may do or not do."[96]

Vermeulen, former president of the European Union of Arabists and Islamicists,[97] says Islam is only 10 percent religion, while 90 percent deals with how people have to behave in accordance with Islamic law based on divine revelations Muhammad received when he was a political leader in Medina. While there is no problem with setting rules about how people should pray and how they should fast, Vermeulen says, Islam becomes problematic when it tries to impose—as Allah says it must—Islamic holy law on the whole of society, including on non-Muslims.[98] He explains, "In Islam you can't eat *à la carte*, you have to take the whole menu."[99]

"Islam classically demands a political realization, and specifically one in which Islam rules over all other religions, ideologies and competing political visions," writes Australian theologian Mark Durie. He adds, "Islam is not unique in having a political vision or speaking to politics, but it is unique in demanding that it alone must rule the political sphere."[100]

The influential twentieth-century Islamic spiritual leader Abul Ala Maududi freely acknowledged that "Islam is an ideology" because it demands that the state be regulated according to Islamic law. "The five pillars of Islam," Maududi said, "cry out for a State to exist in order for their full establishment to be achieved. This is the nature of Islam as it is an ideology."[101]

Using Islamic prayer as an example, Maududi complained that "today, no ruler in the world treats the prayer as an obligation protected by the state's law and enforced by the judiciary and police. Rather the principles of 'free-choice' and 'freedom of worship' are preferred over Allah's command. This only proves that for the prayer to be fully implemented requires the apparatus of the state which creates the atmosphere where prayer is understood to be an obligation and not optional."[102] Indeed, Islam's most important goal, its ultimate ambition, is the establishment of a worldly state, a global political empire: the Caliphate, to whose authority all of mankind—Muslims and non-Muslims alike—are subjected.

The fact that Islam is more a political ideology than a religion also explains why theology is not popular in Islam. Vermeulen points out that at al-Azhar, the teaching of philosophy is explicitly forbidden because it "leads the faithful astray from the right path of faith."[103] In Islam, theology and philosophy are widely rejected, as are rationalism and the spirit of free inquiry. These only lead to *fitna*, the Arabic word for a "test of faith" or "confusion." American scholar Daniel Pipes, director of the Middle East Forum, writes that "the adage 'better a 100 years of repression than a day of anarchy' sums up the dread of anarchy (*fitna*) that lies deep in Islamic civilization."[104]

Though at the time I was not familiar with the concept, I caused a lot of *fitna* on a 1994 visit to Iran. In those days, I was working as a policy advisor to the Dutch Liberal Party, or VVD. The Dutch embassy in Tehran arranged some meetings for me with local politicians, journalists, and academics. One Iranian official asked me to give a 30-minute talk at a Tehran school for diplomats and military cadets. I accepted on condition that I could speak freely. He agreed.

In my speech to those aspiring diplomats and officers, I strongly criticized Iran's human rights record. I also argued that the Iranian regime's policies were not in its people's best interests, which would be better served if Iran would drop its hostility toward the West and toward Israel. My listeners were outraged by my remarks; some stood up, gesticulating and shouting that I was a friend of the Great Satan (the U.S.) and the Little Satan (Israel). It was not a pleasant experience, but I wondered if my audience really believed the ridiculous slogans they yelled at me, or if the students simply thought they'd get good marks from their instructors by confronting a pro-American, Zionist visitor.

The following day, I was surprised to find I had made the front page of *Iran News*. That same morning, I had an appointment with the Director General of the Justice Department. Like the secret services, the army, and the Defense Ministry, the Justice Department is a stronghold of Iranian hardliners. Besides the Director General, three other Iranians attended the meeting. One of them, a short fat man, introduced himself as a judge. He clearly outranked the Director General, because when he screamed at me, the Director General did not interfere even though he was visibly annoyed. It was quite a performance; as I sat on a couch, the judge stood in front of me and shouted at me in English with a high-pitched voice, occasionally spitting. He said that I had insulted Iran and that my comments were intolerable. "If you ever again criticize our human rights record," he yelled, "I will have you experience the way we deal with human rights! I will make you an Iranian human rights expert!"

In light of the judge's threats, I returned to my hotel after the meeting and decided to leave the country at once. An embassy car took me to the airport, where embassy officials accompanied me to the gate. There I waited for almost ninety minutes as Iranian armed guards kept a close watch. They asked for my papers, looked at them, talked to each other in Farsi, and handed them back to me. This happened at least five times. Finally, I boarded my Iran Air flight and left for Istanbul, where I had to change planes on my way back to Europe. Upon arriving in Turkey, I literally kissed the ground, as if I were the pope.

Undeterred by that experience, I later made two more visits to Iran.

CHAPTER FIVE

The Yoke of Ishmael

But you must remember, my fellow-citizens, that eternal
vigilance by the people is the price of liberty, and that you
must pay the price if you wish to secure the blessing.

—Andrew Jackson

In 1981, after finishing high school, I decided to leave the Netherlands and discover the world.

I wanted to go to Australia. That country appealed to me. When I was a young boy I had read a book relating how Dutch navigator Willem Janszoon, aboard his ship the *Duyfken* (Little Dove), discovered Australia in 1606, and how Dutch explorers Dirk Hartog, Abel Tasman, and Willem de Vlamingh had made further voyages to New Holland (as Australia was called at the time) and Van Diemen's Land (present-day Tasmania).

My plan was to earn enough money to buy a one-way ticket to Australia and then find a job there, perhaps on a ranch in the outback. So I went to work at Kühne, a gherkin factory in Straelen, Germany, which was only three miles from our home in the border town of Venlo. My job was simple; I had to ensure that every jar of gherkins, which are a kind of cucumber, had the right weight by hitting the last gherkin into the jar. The salary was good, but that was the only nice thing about

Kühne. The factory was highly regimented, with German supervisors walking around in gray, brown, blue, or white jackets according to their rank. The higher ranks barked orders at those below them, and the lower ranks barked at me. At the end of the summer I quit.

Since I had not yet saved enough money for Australia, I decided to go to Israel, which was the only foreign country apart from Australia where I could legally work. I felt at home as soon as I landed at Ben Gurion Airport in Tel Aviv. The country's green, clean surroundings felt familiar. I was happy and relaxed, enjoying my first voyage on my own. I have since returned to Israel over fifty times, at least once a year, sometimes even three times. It always feels good to be back there.

I remember being surrounded by tourists, machine gun-toting Israeli soldiers, and an old lady with a concentration camp number tattooed on her arm during my first bus trip from the airport to Jerusalem, which in my opinion is the most beautiful city in the world. After six weeks, I ran out of money and went looking for a job. I did all sorts of things. I worked in a bread factory in Jerusalem, in a kibbutz and a moshav, and in a greenhouse where I loaded crates of flowers onto a truck. I also worked as a beekeeper and I worked on the land, harvesting bell peppers, eggplants, honeydew melons, grapes, and onions.

It's great to be a guest at a kibbutz, but I would never want to live there. I disliked the collectivism, and it didn't help that the kibbutz did not pay wages, just room and board. I worked for just one week at Yad Mordechai kibbutz near Ashkelon, on the border with Gaza, then stayed for half a year on the Tomer moshav, thirteen miles north of Jericho in the Jordan Valley, on the West Bank. While a kibbutz is a collective agricultural community, the farms in a moshav are individually owned, meaning that I got room and board in Tomer but also earned a few dollars. Working the fields near the Jordan River, I could see the Kingdom of Jordan on the other side. In fact, the Jordanian capital Amman was closer to the moshav than Jerusalem was.

Israeli border patrols often passed by, looking for armed Palestinians who occasionally infiltrated from Jordan. When there were nighttime infiltrations, the Israeli air force lit flares to illuminate the intruders, who were subsequently shot.

For a teenager this was all very exciting. But I did not realize that I was witnessing a skirmish on the frontline of a war that had been raging for fourteen centuries. It is the war between the jihadists of the *Umma* and the valiant defenders of the non-Islamic world. The heroes of this war form a long line, from Charles Martel to the army of Constantinople to John III Sobieski to the vigilant Israeli soldiers patrolling around the Tomer moshav.

After Muhammad's death in 632, the Muslims chose a leader in accordance with a command issued by their prophet: "*Bani Israel* (the children of Israel) were ruled over by the Prophets. When one Prophet died, another succeeded him; but after me there is no prophet and there will be caliphs and they will be quite large in number."[1] Named after the Arabic word *khalifa*, which means "successor," the Caliph was to replace Muhammad as the *Umma's* supreme leader, with all the powers of Muhammad but without the attributes of prophecy. The Caliph's duty was to maintain the realm of Islam and extend its power and territory, but he had no mandate to change the ideology.

The first three Caliphs—Abu Bakr, Umar, and Uthman—had been companions of Muhammad, early converts to Islam who had accompanied their prophet on his *hijra* from Mecca to Yathrib. The same goes for Ali ibn Talib, the fourth Caliph, who was Muhammad's paternal cousin and son-in-law. By the time of Ali's accession in 656, Islam's warriors had conquered all of north Africa, the Near East, and Persia. However, Ali was murdered in 661 and succeeded as Caliph by the son of Abu Sufyan, the erstwhile Quraishi leader who had initially opposed Muhammad but later surrendered Mecca to the Muslims. Abu Sufyan's son became the first Caliph of the Umayyad dynasty, which ruled the *Umma* until 750.

The murder of Ali and the accession of the Umayyads mark the great schism in Islam between Sunni and Shiite Muslims. Venerating Ali as a saint, the Shiites (from the Arabic word *shia*, meaning "faction") did not recognize the Umayyads. To this day they regard Ali as the first Caliph, disputing the legitimacy of his three predecessors because they had not been close blood relatives of Muhammad.

The Shiites are dominant in Iran and southern Iraq. They represent about 15 percent of all Muslims worldwide, while the Sunnis comprise most of the remaining 85 percent. The Shiites have religious leaders, called ayatollahs, who are a kind of Islamic bishop. There are no ayatollahs in Sunni Islam, which has no religious hierarchy, though the secular authorities in Islamic countries sometimes appoint a *mufti* ("wise civilian") or *sheikh* ("wise old man") as a spokesman for the religious community.

From the Umayyads, the Caliphate descended via the Abbasid and the Fatimid dynasties to the Turkish Ottoman dynasty. The Ottomans ruled over most of the Islamic world, including Arabia, until the end of World War I, when the victorious Allies dismantled their empire. On March 3, 1924, Turkish General Mustafa Kemal, alias "Atatürk" (Father of the Turks), abolished the Caliphate and founded the secular Republic of Turkey. "Islam, this theology of an immoral Arab, is a dead thing," declared Kemal.[2] He was wrong. Two days later the title of Caliph was claimed by Hussein bin Ali, the Emir of Mecca. In 1917, after the ousting of the Turks, he had become King of Hejaz, the province encompassing Mecca and Medina.

Hussein, a direct descendant of Muhammad, was the hereditary leader of the Banu Hashim, the Hashemite clan of the Meccan Quraishi tribe. By claiming the title of Caliph, he indicated that he aimed to unite all Muslims under his leadership. Hussein's claim, however, did not make much of an impression. Abdul Aziz Ibn Saud, a chieftain from the Arabian city of Riyadh, marched on Mecca, defeated Hussein, and annexed Hejaz to Saudi Arabia. Hussein fled to Palestine, where the British had installed his son Abdullah as emir of Transjordan. Later becoming King of Jordan, the cautious Abdullah wisely decided not to claim the Caliphate. Abdullah's great-grandson, Abdullah II, is the present Hashemite King of Jordan.

The Saudi kings did not claim to be Caliphs either, but since 1986 they have assumed the title of "Custodian of the Two Holy Mosques," realizing that the role of "Custodian" of Mecca and Medina is a traditional role of the Caliph.

The Saudis adhere to Salafism, a movement of Sunnis who attempt to live as much as possible like Muhammad and his earliest companions did, as described in the Koran and the Hadith. They are also called Wahhabists after Muhammad Ibn Abdul Wahhab, an eighteenth-century imam who helped establish the first Saudi state. Salafists/Wahhabists want to re-establish the universal Islamic Caliphate, though obviously not under the control of the rival Hashemites.

The Shiites, too, want to restore the Caliphate. They believe Ali's rightful line did not end with him but went underground. The Shiites are now awaiting an Islamic messiah, known as the "twelfth Caliph," or the *Mahdi*.[3] He is also called the "Hidden Imam," because he is said to have already been with them for centuries but that Allah has kept him hidden.

According to Shia eschatology, the *Mahdi* is a descendant of Muhammad and, together with Iesa (Jesus), he will reinstitute the Caliphate and reign for forty years. He will also wage war against Israel and eliminate the Jews. When Ayatollah Ruhollah Khomeini was at the pinnacle of his power in the early 1980s, many Shiites thought he was the *Mahdi* who would reunite all Muslims. Even some Sunnis hailed him as such.[4]

Many Muslims demand a new Caliphate because Muhammad himself ordered them to choose a single leader of the *Umma*. Muhammad was clear that the Muslims cannot have two rulers simultaneously: "When oath of allegiance [sic] has been taken for two caliphs, kill the one for whom the oath was taken later."[5] Abu Bakr, the first Caliph, warned that having two leaders would impede Muslim unity: "The Sunnah [the Way of Islam] would then be abandoned, the bida'a (innovations) would spread and Fitna [confusion, chaos] would grow, and that is in no one's interest."[6]

Many Islamic groups explicitly seek to re-establish the Caliphate. Some of these groups, such as Tablighi Jamaat (the Society for Spreading Faith, founded in 1866 in India),[7] Ikhwan al-Muslimin (the Muslim Brotherhood, founded in 1928 in Egypt),[8] and Hizb ut-Tahrir (the Party of Liberation, founded in 1953 in Jerusalem),[9] have branches in Western countries.[10] These organizations want to replace existing political institutions with a worldwide Caliphate.

The goal of uniting all Muslims worldwide, including those living in Western countries, under one political authority is a radical one. Yet "the caliphate is also esteemed by many ordinary Muslims," Karl Vick of the *Washington Post* noted. He explained, "Muslims regard themselves as members of the *umma*, or community of believers, that forms the heart of Islam. And as earthly head of that community, the caliph is cherished both as memory and ideal, interviews indicate."[11]

In short, the Caliph is the political and military leader of the *Umma* tasked with leading the "nation of Islam" in conquering the world and establishing a global Islamic state. This can be achieved by converting unbelievers through *dawa* (preaching),[12] but that is of secondary importance. Islam realizes that most non-Muslims will not voluntarily accept Islamic rule. Consequently, Islam admonishes pious Muslims to prepare themselves for jihad, the holy war to bring the whole world under Allah's domination.

That is the crux of Islam: it is an ideology of global war. It advocates the incorporation of the non-Islamic *Dar al-Harb*, or "House of War," into the *Dar al-Islam*, or "House of Submission," so that the former will cease to exist and the whole world, united under Muslim rule, will become *Dar al-Salam*, the "House of Peace." Note that *islam* (submission) and *salam* (peace) have the same verbal root, indicating that peace is only possible after the submission of the enemy to the army of Allah.

"It follows," wrote the Islamic scholar Majid Khadduri, professor of the Middle East Studies Program at Johns Hopkins University, "that the existence of a dar al-harb is ultimately outlawed under the Islamic jural order; that the dar al-Islam is permanently under jihad obligation until the dar al-harb is reduced to non-existence.... The universality of Islam, in all its embracing creed, is imposed on the believers as a continuous process of warfare, psychological and political if not strictly military."[13]

In 1939 Abul Ala Maududi, founder of the Pakistani Jamaat-e-Islami (Party of Islam), explained, "The objective of Islamic 'Jihad' is to eliminate the rule of an un-Islamic system and establish in its stead an Islamic system of state rule. Islam does not intend to confine this revolution to a single state or a few countries; the aim of Islam is to bring about a universal revolution."[14] Maududi, one of the most influential Salafist ideologues of the twentieth century, added that jihadists include not only those who actively fight for Allah, but everyone who helps them achieve their goal of worldwide Islamic domination: "In the jihad in the way of Allah, active combat is not always the role on the battlefield, nor can everyone fight in the front line. Just for one single battle preparations have often to be made for decades on end and the plan deeply laid, and while only some thousands fight in the front line there are behind them millions engaged in various tasks which, though small themselves, contribute directly to the supreme effort."[15]

Former New York City Mayor Ed Koch told Fox News in early January 2010, "Of course the vast majority of Muslims—there are 1.4 billion—are not terrorists, but there are hundreds of millions who are."[16] If one thinks of terrorists or jihadists as not just active fighters but also their supporters, one sees that Mayor Koch's message is largely the same as Maududi's seventy years ago.

Since Islam is bent on destroying our constitutional system and its attendant liberties, we should not extend to it the leeway that we allow religions in general. Indeed, we put all of Western civilization at risk if we fail to recognize Islam for what it really is: an aggressive enemy of freedom. As President Andrew Jackson proclaimed in his farewell address, "But you must remember, my fellow-citizens, that eternal vigilance by the people is the price of liberty, and that you must pay the price if you wish to secure the blessing."[17]

We must be vigilant. We should listen to the famous twentieth-century Swiss theologian Karl Barth, who wrote, "It is impossible to understand national socialism unless we see it in fact as a new Islam, its myth as a new Allah, and Hitler as this new Allah's prophet."[18] And we should listen to one of the great scholarly authorities on the Middle East, Professor Bernard Lewis, who compared Islam to another totalitarian ideology: "The traditional Islamic division of the world into the House of Islam and the House of War...has obvious parallels in the Communist view of world affairs.... The aggressive fanaticism of the believer is the same."[19]

We should not be deceived by the few aspects of Islam that resemble other religions. Instead, we must focus on the many dangerous threats this ideology poses to the entire world.

When I was in Israel, I made a lot of new friends—Israelis, Europeans, and Americans. One European friend was more interested in politics than I was. He asked the Israelis what they thought of the Arabs, and the Arabs how they felt about the Israelis. Afterward, he liked to mull over those conversations with me, asking, "Hey, Geert, did you hear what he said?" or "What do you think he meant?"

We both noticed that Israelis often had negative political opinions about Arabs, but they did not feel offended by the Arabs' mere existence. Even Israelis who had lost relatives to Arab terrorists had the same attitude. Obviously, the Israelis had a problem with terrorists, but they did not seem to have a problem with Arabs or Muslims *per se*. The Arab sentiment was different. When I visited Egypt, I was surprised to notice that even there, notwithstanding the Egyptians' immense kindness and generosity, the mention of Israel inevitably produced an outburst of vitriolic hatred. Their wrath was not confined to Israeli soldiers or politicians or to Israelis who had done them personal harm. No, this was hatred against all Jews, even children.

I never heard an Israeli talk that way about Muslims, but it was hard to find an Arab who spoke about Jews with anything but unconcealed contempt. Their views were encapsulated by a statement made by Muhammad Sayyid Tantawi, the Grand Sheikh of Cairo's al-Azhar University, who was President Obama's host during his Cairo visit. "All Jews are not the same," declared Tantawi. "The good ones become Muslims, the bad ones do not."[20] Tantawi, who died in March 2010, was generally considered a moderate by Western policymakers and media outlets despite his habitual anti-Jewish exclamations.[21] In another typical display, in 2002 he told a delegation of Palestinian Muslims they should intensify suicide attacks against Israelis "including children, women, and teenagers."[22]

I quickly learned during my first foray in the Middle East that it's better and safer to live as a Muslim in Israel than as a Jew in Egypt. Muslims in Israel have mosques, they have the right to vote, and they have representatives in the Knesset, the Israeli Parliament. Jews in Egypt and other Arab countries—though they have been living there for more than twenty-five centuries, almost twice as long as Muslims have inhabited the land of Israel—have virtually no rights at all.

The victimization of Jews in the Middle East is nothing new. In January 1915, the *New York Times* reported from British-controlled Egypt, "Nearly all the [7,000] Jewish refugees in Alexandria come from Jerusalem and other large towns [in Palestine]."[23] Indeed, the Jews of Palestine had long been persecuted by their Muslim neighbors, falling prey to pogroms in 1920, 1929, and 1936–39 that were organized by the British-appointed Grand Mufti of Jerusalem. The 1929 attacks included the murder of sixty Jews in Hebron, including women and children, whose families had lived in the area for centuries.

Sadly, the plight of Palestine's Jews was not unique; in 1912 and 1942 there were anti-Jewish pogroms in Morocco; in 1917, 1940, and 1941 in Tunisia; in 1933 and 1947 in Yemen; in 1934 in Algeria; and in 1936, 1941, and 1946–47 in Iraq. There were also pogroms in 1942 and 1945 in Libya,[24] where at the time a quarter of Tripoli's population was Jewish. Today, there is not a single Jew left there. One Jewish man returned to Tripoli in 2011 after Moamar Gaddafi was overthrown and tried to re-open an abandoned synagogue; he was quickly hounded out of the country by mobs that tried to storm his hotel room while carrying signs declaring, "There is no place for the Jews in Libya."[25] There were further pogroms in 1945 in Egypt; in 1945–47 in Syria; and in 1947 in Bahrain.[26] Jews had been indigenous to all these lands for hundreds of years before the Islamic conquest.

The birth of the modern state of Israel in 1948 provoked a shocking campaign of ethnic cleansing throughout the Islamic world, as Jews were expelled *en masse* from their homes and had their properties confiscated. In 1948, there were 75,000 Jews in Egypt and almost 1 million in the Arab countries combined, including more than a quarter million in

Morocco. Today, there are only 100 Jews left in Egypt and less than 8,000 in the entire Arab world, of whom just 6,000 remain in Morocco. It's a little-known fact that more Jews became refugees from Arab countries in 1948 than the estimated 710,000 Arabs who fled the newly created state of Israel that year.[27]

No one talks about the Jewish refugees anymore because they quickly made new lives for themselves in Israel, Europe, and America, even though many of them had arrived penniless. This is a relatively common phenomenon in recent history. The Germans who were expelled from the Sudetenland and the lands east of the Oder and Neisse rivers, the Greeks who were ejected from the Aegean coast of Anatolia, the Hindus who fled the Punjab—all of them resettled somewhere and started over. World War II produced 50 million refugees who began anew in different countries.

Today, all the refugee problems predating the 1950s have been solved with one exception: the Palestinians. Instead of granting citizenship to their fellow Arabs, Arab regimes in Lebanon, Syria, and elsewhere stripped Palestinian refugees of their basic rights and locked them into refugee camps. This created a permanent underclass of disenfranchised refugees who have been used for sixty years by their Arab rulers as pawns in the conflict with Israel.

The blame lies not just with the opportunistic Arab governments, but with the international community as well. According to international practice, the status of "refugee" or "displaced person" only applies to first-generation refugees—in other words, to a person who himself is actually displaced—but the United Nations makes an exception for Palestinians, who are defined as refugees even if they are descendants of refugees. Consequently, the number of so-called Palestinian refugees registered with the UN increased from just over 700,000 in 1950 to 5 million in 2011.[28]

This all comports with a strong characteristic of Islam: it nurtures resentment, passing it on from generation to generation. Islam still complains about the Crusades, as if France would still moan about the Hundred Years' War or America would seethe over the War of 1812. What's more, it's not just the actual victims of some supposed injustice who burn with resentment, but also people who live half a world away and were never, directly or indirectly, part of the original conflict, whether it be the Crusader conquest of Jerusalem in 1099 or the foundation of Israel in 1948.

Islam denounces Israel's Jews as usurpers—recent arrivals who stole the country from its rightful owners—and the *Umma* crudely falsifies history to justify Islam's exclusive claim to the land. Islam ignores or denies the Jews' nearly 4,000-year presence in the region, which continued to various extents even after the Romans' expulsion of most Jews from ancient Israel in 70 AD. In fact, contrary to popular belief, the only autonomous states that ever existed in the land of Israel were Jewish ones.

It is a cardinal belief of Islam today that Israelis stole the land of Palestine. In reality, the British partitioned the territory of the British Mandate for Palestine in 1922 into Cisjordan in the West and Transjordan in the East. The largest part, Transjordan, comprising 78 percent of the territory, was handed over to Hashemite strongman Abdullah ibn Hussein. In 1948, the United Nations partitioned the remainder—Cisjordanian Palestine—into a Jewish and an Arab part. Although the Jews accepted the tiny slice of land they were allotted, the Arabs rejected the UN ruling and invaded Israel in order to drive the Jews into the sea.

After the tiny, fledgling Jewish state defeated troops from approximately a dozen Arab nations plus Palestinian irregulars, the Arabs took revenge on the Jews in East Jerusalem and in the provinces of Judea and Samaria (the so-called West Bank), areas which the Arab forces retained after the war. All the Jews were evicted from these regions and all their synagogues were destroyed, including the ancient Hurva Synagogue in the Old City of Jerusalem. Those lands were then assigned to the Hashemite Kingdom of Transjordan, later known simply as Jordan. Notably, when the Israelis liberated these territories in 1967, they did not return the favor by systematically destroying mosques or expelling all the Muslim residents.

Following the 1967 liberation, Jewish settlers returned to Judea and Samaria. They turned barren land into flourishing fields, gardens, and orchards in places like Tomer, near age-old towns that bear the mark of millennia of continuous Jewish history, from 1500 BC until 1948. I respect these settlers. Their spirit is the spirit of the West, the spirit of the pioneers who settled America and spilt "their own blood...in acquiring lands for their settlement," as Thomas Jefferson wrote in 1774. These settlers, Jefferson noted, expended "their own fortunes...in making that settlement effectual; for themselves they fought...and for themselves alone they have right to hold."[29] That also applies to today's Israeli settlers, whom the international media, unthinkingly regurgitating Islamic propaganda, has unfairly demonized

This all explains why I always feel at home in Israel: it is animated by the same spirit that made Western civilization great—that of the soldier protecting the frontier and the pioneer settling the land. Israel is, indeed, a vital outpost of Western civilization. That is a big reason why Islam conditions the faithful to hate the Jewish state and to view its destruction as a religious imperative.

According to the Islamic doctrine of *tawhid*, or "Oneness," every country where even a single Muslim lives must be brought under Islamic rule; Muslims should not be ruled by infidels since, as the Koran says, "You [Muslims] are the best nation."[30] Islam also demands that every country that becomes part of *Dar al-Islam*, the "House of Islam," remain so forever. Finally, Islam demands that areas without any Muslims be brought under Islamic rule, because it is an insult to Allah that some countries are not ruled in his name.

Hence, Israel is a triple insult to Islam: it should be Islamic because the whole world belongs to Allah, because it has Muslim inhabitants, and because it was conquered by the *Umma* in 636. That last reason was stressed by Osama bin Laden, who demanded that every nation that has ever fallen to Islam return to Islam. In 1994 the al Qaeda leader declared, "The banner of jihad is raised up high to restore to our umma...every stolen Islamic land, from Palestine to Al-Andalus [Spain] and other Islamic lands that were lost."[31]

Consequently it is simply impossible for Islam to tolerate Israel's existence. There can be no compromise or accommodation. Israel is a thorn in the side of the Islamic body that must be destroyed.

Islam also regards Jewish control of Jerusalem as a mortal insult. Although it is claimed that the city is Islam's third holiest after Mecca and Medina, Islam's theological connection to Jerusalem is weak. The city is not mentioned anywhere in the Koran, in contrast to the hundreds of references to it found in the Bible. Furthermore, there is no proof that Muhammad ever set foot in Jerusalem, although it's possible he visited the city in his young, pre-prophetic days when he accompanied his wife Khadija's trading caravans to Syria.

Islam's theological claim to the city stems from a Koranic verse and various Islamic traditions relating that Muhammad once traveled from Mecca seated on *Buraq*, a winged horse with a woman's face, which took him to the *Masjid al-Aqsa*, or "the Farthest Mosque." From there, Muhammad ascended into heaven for an audience with Allah before the *Buraq* returned him to Mecca. The next morning, Muhammad told the Meccans he had taken a long journey on a winged horse with a woman's face. Unsurprisingly, the Meccans said he was crazy and complained about the absurd story to Abu Bakr, later the first Caliph, who simply replied that if Muhammad said it was true, it had to be true.

The Koran never specifies the location of the "Farthest Mosque," but Islamic traditions soon identified it as Jerusalem. However, there were no mosques in Jerusalem in 620, the year of Muhammad's supposed night visit. In fact, there weren't any mosques anywhere—the first mosque was built in Medina in 622.[32] Nevertheless, when the Arabs conquered Jerusalem in 636, they sought out the mythical "Farthest Mosque." Failing to find it, they proclaimed that it must have stood on the Temple Mount, the holiest site in Judaism, where the first two Jewish temples had been located.

Building the Al-Aqsa Mosque on the Temple Mount along with a shrine (the Dome of the Rock), the Muslims in typical Islamic fashion claimed the Jews' holiest site for themselves. The mosque was transformed into a church after the Crusaders liberated Jerusalem from Islamic rule in 1099, then back into a mosque after Saladin recaptured the city for Islam in 1187. When the Israelis finally liberated Jerusalem's Old City in 1967, they left the Temple Mount under Islamic rule, even enforcing a ban on prayer by non-Muslim visitors.[33] This, then, is the consequence of Muhammad's widely disbelieved story of visiting a non-existent mosque on a flying horse with a woman's face—1,400 years later, Israel prevents Jews from praying at their own holiest site.

Despite Israel's groveling to Islamic sensitivities in a manner that Islam does not reciprocate toward other faiths (non-Muslims are not even allowed to *enter* Mecca), the Jewish state's gestures have not made the *Umma* respect Israel. The mere fact that the Temple Mount, and indeed any part of Israel, remains under Jewish sovereignty is considered an unforgivable affront to Islam.

Just as Muhammad's revelation blamed the Muslims' loss in the Battle of Mount Uhud on their disobedience to him and their greed for loot, so too Islam attributes its string of humiliating military defeats by Israel to Allah's anger over Muslims' sinfulness. The *Umma* can only redeem itself by annulling the defeats with the blood of jihadi martyrdom. A negotiated two-state solution is out of the question.

Islamic regimes want the Palestinians to stay in refugee camps for generations until the agonizing stain of defeat has been atoned for with a final, decisive victory over Israel and the liquidation of the Jews there. I, on the other hand, would like to see these refugees permanently settled in their own homeland, so they can start anew. That's why I drew up a proposal to consider Jordan as the Palestinian homeland and to allow the "refugees" to voluntarily resettle there.[34] My suggestion was condemned throughout the Islamic world, including in Jordan,[35] despite the fact that as late as 1981 Jordan's King Hussein admitted that "Jordan is Palestine and Palestine is Jordan," and that in March 1971, the Palestine National Council stated that "what links Jordan to Palestine is a national bond...formed, since time immemorial, by history and culture."[36] What Islam demands for the Palestinians is not peace or freedom or opportunity, but *revenge* for the insult of losing to the Jews. Until the international community acknowledges this reality, all their peace proposals are doomed to failure.

Islam's militant zeal is evident in the jihadi warriors who regard Muhammad's blood-soaked life as the ideal example for all Muslims to emulate. The instructions they follow about how to wage war and what to do with their defeated enemies are found in the Koran, the Hadith, and the *Sira*. According to these traditions, in jihad the end always justifies the means. Terrorism, atrocities, betrayal, deception, deceit, assassination, and hostage-taking are all *halal* (permitted) because Muhammad himself set the "good" example. All this is explained extensively in the essential book *The Legacy of Jihad: Islamic Holy War and the Fate of Non-Muslims*, edited by Dr. Andrew Bostom.[37]

Muhammad and his followers gained many of their victories through deception. The Islamic principle of *taqiyya*—lying for the sake of Allah— allows a believer to conceal his true intentions in order to advance the cause of Islam.[38] Islam has used *taqiyya* since the seventh century to confound and confuse unbelievers. In Islamic jurisprudence, the use of *taqiyya* is regarded as a virtue and a religious duty. "None invents falsehoods save those who disbelieve the revelations of Allah; they alone are the liars," says the Koran.[39]

Taqiyya includes lying under oath in testimony before a court. Muhammad told his followers, "If I take an oath and later find something else better than that, then I do what is better and expiate my oath."[40] His wife Aisha recalled "that her father [Abu Bakr, the first Caliph] never broke his oath till Allah revealed the order of the legal expiation for oath."[41]

A favored *taqiyya* tactic is persuading the enemy that preparations for war are not aimed at him but at another target. Another common ruse is to deny there is any jihad at all. Yet another ploy is the *hudna*,[42] which is a deceptive truce, armistice, or peace agreement. If an enemy proves too strong for Islam, rather than continuing a war and suffering defeat, the *Umma* should conclude a truce with the infidels. The terms of this agreement are unimportant, since the faithful are obliged to violate it and resume hostilities once they have strengthened their forces and are capable of victory. The model is the ten-year truce Muhammad signed with the Meccans after his defeat at Mount Uhud, which he broke two years later when his army was strong enough to conquer Mecca.

Taqiyya also allows jihadists to take the shape of the enemy or assume whatever identity is necessary to fool the infidels. They are allowed to wear Western clothes, drink alcohol, eat during Ramadan or eat non-*halal* food, or even pretend to be Jews, Christians, or atheists, if the subterfuge is aimed at harming the infidels.

In one shocking, failed attempt at *taqiyya*, in 1986, Nizar Hindawi, a 32-year-old Jordanian of Palestinian origin, planted a bomb in the suitcase of his pregnant Irish fiancée, Ann-Marie Doreen Murphy, then sent her unknowingly to blow up an Israeli airline flight from London to Tel Aviv.[43] "Though one sickens and unequivocally condemns the method of revenge taking, the hatred and frustration that lay behind it can be understood," writer Mervyn Hiskett declared in a typical apologia for Palestinian savagery.[44] Somehow, I doubt the international media would show as much understanding if it were an Israeli who sent a pregnant woman on a plane to act as a human bomb.

It's important to understand that Islamic imperatives guide these terrorists' actions. During his trial, Mohammed Bouyeri, Theo van Gogh's assassin, argued that van Gogh's blood was *halal*. "We are talking about the fundamentals of Islam," he told the court. "There is no doubt that the blood of a kafir [infidel] is halal. That is obvious. It is written in the law [of Islam]. No-one can disagree with that. You will find this in the Koran and the Sunna.... The problem is that you are asking Muslims to disapprove of such an act. That is impossible, because then they would contradict the law."[45]

Bouyeri belonged to Hofstadgroep, a group of young Dutch jihadists from the Hofstad borough in The Hague, whose beliefs are exemplified in the following online exchange: "the government, ministries, police, etc., their blood and possessions are halal because they declare war on

Islam.... It is now allowed for me to slaughter every policeman, minister, soldier, officer."[46] Hofstad members studied al Qaeda videos of people being ritually beheaded, which they use as recruitment tools.

Hostage-taking is another ancient Islamic tradition. Hostages are seized either for ransom or to be used as human shields in battle. In 624, Muhammad captured prisoners in a raid on a Meccan caravan at Badr. He murdered the men and intended to sell the women back to their families. Muhammad's men asked permission to rape the hostages, suggesting coitus interruptus be practiced so the women could still be returned in their original condition, thus maximizing the possible ransom. But Muhammad told them not to worry about such trivialities: "There is no harm if you do not practice it, for every soul that is to be born up to the Day of Resurrection will be born."[47] Thus the Prophet condoned rape as well as hostage-taking.

Enjoying full religious sanction, Islamic zealots throughout history have committed unspeakably heinous atrocities against non-Muslims. "The Islamic conquest of India is probably the bloodiest story in history," wrote historian Will Durant. "It is a discouraging tale, for its evident moral is that civilization is a precious good, whose delicate complex order and freedom can at any moment be overthrown by barbarians invading from without and multiplying from within."[48] Indian historian K. S. Lal calculated that the population of India dropped from 200 million in 1000 AD to 170 million in 1500, with 60 to 80 million Indians dying as a direct result of jihad.[49]

While Islam still burns with indignation over the Crusaders' attacks, the *Umma* champions those who have slaughtered non-Muslims, claiming the atrocities demonstrate their devotion to the work of Allah. Mahmud (971–1030), Sultan of Ghazni, in present-day Afghanistan, had 50,000 Hindus slain near the Hindu temple of Somnath, which he destroyed. Muslims in Afghanistan, Iran, and Pakistan still celebrate Mahmud as a paragon of virtue and piety. His scribes relate how the Sultan went "on holy expedition." They described how "the Sultan zealous for the Muhammadan religion...stretched out...the hand of slaughter, imprisonment, pillage, depopulation, and fire.... Thus did the infidels meet with the punishment and loss due to their deserts. The standards of the Sultan then returned happy and victorious to Ghazni, the face of Islam was made resplendent by his exertions, the teeth of the true faith displayed themselves in their laughter, the breasts of religion expanded, and the back of idolatry was broken."[50]

Similarly, Alauddin Khilji (d. 1316), the Sultan of Delhi, beheaded infidels because, the Muslim chroniclers wrote, in him "the vein of the zeal of religion beat high for the subjection of infidelity." He fought "with a view of holy war, and not in the lust of conquest." He "kill[ed] and slaughter[ed] on the right and on the left unmercifully, throughout the impure land, for the sake of Islam."[51]

The Muslim traveler Ibn Battuta (1304–68) described how Sultan Ghiyasuddin of Madurai waged a horrific jihad in 1345. "In the morning, the Hindus who had been made prisoners the day before, were divided into four groups, and each of these was led to one of the four gates of the main enclosure. There they were impaled on the posts they had themselves carried. Afterwards their wives were butchered and tied to the stakes by their hair. The children were massacred on the bosoms of their mothers."[52]

Another great jihadist was Turko-Mongol conqueror Timur (1336–1405). He was an educated man who kept a diary relating how, following Muhammad's example, he led *razzias* against the infidels. "About this time there arose in my heart a desire to lead an expedition against the infidels, and to become a ghazi; for it had reached my ears that the slayer of infidels is a ghazi, and if he is slain he becomes a martyr," he wrote.[53] With great ferocity, Timur invaded Hindustan, aiming to slaughter everyone who refused to convert to Islam. He relates that he once had 10,000 prisoners decapitated in a single hour—"the sword of Islam was washed in the blood of the infidels"—and that on another occasion he had 100,000 prisoners killed in one day. The Bahmani Sultanate, a fifteenth-century kingdom in southern India that habitually massacred 100,000 Hindus each year, was small fry compared to Timur, whose descendants founded the Mughal Empire.

While Islam committed innumerable massacres as it swept through Asia and the Middle East, it should be noted that the Crusaders committed their own excesses in Palestine. But the difference is that Christians did not find sanction for their atrocities in Christian scripture; neither the Bible nor the example of Christ's life command Christians to kill unbelievers. The Koran and the example of Muhammad's life, however, do.

"Unlike Christianity, which preached a peace that it never achieved, Islam unashamedly came with a sword," British historian Steven Runciman wrote in his work *A History of the Crusades*.[54] Although Islam today ceaselessly professes its peacefulness to the West—and, ironically, threatens to kill those like me who say otherwise—it was not always so concerned with its image. For example, medieval Muslim historian and jurist Ibn Khaldun (1332–1406) wrote clearly about the unique aggression of Islam. "The holy war is a religious duty, because of the universalism of the [Islamic] mission and [the obligation to] convert everybody to Islam either by persuasion or by force," he argued. "Therefore, caliphate and royal authority are united, so that the person in charge can devote the available strength to [religion and politics] at the same time. The other religious groups [do] not have a universal mission, and the holy war [is] not a religious duty for them, save only for purposes of defense."[55]

The Jews of Palestine realized this uniqueness, too. Isaac ben Samuel of Acre (1270–1350), who lived under both Christian and Muslim rule, wrote in reference to a Talmudic verse, "Our rabbis of blessed memory have said, 'Rather beneath the yoke of Edom [Christendom] than that of Ishmael [Islam].' They plead for mercy before the Holy One, Blessed be He, saying, 'Master of the World, either let us live beneath Thy shadow or else beneath that of the children of Edom.'"[56]

Writing in 1630 about the Islamic Mughal Empire, Pieter van den Broecke, Director General of the *Vereenigde Oost-Indische Compagnie* (the Dutch United East India Company), voiced doubts whether an empire "won by so many crimes and the slaughter of so many innocent victims" could prosper.[57] Van den Broecke was perceptive; an Islamic society lives off the wealth created by others; its lords, or *pashas*, cannot live as parasites forever. By killing off the host society, they doom themselves—without *bida* (innovation), which Islam resolutely rejects, every society will fall sooner or later.

Van den Broecke's son Paulus became a nutmeg plantation owner on the Banda Islands in present-day Indonesia. The van den Broecke family continued to live on Banda for fourteen generations, until April 19, 1999, when jihadists armed with machetes cut the throats of five members of the family and burnt down their house.[58] The incident marked a bloody end to the van den Broeckes' 375-year presence on the islands.

There is no escape from the yoke of Ishmael. Two and a half years after the van den Broeckes discovered that fact on Banda, the United States too realized it on a sunny day in Manhattan.

CHAPTER SIX

Tears of Babylon

Those who deny freedom to others,
deserve it not for themselves.

—Abraham Lincoln

In 1957, two years after Egypt's government revoked her citizenship for the crime of being Jewish, a young woman and her parents fled Cairo for Britain, arriving as stateless refugees. Later gaining British citizenship through marriage, the woman studied history and adopted the pseudonym Bat Ye'or—"Daughter of the Nile"—under which she became the world's foremost expert on the history of non-Muslims living under Islamic rule.

It was her life experience that compelled her to write about this topic. According to Bat Ye'or, "I had witnessed the destruction, in a few short years, of a vibrant Jewish community living in Egypt for over 2,600 years.... I saw the disintegration and flight of families, dispossessed and humiliated, the destruction of their synagogues, the bombing of the Jewish quarters and the terrorizing of a peaceful population. I have personally experienced the hardships of exile, the misery of statelessness—and I wanted to get to the root cause of all this."[1]

In one of her books, Bat Ye'or describes the events surrounding the deaths of the five van den Broeke family members on Banda in 1999. At the turn of the century, jihadist warriors declared holy war on the majority Christian population of the Indonesian Moluccas (Maluku) Islands, to which the Banda Archipelago belongs. During 1999 and 2000, jihadists from Indonesia, the Philippines, Afghanistan, Pakistan, and Saudi Arabia attacked Christian villages, one after another, in a coordinated campaign.

Thousands were killed as the jihadists committed countless acts of savagery. Kids were tied together and dragged to their deaths behind speeding cars. Women and children were abducted. Masses of people were forced to convert to Islam. Both men and women were forcibly circumcised without painkillers or antiseptics. Those who resisted were beheaded. Half a million people fled as 40 percent of the Maluku capital, Ambon City, was reduced to ashes.[2]

The fate of Ambon City does not stand out in history—it is simply one of countless Islamic massacres going back to the time of Muhammad himself. It was his "revelations" and his example that laid the basis for Islam's eternal persecution of non-Muslims.

Barely eighty years after Muhammad's death, Muslim armies had subdued Persia, the Middle East, north Africa, Spain, and Portugal, bringing large numbers of Jews, Christians, and pagans under the authority of the rapidly expanding Caliphate. For the unbelievers, the Islamic conquest meant, first and foremost, their disenfranchisement, since citizenship in the Caliphate is reserved strictly for Muslims. In many places, immigrant Arab conquerors came to rule over indigenous majorities who no longer had any rights at all in their native lands. As Allah ordered, Muslims must be "ruthless to the unbelievers but merciful to one another."[3]

In no less than thirty-two passages, the Koran states that unbelievers are Allah's enemies or "shall become the fuel of hell;" in twenty-three passages the Islamic holy book advocates war against the infidels; and in ten places it forbids Muslims from befriending non-Muslims.[4] Islam offers most *kafirs* a simple choice: convert to Islam or die. For Jews and Christians—the so-called "people of the book"—there is a third option: they are allowed to accept the humiliating status of dhimmitude.

The word dhimmitude is derived from the Arabic word *dhimma*, related to the word for servitude. The dhimma is a "protection pact" in which Muslims agree to protect the lives and properties of Jews and Christians, known as "dhimmis," in return for the dhimmis' payment of the poll tax, the *jizya*.[5]

When Umar, the second Caliph, sent his troops to Mesopotamia in 636, he ordered them, "Summon the people to [Allah]; those who respond to your call, accept it from them, but those who refuse must pay the poll tax out of humiliation and lowliness. If they refuse this, it is the sword without leniency."[6] Umar acted in accordance with the Koranic verse, "Fight against such of those to whom the Scriptures were given...and do not embrace the true faith, until they pay tribute out of hand and are utterly subdued."[7]

As Umar indicated, the status of dhimma and the payment of the *jizya* were meant to degrade non-Muslims. Many unbelievers accepted these conditions because, at least in theory, subservient dhimmis were guaranteed a few fundamental protections, such as the right not to be slaughtered. However, Islam allows Muslims to revoke the dhimma pact at any moment. In his *History of the Jews*, Paul Johnson explains that many Jews from Islamic Spain and the Near East fled north into Christian territory because under Islam their right to practice their religion, and even their right to live, might be arbitrarily withdrawn at any time.[8]

Dhimmitude served an essential function in the Caliphate related to Islam's wariness of *bida* (innovation). Innovation, of course, is vital to technological progress, economic growth, and wealth creation. Because Islam generally condemns *bida* as something that risks diverting Muslims from the example of Muhammad, Islamic societies had problems creating their own wealth. But they needed to find *some* source of income, so they extorted *jizya* payments from non-Muslims. These taxes, in fact, were the Caliphate's most important source of income from its inception. Islamic rulers extracted them from non-Muslims with great ferocity and relentlessness, with punishments including torture and making relatives responsible for defaulters.

Although the Caliphate needed the dhimmis' special taxes, it treated
non-Muslims so badly that masses of them either fled or converted to
Islam in order to join the privileged, wealth-consuming class.[9] "The men
scattered, they became wanderers everywhere," an eighth-century monk
wrote about the fate of the dhimmis in Islamic Mesopotamia. "The fields
were laid waste, the countryside pillaged; the people went from one land
to another."[10] Under Islamic rule, the non-Muslim population also
declined because, according to Islamic law, when a Muslim man marries
a non-Muslim woman (the opposite is forbidden), the children have to
be raised as Muslims.[11] Thus, dhimmitude—the status of permanent
humiliation, degradation, and insecurity—led to the asphyxiation of
Christian and Jewish life in the Islamic world, consigning Islamic society
to poverty and backwardness, forcing it to constantly conquer new lands
in order to capture more economically productive dhimmis.

Reliant on forced *jizya* payments from ever dwindling numbers of
dhimmis, Islamic rule was parasitic and economically disastrous. Professor Bernard Lewis found that it even led to the near disappearance of the
wheel in the pre-modern Middle East. As Lewis explains, "A cart is large
and, for a peasant, relatively costly. It is difficult to conceal and easy for
requisition. At a time and place where neither law nor custom restricted
the powers of even local authorities, visible and mobile assets were a poor
investment."[12] Indeed, the fear of predatory Islamic authority impover-
ished much of the Middle East, north Africa, Anatolia, and Persia.

"The Muslims are not the sons but the fathers of the desert," Jean-
Claude Barreau, head of the French government bureau for international
migration, wrote in his 1991 book *De l'Islam en général et du monde
moderne en particulier* (On Islam in General and the Modern World in
Particular).[13] Calling the spread of Islam "one of the great catastrophes
in history," Barreau observed that wherever populations become Islamic,
agriculture collapses and the economy and science stagnate. In a textbook
example of punishing the messenger, the French government fired Barreau
for writing his book. Like Barreau, those who oversee the West's immigration policies know the truth but are not allowed to speak it.

Dhimmis who chose not to flee Islamic rule faced a wide range of incentives to convert to Islam. Some converted to end their own persecution and to eliminate the risk of themselves or their families being randomly enslaved or killed. Ambitious dhimmis also converted to gain access to the many trades and professions that were off-limits to non-Muslims. Furthermore, conversions occurred due to Islam's prohibition on dhimmis testifying against Muslims; in Islam, non-Muslims always lose their court case to Muslims unless the unbelievers themselves become Muslims.[14]

Of course, dhimmis also converted to escape the crushing tax burden imposed on non-Muslims. Officially, the *jizya* no longer exists in Islamic countries, though Islamic extremists sometimes extort money from non-Muslims and defend the crime as a form of *jizya*.[15] But other traditional restrictions on dhimmis persist today, including the Islamic prohibition against the proselytizing of Christianity or Judaism to Muslims. In Morocco, Christians are free to practice their religion, but converting Muslims to another religion is punishable by up to three years in prison.[16] This is not some arcane legal technicality, but an actively enforced law. In March 2010, sixteen Dutch and American citizens who ran an orphanage in Morocco were deported for allowing children to read from a children's Bible. These were "stories of Noah and the Ark and Jonas and the whale. Stories that appear in the Koran as well," said Herman Boonstra, one of the expelled Dutchmen, who added that the children "got Koran lessons all the same." Nevertheless, the Moroccan government announced that it would "continue to take stern action against everyone belittling religious values."[17] In light of these events, the dhimmified Catholic and Evangelical churches of Morocco issued a joint statement denouncing the "deplorable" activities of the deported Christians.[18]

Islam is always finding new, creative ways to humiliate non-Muslims, providing yet another incentive for dhimmis to convert. The Caliphate's dhimmis had to allow Muslims into their house whenever Muslims demanded. They were not allowed to carry arms or ride horses or mules. They had to wear identifying badges (though they were banned from wearing their own religious symbols) and refrain from dressing like a

Muslim.[19] A dhimmi was also forbidden from employing Muslim servants. In 1880 in Entifa, Morocco, draconian punishment was meted out to an elderly Jewish man who hired a poor Muslim woman to work for him and his wife: he was nailed to the ground and beaten to death, his property was confiscated, and the Jewish community had to pay a ransom to retrieve his corpse for burial.[20]

Jews indeed met a grim fate under Islamic rule, despite the popular myth today that the Caliphate was a beacon of religious tolerance. A Jewish document of 1121 describes how a Jew in Baghdad had to wear "two yellow badges...a piece of lead weighing [3 grammes] with the word *dhimmi* on it [and] a belt around his waist. The women have to wear one red and one black shoe and have a small bell on their necks or shoes.... The vizier appointed brutal Muslim men to supervise the [Jews] and hurt them with curses and humiliations.... The Moslems were mocking the Jews and the mob and youths were beating them up in all the streets of Baghdad."[21]

Seven hundred years later, not much had changed. William Shaler, the American consul general in Algiers from 1816 to 1828, wrote that the Jews of Algiers, who constituted a quarter of the city's population, were "a most oppressed people; they are not permitted to resist any personal violence of whatever nature, from a Mussulman; they are compelled to wear clothing of a black or dark colour.... They are pelted in the streets even by children.... They learn submission from infancy, and practice it throughout their lives.... It appears to me that the Jews at this day in Algiers constitute one of the least fortunate remnants of Israel existing."[22]

In 1854, Karl Marx wrote in the *New York Daily Tribune* about the plight of the Jews in Jerusalem. The city's population numbered 15,500 souls, he wrote, comprising 3,500 Christians, 4,000 Muslims, and 8,000 Jews. "Nothing equals the misery and the sufferings of the Jews at Jerusalem," Marx said. "[They are] the constant objects of Mussulman oppression and intolerance...living only on the scanty alms transmitted by their European brethren."[23] Islam subjected Christians to similar humiliation. In 1909, the British vice consul in Mosul, Iraq, noted that "almost any Christian submissively makes way even for a Moslem child."[24]

Some of the classic restrictions against dhimmis were outlined in the seventh-century "Pact of Umar," in which Caliph Umar demanded that Syrian Christians meet numerous conditions in exchange for his "protection."[25] One of these conditions was a ban on renovating churches—if their churches collapsed, Christians were not allowed to rebuild them. The Pact of Umar is reproduced on various Islamic websites today and is still taken seriously by some.[26] Notably, on September 30, 2011, after attending Friday prayers at local mosques in the village of Elmarinab, Egypt, an Islamic mob destroyed St. George's church because it was being renovated.[27]

Having faced harsh discrimination ever since the seventh-century Islamic conquest, Jewish communities in the Middle East were all but wiped out after World War II. Christians have fared slightly better under Islam, but not by much; until the end of the eleventh century, half the Christians in the world lived under Islamic rule.[28] Christians remained a majority in Egypt and Syria until the thirteenth century, but now they're a small minority in both countries. In Turkey, 30 percent of the population was still Christian in the early 1900s, but that community was devastated when the Turks massacred 1.5 million Armenians in the genocide of 1915, expelled 1.5 million more from Asia Minor in the early 1920s, and chased out 130,000 from Istanbul through the anti-Greek pogrom of 1955. In Iraq, the Christian population has shrunk from 2.5 million to 1.5 million just in the last decade due to violent attacks and intimidation by Islamic terrorists.[29]

Whenever Islam becomes empowered, the non-Muslim population suffers. That's something to keep in mind as Islam relentlessly expands throughout the West.

The *jizya* was not the only—or even the worst—dhimmi tax. In the Balkans and in Greece, the Ottoman Turks levied a blood tax, the so-called *devshirme*, or boy tribute. Every three years an Ottoman tribute officer visited Christian villages to select the strongest and smartest male children. The most talented and promising boys were forcibly taken from their families, converted to Islam, and enrolled for service in the administration of the Ottoman Empire. Other times they were conscripted into the army, where they formed the Janissary regiments that were used to subdue the communities from which the boys were stolen.

Janissaries were allowed to marry. Since no one who was born Muslim could be enslaved, however, their own sons were barred from joining the regiments, which constantly had to be replenished with new slave boys. As a result, the boy tribute forced Christian communities such as the Balkan Slavs, Albanians, and Greeks to surrender about one-fifth of their own sons. A dhimmi family could only prevent the theft of its sons by converting to Islam.

"The boy tribute fulfilled the logic of an empire geared for war," writes historian Jason Goodwin. "Just as war booty financed the next assault, so the borderlands could be made to furnish the men who, being raised to perfection in the capital, were turned out again to rule the empire and to expand the frontiers of the state."[30] Although the Ottomans put their own stamp on this system, the basic practice was not their invention; Islamic nations used slave armies from the ninth century until as late as the mid-1800s. In 1863, Mohammed Said Pasha, the Ottoman viceroy of Egypt, sent an army of Sudanese slaves to Mexico at the behest of French Emperor Napoleon III.[31]

As the number of tax-paying dhimmis dropped, slavery became crucial to the Caliphate's economy. Here, too, a continuous supply of new slaves was needed because, like the Janissaries, the slaves were forcibly converted to Islam, meaning their children were born Muslims and could not be enslaved. In most cases, however, Muslims ensured their slaves had no children by castrating them. The Janissaries were spared this fate because the Ottomans believed castration weakened their fighting ability.

Tropical Africa was the principal area for procuring the Caliphate's slaves. Muslims dominated that continent's slave trade, including in West Africa, where Muslims sold slaves to Europeans who shipped them to the Americas.[32] By contrast, in Western Europe, with the exception of Islam-occupied Spain, slavery had largely disappeared by the end of the fifteenth century. The re-conquest of Spain, however, reacquainted Europeans with the wretched institution.[33] In the following decades and centuries, as the Spaniards, followed by other European nations, began to colonize the New World, they shipped millions of African slaves across the Atlantic Ocean. Most of these slaves were purchased from Arab raiders in West Africa.[34]

The bulk of Africa's slaves was sent to the Islamic world. In the ninth century, half the population of lower Iraq consisted of *Zanj*, or black slaves. They worked in saltpeter mines around Basra and on sugar cane plantations in the marshlands of the Tigris and Euphrates delta. The largest slave rebellion in history happened in southern Iraq between 868 and 883. Involving over 500,000 black slaves, the revolt lasted fifteen years until it was finally suppressed by large Arab armies. Unlike the rebellion of Spartacus, which involved a comparatively small group of 120,000 slaves and took the Roman Empire just three years to subdue, the massive Zanj Rebellion against the Abbasid Caliphate has not attracted the attention of Hollywood, though it is a tale of great sacrifice and heroism.

Today, nearly two million of Iraq's 27 million people are blacks. Widely overlooked by the international media, they have hardly any political representation, suffer severe job discrimination, and are reportedly forced to sit in the back of school classrooms and banned from marrying Arab girls. They say they are "still seen as slaves,"[35] and some even claim that sheiks still keep blacks as slaves today.[36] When Barack Obama was elected president, this oppressed minority hoped he would speak out on their behalf.[37] In his Cairo speech, however, Obama only referenced the past oppression of American blacks, not the current oppression of blacks in the Islamic world.

American author Thomas Sowell, himself a descendant of slaves, notes an interesting anomaly: "Although the Islamic countries of the Middle East and North Africa imported more slaves from sub-Saharan Africa than did the European off-shoot nations of the Western Hemisphere, there are in those Moslem countries today no such large, discrete and self-conscious groups of black African descent as the 60 million

Negroes currently living in the Western Hemisphere." He explains, "What is known, is that there was an extremely low reproduction rate among the Africans enslaved in the Moslem countries."[38]

This was largely because Islamic slave masters suppressed both marriage and sex among slaves.[39] They also castrated hundreds of thousands of black boys and men in a gruesome procedure that killed an estimated 90 percent of those subjected to it. In this operation, a slave's testicles and penis were swept off with a single cut of a sickle; a tin or wooden spigot was set in the urethra; and the wound was cauterized with boiling oil and bandaged. Unable to relieve himself, the victim suffered intense pain for three days before the bandage and spigot were removed. If the sufferer could then relieve himself, he was typically out of danger; if he could not, he was usually doomed to an agonizing death from a burst bladder.[40]

This kind of male genital mutilation was confined to slaves. In contrast, female genital mutilation (sometimes called FGM, cliterodectomy, or female circumcision) was—and still is—widely performed on Muslim girls. The procedure, which involves cutting out the clitoris, was sanctioned by Muhammad, though he thoughtfully ordered Muslims not to cut off the *whole* clitoris. "Do not cut severely as that is better for a woman and more desirable for a husband," he said.[41]

Eunuchs brought far higher prices than other slaves in the Caliphate. The tenth-century court of the Caliph in Baghdad included 7,000 black eunuchs and 4,000 white ones.[42] Because the blacks were "clean-shaven," meaning they lacked all genitalia, they served in the harem. The whites, who had their testicles removed but retained their penis, served in the administration or in other places away from women. Thus, most of the key elements of the Caliphate, from its finances to its economy to its military to its governmental administration, relied on slavery.

The cruel fate of many blacks in the Caliphate was connected to the inveterate racism that has always run deep in Islamic societies. This was demonstrated in the writings of many Islamic historians. For example, Al-Masudi (896–956), one of early Islam's pioneering historians, wrote that Sudanese have "kinky hair, thin eyebrows, broad noses, thick lips, sharp teeth, malodorous skin, dark pupils, clefty hands and feet, elongated penises and excessive merriment.... Surely the dark complexion person is overwhelmed by merriment due to the imperfection of his brain; therefore, his intellect is weak."[43] Similarly, Ibn Qutayba (828–89), a renowned Islamic scholar from Baghdad, argued that blacks "are ugly and misshapen, because they live in a hot country. The heat overcooks them in the womb." (Qutayba contrasted blacks with Europeans, who he claimed "are undercooked in the womb.")[44] Persian philosopher Nasir al-Din al-Tusi (1201–74) remarked that "the ape is more teachable and more intelligent than the Zanji [blacks]." Ibn Khaldun (1332–1406) from Tunis, widely considered the greatest Islamic scholar of all time, wrote that "the Negro nations are, as a rule, submissive to slavery because [Negroes]...are quite similar to...dumb animals."[45]

The *Umma* took white slaves, too, who were stolen by Islamic pirates from ships in the Mediterranean and the Atlantic. This included 130 American seamen seized in the Atlantic between 1785 and 1793. They also raided European coastal areas, depopulating towns from Sicily to Cornwall.[46]

One notorious seventeenth-century Islamic pirate was Murad Reis. Previously known as Jan Jansen van Haarlem, Reis was a Dutch sailor, born in Haarlem near Amsterdam, who had been captured by the Barbary pirates. He subsequently converted to Islam and became a steersman of Sulayman Reis, another Dutchman who had converted to Islam and become a Barbary pirate. Sulayman began his career as a corsair under yet another Dutch pirate who worked for the Bey of Algiers.[47]

In July 1627, Murad Reis raided Iceland and kidnapped 242 men, women, and children. On the way back, he captured a Dutch vessel and seized more unfortunates destined for servitude in the Islamic world. On June 20, 1631, Reis and his crew of Dutch, Algerian, and Turkish pirates attacked the village of Baltimore on the southwest coast of Ireland, where they captured 108 people.[48] The event was memorialized in the poem "The Sack of Baltimore" by the early nineteenth-century Irish poet Thomas Osborne Davis, who wrote,

The yell of "Allah!" breaks above the prayer, and shriek,
and roar: O blessed God! the Algerine is lord of Baltimore![49]

★   ★   ★

Influenced by the Scottish Enlightenment, Anglo-Saxon philanthropists such as William Wilberforce (1759–1833) created the abolitionist movement in the late eighteenth century to free slaves and end the slave trade. The forces of slavery soon found determined foes throughout the West, especially the British Empire, which banned the slave trade in 1807 and employed the might of the British Navy to fight it.[50] Before it plunged into a civil war partly sparked by revulsion at the slave trade, the United States waged two naval wars against the Barbary pirates in Morocco, Algeria, Tunisia, and Libya. In 1816, the British and the Dutch navies shelled Algiers to dissuade it from attacking non-Muslim vessels and to force it to free Christian slaves. In 1830, with wide Western support, France decided to invade, occupy, colonize, and annex Algeria in order to exterminate piracy in the Mediterranean.

Western abolitionist pressure forced the Ottoman Empire to shut down the slave market in Istanbul, the world's largest. It was officially closed in 1847, but it simply moved underground, where it endured with the tacit permission of the Ottoman authorities.[51] Ottoman slavery ended only after the empire was abolished and Atatürk established the secular Turkish state.

When the British colonized Sudan in the late nineteenth century, they cracked down on the slave trade and put a stop to the widespread castration of black youths by Arabs. Despite their best efforts, however, the British never could completely eradicate Arab slave dealing, which resumed immediately after Sudan's decolonization in 1956.[52]

In the early 1960s, author Sean O'Callaghan toured slave markets throughout the Horn of Africa and the Middle East. In Djibouti he saw ten naked boys "and I saw with horror that five had been castrated. The [slave dealer] said that usually 10 per cent of the boys are castrated, being purchased by Saudi homosexuals, or by Yemenis, who own harems."[53] In Yemen, O'Callaghan witnessed a girl being punished for attempting to escape from the harem. "Punishment was administered by a eunuch, a huge powerful Negro who seemed to enjoy his task. 70 lashes were given.... The eunuch often has his penis removed as well as his testicles."[54]

In Saudi Arabia, O'Callaghan visited a slave auction in the supposedly holy city of Mecca. "As the next slave was led in, a murmur of excitement went up among the buyers.... He was a slender boy of about 12 years old with beautiful classical Arab features.... There is an old saying among the Bedouin: A goat for use, a girl for enjoyment, but a boy for ecstasy."[55] The fact that pedophilia is widely condoned in Islamic culture is unsurprising, considering Muhammad had sex with Aisha when she was nine. And the prophet's example has been followed long after his death, as O'Callaghan discovered. "We tell the girls from a very early age that they are made for love," a Djibouti slave dealer told him. "At age nine we let them practice with each other, and a year later with the boys."[56]

Slavery still persists today across the Islamic world, especially in the former French colonies of Islamic West Africa. The French were unable to snuff out the institution, and the post-colonial regimes were clearly unwilling to do so. Mauritania officially abolished slavery in 1981, but it still exists, with slaves regarded as "domesticated animals."[57] In Chad, children abducted by Islamic raiders are forced to abandon their native language and Christian religion for Arabic and Islam.[58] In Niger, almost 8 percent of the population is estimated to be slaves.[59] In Mali, a reporter for the National Geographic Society bought two slaves in 2002 in order to free them.[60] Overall, slavery is so prevalent today that slaves are now cheaper than ever before in history. Dr. Kevin Bales, an expert on modern slavery, calculated that the enslaved fieldworker who cost the equivalent of $40,000 in 1850 costs on average less than $100 today, with some as cheap as $5 or $10.[61]

Many Americans may not know that some of their fellow countrymen today are former slaves—not descendants of slaves, but former slaves themselves. Take Sudanese-born Simon Deng, a lifeguard at Coney Island. Born in 1957 in a Christian village of southern Sudan, Deng spent several years as a slave before escaping to America. "When I was nine years old, my village was raided by Arab troops in the pay of Khartoum," he recalls. "As we ran into the bush to escape I watched as childhood friends were shot dead and the old and the weak who were unable to run were burned alive in their huts. I was abducted and given to an Arab family as a 'gift.'... I lived as a slave for several years. I was beaten time and time again for no reason at all—even the whim of my 'master's' children could produce these beatings. I was subjected to harsh labor and indignities of every sort."[62]

It's unlikely slavery will disappear from the Islamic world in our lifetimes, if ever. It's an intrinsic part of Islam sanctioned by Muhammad himself. As Sheikh Saleh Al-Fawzan, a member of the Senior Council of Clerics, Saudi Arabia's highest religious body, proclaimed in 2003, "Slavery is part of jihad, and jihad will remain [as] long there is Islam."[63]

In Islam's petro-states, foreign guest workers ranging from *au pairs* to manual laborers often work in slave-like conditions. Consider this report on Saudi Arabia from the U.S. State Department's Trafficking in Persons Report of June 2011:

> Saudi Arabia is a destination country for men and women subjected to forced labor.... Men and women from Bangladesh, India, Sri Lanka, Nepal, Pakistan, the Philippines, Indonesia, Sudan, Ethiopia, Kenya, and many other countries voluntarily travel to Saudi Arabia as domestic servants or other low-skilled laborers, but some subsequently face conditions indicative of involuntary servitude, including nonpayment of wages, long working hours without rest, deprivation of food, threats, physical or sexual abuse, and restrictions on movement, such as the withholding of passports or confinement to the workplace. Recent reports of abuse include the driving of nails into a domestic worker's body.
>
> ... Women, primarily from Asian and African countries, were believed to have been forced into prostitution in Saudi Arabia; others were reportedly kidnapped and forced into prostitution after running away from abusive employers.... Saudi Arabia made limited progress in protecting victims, but

its overall efforts remained inadequate during the reporting period.... As a result, many victims of trafficking are likely punished for acts committed as a result of being trafficked. Under Saudi law, foreign workers may be detained, deported, or in some cases, corporally punished for running away from their employers.... Women arrested for prostitution offenses face prosecution and, if convicted, imprisonment or corporal punishment, even if they are victims of trafficking.[64]

Although the international media rarely reports on the plight of these poor souls, some journalists took note when south Asian workers in Dubai, UAE, went on strike and even rioted in March 2006 and October 2007. The strikes provoked some rare reporting on the conditions these workers endure: they toil twelve hours a day for $4, often in hazardous conditions with a high risk of injury and death, as they build the city's skyscrapers, luxury homes, shopping malls, artificial islands, indoor ski resorts, and airport terminals. Dubai's "guest workers" are housed in dismal conditions, their pay is often withheld, and their employers sometimes confiscate or "lose" their passports to stop them from returning home.[65]

Western countries are increasingly confronted with this kind of exploitation on their own soil. In 2004, a Saudi couple in Aurora, Colorado, was arrested for keeping a 24-year-old Indonesian woman as their slave. For four years, when the woman was not working, the couple kept her locked in an unheated basement with just a mattress. When she was allowed out of her hovel, she had to cook, clean, care for the children, perform sex acts on her master, and was sometimes loaned out to other families.[66]

In July 2008, Belgian police liberated fourteen girls kept as slaves for eight months by an Arab royal family who had rented an entire floor of a luxury hotel in Brussels. The royals had confiscated the passports of their slaves—who came from the Philippines, India, Egypt, Turkey, Iraq, Morocco, and Syria—upon their arrival in Belgium. Police intervened after four girls attempted to escape; three of them were captured by their masters' security staff, but the fourth managed to alert the authorities.

Though most of the fifty-three rooms on the hotel floor were empty, the slaves had to sleep on the hallway floor. They were given almost nothing to eat and frequently burned their hands bringing their masters hot coffee, which they had to carry in cups without saucers.[67]

In February 2010, Bandar Abdulaziz, the servant of another royal Arab family, was found strangled to death in a hotel in central London.[68] Eight months later, a British court convicted an Arab prince of the murder. Britain's *Guardian* reported, "The court had heard that the murder of Abdulaziz was the final act in a 'deeply abusive' master-servant relationship in which the prince carried out frequent attacks on his aide 'for his own personal gratification.' Jurors were told that by the early hours of 15 February, Abdulaziz was so worn down and injured—having suffered a 'cauliflower' ear and swollen eye from previous assaults—that he let [the prince] kill him without a fight."[69]

A former top London hotelier told the *Sunday Times* that the crime reminded him of a disturbing event a few years earlier: "Soon after a relative of the king of Saudi Arabia took over the sixth floor…a man working in the loading bay called me to say that there was a Moroccan girl curled up in a ball underneath the desk in a nearby office…. In broken English the girl told me she had been travelling round the world with the Saudi prince for the past two years and was the personal slave of a princess [who] had whipped her…. When she lifted her blouse to show me her back, it was like a scene from a horror movie. There were five or six long slashes and underneath the wounds were old scars."[70]

Slavery has always existed in Islamic societies and it continues to exist in many Islamic nations today. Islam does not and *cannot* apologize for slavery, nor can it abolish the institution, because the Koran allows the faithful to enslave their enemies.[71] Moreover, the Koran condones sex slavery by granting men sexual access to "what their right hands possess" (meaning female captives or slaves) and to "the slave girls whom Allah has given you as booty."[72] Thus, admitting that slavery is morally wrong would be tantamount to acknowledging the fallibility of the Koran, which is impossible since Allah himself supposedly wrote it.

Moreover, Muhammad, the perfect man whose example all Muslims must follow, was a slave trader who owned many slaves, including female concubines such as Mary the Copt. He bought some of them, received others as presents, and seized still others as war booty. Some he kept, some he sold, and some, such as Mary's sister Shirin, he gave to others as gifts. When a woman told Muhammad she had freed her slave girl, he told her she would have been better rewarded if she had given the girl to one of her uncles.[73]

Islamic apologists refer to Koranic verses that instruct Muslims to treat their slaves well, such as sura 24:34, which tells Muslims not to force their female slaves into prostitution. However, while a Muslim is not permitted to earn money by letting other men have sex with his slave, the Koran allows *him* to have sex with her as much as he likes (suras 23:5–6, 33:50, 70:29–30).

The Koran also teaches that Allah will reward those who free a slave.[74] On the website Answering Islam, Silas, a former Muslim, sardonically describes how this injunction is often observed: "As the slaves get too old to perform service or sexually satisfy their masters, their masters 'manumit' [free] the slaves. Now, aged, worn out, they are put out on the streets to fend for themselves. Their former owner has committed a great, righteous act in freeing a slave! He gets rid of the burdensome slave, and gets a bonus in heaven. What a religion!"[75]

Although the West was responsible for ending the slave trade in much of the world, Western nations bow to endless demands to apologize for their prior participation in slavery, and for the racism and "Islamophobia" that allegedly plague our societies. The Organization of Islamic Cooperation (OIC) and its "Islamophobia Observatory" are especially critical of the West; as detailed in chapter seven, their current goal is to criminalize any criticism or satire of Islam worldwide. The Islamic world hurls these accusations and makes these demands even as slavery is found, to this very day, within its own borders, and as the most virulent racism still permeates much of the Arab world.

CHAPTER SEVEN

Survival

Our goal is not the victory of might,
but the vindication of right.

—John F. Kennedy

After the fall of Mecca in January 630 AD, Islam took over a third of the known world in less than two centuries. Sealing Europe off from the south and southeast, Islam became an impregnable rock, its adherents confident of their cultural superiority and military invincibility. The Crusaders' re-conquest of Jerusalem in 1099, however, caused *fitna* (confusion), and had a lasting impact on the collective memory of the *Umma*, the worldwide Islamic community.

Nevertheless, the Crusaders' victory proved short-lived, as Saladin recaptured Jerusalem for Islam in 1187. This brought a new impetus to Islamic expansion, culminating in the fall of Constantinople in 1453—a cataclysmic event for Christianity. Three years later, a 70-year-old Roman Catholic monk, the Italian John of Capistrano, helped stop the invading Ottomans at Belgrade. But the Christians could not resist the rising tide of Islam for long; in 1521, Belgrade fell to the Ottomans, and Serbia and Hungary were overrun.

Islam encountered a new setback in 1571, when Don Juan of Austria, commander of a united navy comprising Spain, Venice, Genoa, and the Knights of Malta, defeated the Ottoman fleet at Lepanto, off the coast of Greece. The victory at Lepanto was an omen, for the Muslims were defeated there by the West's superior naval and military technology.

The tide turned definitively against Islam at the gates of Vienna on September 11, 1683, when Polish King John III Sobieski—with only 84,000 men (Austrians, Germans, Poles, Lithuanians, Ukrainians, and Italians) and 152 cannon—defeated a vastly larger Ottoman army of 300,000 troops, 20,000 Janissaries, and 300 heavy cannon. In a sense, the fateful date of 9/11, 1683 marked the end of the 1,000-year reign of Islam. A thousand years of darkness seemed to draw to a close. The lack of innovation—the *bida* that Islam dreaded—and the near-disappearance of the wealth-creating dhimmi population that sustained the *Umma* had exhausted and depleted Islam.

The following 250 years were catastrophic for the *Umma*. The entire Islamic world except for contemporary Turkey, Iran, Afghanistan, and Saudi Arabia fell to the infidels. A tiny part of the *Umma* even briefly came under American rule. From 1899 until 1913, the U.S. Army fought the Moro Rebellion on the Philippine island of Mindanao, where Muslims (or *Moros*) form a third of the population. When the *Moros* resorted to suicide attacks, the Americans did not profess their immense respect for Islam or marvel about Islam's contributions to world civilization. No, they adopted a different approach—they wrapped dead jihadists in pig skin and stuffed their mouths with pork. Since pigs are anathema in Islam, the *Moros* were convinced that this "unspeakable defilement" would prevent the Islamic "martyrs" from entering paradise.[1]

The outlook was bleak for Islam as its lands fell to Russia, Britain, France, Italy, Spain, and the Netherlands. Given that the Koran insists Islam is the "best nation" and that Allah has vowed to protect it, in the Islamic view, this was not supposed to happen. And yet, it did. When all seemed lost, however, Allah saved Islam, orchestrating what in Islamic eyes must look like two miraculous events: the outbreak of the French Revolution and the West's development of an unquenchable thirst for oil.

The French Revolution was a huge jolt, setting in motion events that ultimately raised the *Umma* out of its lethargy. French revolutionary troops, led by General Napoleon Bonaparte, invaded Egypt in 1798 for the greater glory of the French state and its geopolitical goal of building a canal as a gateway to India. The arrival of the French revolutionaries revamped Islam at a crucial moment when its resources were diminishing due to its lack of innovation, the decline of its dhimmi population, and dwindling influxes of new slaves.

Napoleon's invasion of Egypt was the first major European penetration into the heart of Islamic territory since the Crusades seven centuries earlier. Upon his arrival in Alexandria on July 1, 1789, Napoleon issued a proclamation. "People of Egypt, they tell you that I have come to destroy your religion; do not believe them," he declared. "I respect God, his Prophet and the Koran." He added, referring to the French army, that "the French, too, are true Muslims. Proof of this is that they went to Rome and overturned the government of the Pope, who always pressed Christians to wage war against Muslims. Next they went to Malta and destroyed the Knights who claimed that God ordered them to go to war against Muslims."[2]

Napoleon's words impressed less than his deeds. The French general crushed the Egyptian army, exposing the weakness of Islamic rule. This came as a blow to young Muslims, who became convinced of the need for political revolution along with military and administrative modernization.

Insisting that individuals completely submit to the state, the French revolutionaries were alluring to Islam, echoing Islamic commandments that the individual must be subordinated, if necessary by force, to an all-powerful Islamic state. In a sense, Islam encountered a "kindred soul" in Western totalitarian revolutionary thinking. Some argue this thinking became a model for Islamic modernists, but in fact these ideas merely encouraged Islam to return to its own totalitarian roots.

Napoleon's invasion of Egypt also influenced Islam in another way. This humiliating military defeat, followed by 150 more years of continual Western colonization of the Islamic world, forced Islamic ideologues to realize they had to master the instruments of their own defeat; they—so to speak—had to use Satan to cast out Satan. Ending its thousand-year ostracism of the West, Islam from the nineteenth century onward began parroting Western revolutionary jargon, adopting Western technological and scientific innovations, and embracing the belated industrial revolution that Western colonial administration was bringing to the Islamic world—all with the goal of advancing jihad and world domination.

Paradoxically, Islam's reliance on Western innovations further heightened the *Umma's* anti-Western envy and resentment, turning the ideology even more belligerent. "Islam is not merely a religious creed [but] a revolutionary ideology," Pakistani Salafist leader Syed Abul Ala Maududi declared, "and jihad refers to that revolutionary struggle...to destroy all states and governments anywhere on the face of the earth, which are opposed to the ideology and program of Islam."[3] Demonstrating the strange hypocrisy that marks Islam's view of the West, Maududi traveled to the United States for medical care. He died in 1979 in a hospital in Buffalo, New York, where his son worked as a doctor.

Islam's strategy of using Western innovations against the West itself achieved major success thanks to Ayatollah Khomeini, a reactionary madman with the backward mindset of a seventh-century desert dweller. Replacing the Shah of Iran with a clerical dictatorship, Khomeini's revolution was enabled by Western stencil duplicators, telephone lines, transistor radios, and tape recorders that conveyed his sermons to the Iranian masses. Based in a Paris suburb, Khomeini used Western technology to direct an anti-Western revolution 2,600 miles away.

In short, in the last two centuries, Islam realized it needed to find a new target for exploitation due to its diminishing supplies of dhimmis and slaves. The new target became the *harbi*—people from the *Dar al-Harb*, the non-Islamic world. Islam now acts as a parasite of the *harbis*, avidly sucking a continuous flow of alien but necessary goods and services that Islam cannot create for itself. This includes what is currently the biggest source of income for many Islamic nations—oil—a resource that Western nations have discovered and developed, but whose riches mostly flow to Islamic countries simply due to accidents of geography. This process has strengthened and reinvigorated the *Umma* to the point that Islam, thanks to Western technology, now presents a more dire threat to the West than ever before.

Islam still cultivates all its traditional hatreds, including the vilest anti-Semitism, but it is increasingly willing to emulate its enemies in order to defeat and eradicate them. Consider this declaration by Mahathir Mohamad, the reportedly pro-Western former prime minister of Malaysia, from the Tenth Summit of the Organization of the Islamic Conference in 2003:

> The Muslims will forever be oppressed and dominated by the Europeans and the Jews.... It cannot be that there is no other way. 1.3 billion Muslims cannot be defeated by a few million Jews.... The Europeans killed six million Jews out of 12 million. But today the Jews rule this world by proxy.... We are up against a people who think. They survived 2000 years of pogroms not by hitting back, but by thinking. They invited and successfully promoted Socialism, Communism, human rights and democracy so that persecuting them would appear to be wrong, so that they may enjoy equal rights with others. With these they have now gained control of the most powerful countries and they, this tiny community, have become a world power. We cannot fight them through brawn alone. We must use our brains also.[4]

The Wahhabi aristocrats of Saudi Arabia and the Gulf emirates have become experts at deceiving the West. The worldview of these men, like that of Khomeini, is stuck in the seventh century, yet when necessary they talk Western, act Western, dress Western, and worm their way into Western society. The proceeds from oil—Allah's miraculous gift to the Arabs— allow them to acquire all the necessities the Western *harbis* can offer.

Islam was sustained for more than a millennium by non-Muslim dhimmis and slaves. And when Islam seemed doomed in recent times, it was saved by the technology and industry of the non-Muslim West.

Exposure to Islam is ultimately fatal for us, but for Islam, contact with the West is a vital lifeline. Without the West, Islam cannot survive. Western technicians and an army of non-Muslim Asian workers power the economies of Saudi Arabia and the Gulf emirates. Without *harbis*, the Arab princes could not pump their oil or build their extravagant palaces, nor could they fund the worldwide network of Islamic schools, mosques, media outlets, and cultural institutions that advocate overthrowing the West and making Islam supreme everywhere.

"How tremendously European one feels when one has seen these devils in their native muck!" English author Aldous Huxley wrote to a friend in 1925 after spending several months in the Arab world. "And to think that we are busily teaching them all the mechanical arts of peace and war which gave us, in the past, our superiority over their numbers! In fifty years time, it seems to me, Europe can't fail to be wiped out by these monsters."[5]

Huxley identified Islam's Achilles' heel: it is both destructive and self-destructive. Left to itself—deprived of what the young Winston Churchill in 1899 called "the strong arms of science against which [Mohammedanism] had vainly struggled,"[6]—Islam dies in its own deserts. With nothing else to destroy, it destroys itself, as it had nearly done until Western technology saved it.

One of the most dangerous vehicles of Islam today is the Organization of Islamic Cooperation (OIC), based in Jeddah, Saudi Arabia. Founded in 1969 by thirty Islamic states, the group aims to "galvanize the Ummah into a unified body…safeguarding the true values of Islam and the Muslims."[7] The OIC now counts fifty-seven member states, making it the second-largest international organization after the United Nations.

The OIC forms the largest voting bloc in the UN, where it uses this dominance to subvert individual freedom. As mentioned in chapter six, the OIC's current fixation is encouraging international bodies and governments to recognize criticism of Islam as a human rights violation. Its efforts have met with some success, such as the approval in March 2010 by the United Nations Human Rights Council (UNHRC) of a resolution criminalizing "defamation of religions."[8] The resolution, authored by Pakistan on behalf of the OIC, explicitly mentions only one faith: Islam.[9] For the OIC, Islam is the only religion worthy of protection.

The OIC telegraphed decades ago its campaign to undermine traditional human rights and adopt special protections for Islam. In 1990, the organization rejected the UN's iconic Universal Declaration of Human Rights of 1948 and replaced it with the Cairo Declaration on Human Rights in Islam. The Cairo Declaration does not recognize freedom of religion or freedom of speech for non-Muslims, or equal rights for men and women. Instead, it is a document of unabashed Islamic supremacism as established in its preamble, which states that man has the "right to a dignified life in accordance with the Islamic Shari'ah."[10] *Sharia* is Islamic holy law as derived from the Koran and the example set by Muhammad. The Declaration does not mention man's right to live a dignified life *outside* the bounds of Islamic Sharia because the OIC does not believe in that right. This is made clear in numerous passages:

- Article 2 guarantees the right to life of every human being "except for Shari'ah prescribed reason." Likewise, safety from bodily harm is guaranteed unless "a Shari'ah-prescribed reason" dictates otherwise.
- Article 7 restricts parents' rights to those that are "in accordance with the tenets of the shari'ah." Article 12 restricts the rights of free movement "within the framework of the Shari'ah" and further states that the safety of asylum-seekers must be guaranteed "unless asylum is motivated by committing an act regarded by the Shari'ah as a crime."
- Article 16 protects a person's rights to the moral and material interests derived from his scientific, literary, artistic or technical labor "provided it is not contrary to the principles of the Shari'ah." Article 19 states that "there

shall be no crime or punishment except as provided for in
the Shari'ah."

- Article 22 restricts freedom of speech and opinion to "such
  manner as would not be contrary to the principles of the
  Shari'ah." It states that "everyone shall have the right to
  advocate what is right, and propagate what is good, and
  warn against what is wrong and evil according to the
  norms of Islamic Shari'ah." Article 23 guarantees political
  rights as long as they are "in accordance with the provi-
  sions of Shari'ah."

- Article 24 summarizes, "All the rights and freedoms stipulated in this Declaration are subject to the Islamic
  Shari'ah." Article 25 reaffirms that "the Islamic Shari'ah
  is the only source of reference for the explanation and
  clarification of any of the articles of this Declaration."

In short, the OIC's Cairo Declaration limits every human being's
rights and freedoms so fundamentally that nothing remains but the
limited number of liberties granted by the Koran and by Muhammad.
As explained in previous chapters, these few rights and freedoms are
reserved for practicing Muslims, hence they are not universal rights
at all—they are rules for an apartheid society that privileges Muslims
and oppresses non-Muslims.

The Cairo Declaration is such a blatant attack on universal human
rights that states that adhere to it do not belong in the United Nations.
After all, the UN's fundamental document is the 1948 Universal Declaration of Human Rights, which the OIC rejects in favor of the discrimina-
tory Cairo Declaration. Because OIC members have placed themselves
outside the civilized world by rejecting the very concept of human rights,
Western nations should demand that OIC member states be expelled from
the UN until they revoke the Cairo Declaration. The West should stop
paying its financial contributions to the UN as long as the UN accepts
such members.

In a debate in the Dutch Parliament on November 7, 2007, I said that we should limit our bilateral relations with these countries to a minimum and stop our development aid unless they renounce the Cairo Declaration.

I want to contain the further expansion of those who intend to destroy our freedom. As President John F. Kennedy said: "Our goal is not the victory of might, but the vindication of right."[11]

By speaking the truth to the peoples of the *Umma*—as Reagan did to Soviet peoples when he called the Soviet Union an "evil empire"—we will demonstrate our steadfast resolve and our conviction in our own civilization. This show of strength may persuade some in the Islamic world to turn against the Islamic yoke, just as everyday people in Eastern Europe grew disgusted by communism and ultimately overthrew it. As with communism, a Western campaign of constant pressure could expedite the collapse of Islam through its own contradictions.

I am by no means the first to note the similarities between Islam and communism. In a 1956 article, French author and statesman André Malraux wrote,

> The outstanding event of our time is the violence of the advance of Islam. Underestimated by most of our contemporaries, the ascendancy of Islam is analogically comparable to the beginnings of communism at the time of Lenin. The consequences of this phenomenon are still unpredictable. At the outset of the Marxist revolution, people thought they could stem its tide through partial solutions. Neither Christianity nor organizations such as corporations or labor unions found a solution. Likewise today the Western world is hardly prepared to confront the problem of Islam.[12]

Malraux, a valiant veteran of France's anti-Nazi resistance movement, was pessimistic that we could prevail over the Islamic onslaught. "Perhaps partial solutions would have been sufficient to stem the tide of

Islam, if they had been applied in time," he said. "Now it is too late! All that we can do is to become conscious of the gravity of the phenomenon and to try to slow down its progression."[13]

I do not share Malraux's pessimism; in fact, I reject cynicism and despair as vehemently as I reject violence. Our commitment to truth, human dignity, and a just and honorable defense of the West do not permit us to resort to bloodshed or to give in to despondency. I cherish the tradition of Aleksandr Solzhenitsyn, Yelena Bonner, Lech Walesa, and Ronald Reagan, heroes who helped to defeat a totalitarian ideology through the strength of their convictions. As the Islamic apostate Ali Sina declared about his anti-Islam activism, "We don't raise a sword against darkness; we lit a light."[14]

Like his compatriot Malraux, the great French writer and philosopher Alexis de Tocqueville was also acquainted with Islam. "I studied the Koran a great deal," he wrote in an 1843 letter to a friend, "I came away from that study with the conviction there have been few religions in the world as deadly to men as that of Muhammad. So far as I can see, it is the principal cause of the decadence so visible today in the Muslim world and, though less absurd than the polytheism of old, its social and political tendencies are in my opinion to be feared, and I therefore regard it as a form of decadence rather than a form of progress in relation to paganism itself."[15]

Nevertheless, in his seminal book *Democracy in America*, Tocqueville was optimistic that Islam would ultimately be vanquished. "Muhammad brought down from heaven and put into the Koran not religious doctrines only, but political maxims, criminal and civil laws, and scientific theories," he wrote. "The Gospels, on the other hand, deal only with the general relations between man and God and between man and man. Beyond that, they teach nothing and do not oblige people to believe anything. That alone, among a thousand reasons, is enough to show that Islam will not be able to hold its power long in ages of enlightenment and democracy."[16]

On March 2, 2010, a Muslim woman in a *niqab*—Islamic garb that covers the whole body and face except for the eyes—went to buy some stamps at the post office of the main train station in Hamburg, Germany. "I will not wait on you," the female clerk told the mummy in front of her. "You will not be served while veiled. I am face to face with you, so I expect you to do the same for me."[17] The Muslim woman, a 20-year-old German who had converted to Islam the previous year, complained to her Islamic-born husband, who lodged an official complaint with the post office. "This has hurt us deeply," he wailed. "We are not living in Nazi Germany anymore." Following this complaint, the boss of the post office employee warned her that he would not tolerate her "discrimina-tory behavior" and that she was putting her job in jeopardy. "In our office, every customer is treated equally," he told a local newspaper. "If she has a problem with serving veiled people, then she cannot continue working at the counter."[18]

The post office employee, however, should never have been repri-manded. In fact, if Westerners want to preserve our liberty, we should follow her courageous example. She experienced some of the conse-quences that are faced by anyone who takes a peaceful stand against the oppressions of Islam—our jobs are put at risk, we are harassed by the authorities, and our very lives are threatened. And yet, it is our duty to speak the truth, however shocking and politically incorrect it may be.

In that same month of March 2010, Margareta Ritter, mayor of the German town of Monschau, where I had spent some holidays, declared me *persona non grata* and forbade me from entering her town because I had compared the Koran to Adolf Hitler's *Mein Kampf*.[19]

I was not the first to make that comparison. In Winston Churchill's six-volume history *The Second World War*, for which he won the 1953 Nobel Prize for Literature, the great British statesman wrote of *Mein Kampf*, "All was there—the programme of German resurrection, the technique of party propaganda; the plan for combating Marxism; the concept of a National-Socialist State; the rightful position of Germany at the summit of the world. Here was the new Koran of faith and war:

turgid, verbose, shapeless, but pregnant with its message. The main thesis of *Mein Kampf* is simple. Man is a fighting animal; therefore the nation, being a community of fighters, is a fighting unit."[20]

Many Western countries—though not the United States with its First Amendment—prohibit the publication, distribution, sale, or possession of *Mein Kampf*. These include the Netherlands, which outlaws the distribution of Hitler's infamous book. I attracted a lot of attention when I said that if the Netherlands bans *Mein Kampf* as a threat to our society, then it should ban the Koran for the same reason. In reaction to my proposal, a Dutch minister suggested lifting the ban on *Mein Kampf*, but Dutch politicians overwhelmingly rejected his suggestion "out of respect for the victims of the Nazis."[21] I don't understand why the victims of Islam do not deserve the same respect. Why is it hate speech when Hitler calls Jews vermin, but not when the Koran calls them pigs and commands that they be killed?

In Austria, Hitler's native country, it is illegal to possess copies of *Mein Kampf*. Why doesn't the same rule apply to the Koran in Saudi Arabia, Muhammad's native country? Both books propagate an ideology that resulted in the deaths of millions, so why is one legal and the other banned? Because the Saudis believe that the Koran was written by Allah in the seventh heaven? Who can reasonably accept that argument?

In France, publications of *Mein Kampf* must include a warning about its contents, but no similar warning is required for the Koran. Perhaps French authorities believe French readers would take Hitler's words more seriously than Muslims would take the words of Allah. Nevertheless, *Mein Kampf* is not a huge commercial success in France. The same cannot be said for Turkey, where Hitler's treatise is not only legal, it is one of the country's bestselling non-fiction books.[22] The same is true in the territories controlled by the Palestinian Authority and elsewhere in the Arab world.[23]

Most people in the West are fair-minded and educated enough that they can't be incited to commit violence against a group of people just by reading some book. But there is a minority of easily impressionable people who *can* be incited, and this danger is magnified when people believe they are reading a book ordained by God. History teaches that we cannot underestimate the impact a single book can have, from the Bible—which shaped all of Western civilization—to *Uncle Tom's Cabin*—which helped spark the American Civil War.

We must face the fact that some Muslims believe the Koran—and all its oppressive and murderous commands—must be followed because the book relays the immutable word of Allah himself. It is no use arguing to the Koran's adherents that Western norms are better or more progressive or more civilized. In their minds, adopting Western values would require them to cease being Muslims. We must not negotiate with Islam, we must *expose* it by denouncing its endless holy wars, ridiculing its violent reaction to criticism or satire, and banning its chief tools of propaganda. Most important, for the sake of defending our civilization, we should keep those who want to impose Sharia law on our societies as far away from our countries as possible.

Islam considers it blasphemy, punishable by death, to investigate the origin of the Koran; we are all meant to believe, without doubt or discussion, that the book was written before the beginning of time by Allah himself, who has the "Mother of the Book" lying on a table in heaven for all eternity. Studies noting the Persian origin of some words in the Koran are considered sacrilege, as they break the Islamic precept that Arabic is the language of Allah, as Allah himself revealed in the Koran when he said, "Thus have We sent this down—an Arabic Koran."[24]

The few scholars who do this kind of work are subject to death threats, causing many to publish under pseudonyms. Indeed, research into the origin of the Koran and the historical figure of Muhammad is even more threatening to Islam than are cartoons of Muhammad. In 1991 Suliman Bashear, a professor at the Palestinian University in Nablus, was thrown from a second-story window by his own students after he questioned the Koran's historical veracity and argued that Islam developed gradually instead of being revealed by a single prophet.[25]

More recently, in February 2012, Saudi columnist Hamza Kashgari speculated on Twitter about how he'd act if he met Muhammad personally. To Westerners this seems like perfectly innocent contemplation, but in Saudi Arabia, the comments unleashed frenzied accusations of blasphemy. According to the *Wall Street Journal*, "Clerics and thousands of their followers [used] Twitter, YouTube, email and fax to demand the writer's execution." The hysterical response included a deluge of tens of thousands of Tweets that offered bounties for killing Kashgari and posted images of his house. "The speed, number and intensity of messages calling for the death of the writer, Hamza Kashgari, stunned many Saudis," the *Journal* reported. Personifying the absurdly disproportionate reaction, one cleric appeared on a video "shuddering with sobs in outrage at what he said was Mr. Kashgari's insult to the Prophet Muhammad." Kashgari fled the country for Malaysia, where he was promptly arrested at the airport by the Malaysian police and sent back to Saudi Arabia where, according to the *Journal*, "a senior Saudi official said he would likely face a charge of apostasy, which typically carries the death penalty."[26]

Muhammad may be sacred in Islam, but we in the West are entitled to critically research his life and legacy, no matter how deeply it "disturbs," "offends," or "shocks" the bullies in the Islamic world. In fact, it is our *duty* to undertake these kinds of investigations. We should encourage energetic inquiry into this field and vigorously confront Muslims with the findings. Let them *suffer the truth*.

Another prominent Koran expert is a linguist and an expert on Semitic languages who writes under the pseudonym Christoph Luxenberg. He lives in Germany and is probably of Lebanese or Syrian origin. Few people know his real identity. According to Luxenberg, the original language of the Koran is not Arabic, but Syro-Aramaic. These languages are closely related, though their words do not necessarily have the same meaning. Supporting Luxenberg's argument is the fact that Arabic did not turn up as a written language until the late eighth century, 150 years after Muhammad's death.

Luxenberg read the original text of the Koran as if it had been written in Syro-Aramaic rather than in Arabic. By doing so, he discovered that many obscure parts of the Koran that are inexplicable to Arab commentators (they simply state that only Allah can comprehend them) become meaningful, while other parts of the Koran obtain a different meaning altogether. Take, for example, the Koranic verse promising that martyrs in jihad will receive "wide-eyed houris," or virgins, in heaven[27]—a verse cited by Islamic radicals to encourage suicide bombings. In Syro-Aramaic, however, the reading refers not to *houris*, but to "white grapes" or "raisins," which were an iconographic symbol of the Christian hereafter. If Luxenberg's reading is correct, it means Islamic suicide commandos, who think they are heading to the sexual bliss of a heavenly brothel, will be offered a plate of raisins instead of virgins.

In 2003, when *Newsweek* published an article about Luxenberg's thesis,[28] the Pakistani and Bangladeshi governments banned the issue. "The article is insulting to the Koran," the Pakistani Information Minister said.[29]

Luxenberg's thesis is controversial. His suggestion that there was a hiatus in the oral transmission of the Koran and a chronological gap in Muhammad's biography, however, is shared by other scholars who, elaborating on this assumption, doubt whether the historical Muhammad actually existed, or if he did, whether he did much or any of what is ascribed to him in Islamic scripture. The Muhammad who comes to us from the Islamic holy books might be a composite figure, constructed later to give Arab imperialism a foundational mythos. So far, scholars have undertaken little research into these matters—that's unsurprising, considering Islam's violent reaction to unfavorable publicity.

Other Muhammad experts have argued that Muhammad probably did exist as a historical figure. They claim that so many aspects of their prophet's life are acutely embarrassing for Muslims—such as his marriages to a 9-year-old girl and to his own daughter-in-law—that it is "hard to imagine that a pious hagiographer would have invented" these stories.[30] Whether or not the historical Muhammad existed, research into the genesis of Islam is important. Even if Muhammad never existed, 1.5 billion Muslims believe he did.

Consequently, historical, archaeological, and linguistic research into the historical Muhammad and the origins of Islam should be encouraged. It is a potent weapon that could persuade Muslims that the Koran is *not* the literal word of God. This research will help people who were brought up to believe in the basic tenets of Islam to free themselves from their illusions.

We must remember that Islam is not the truth and that we have no obligations to this ideology. We do not have to respect its traditions, convictions, or taboos. We do not have to show deference to its bloody and intolerant history. We should subject its beliefs and arguments to rigorous scrutiny, as we would any other historical claim. Just because Islam may not be able to withstand such scrutiny is no reason to refrain from doing it.

CHAPTER EIGHT

The Amerikabomber

America cannot be an ostrich with its head in the sand.

—Woodrow Wilson

On September 11, 2001, two al Qaeda operatives, the Egyptian Mohamed Atta and Marwan al-Shehhi from the United Arab Emirates, crashed their hijacked planes into the twin towers of Manhattan's World Trade Center, killing more than 2,500 people. A third hijacked plane smashed into the Pentagon, slaughtering around 200 more, while hijackers who faced a passenger rebellion deliberately crashed a fourth airliner into a Pennsylvania field, killing all forty passengers.

Standing at approximately 1,362 feet, the World Trade Center skyscrapers were New York's tallest buildings, having been the tallest buildings in the world until the construction of Chicago's Sears Tower in 1974. Today, the world's tallest building is the *Burj Khalifa* (the Caliph Tower) in Dubai in the United Arab Emirates. The name of the building, which stands at 2,717 feet and houses a mosque on its top floor, proudly refers to the Caliphate, which the 9/11 bombers were serving.

America's skyscrapers symbolize the country's economic power, so it's no coincidence that the nation's enemies seek to destroy them. Sixty years before the 9/11 attacks, the Nazis had laid similar plots. During World War II, they worked on the *Amerikabomber*, an airplane specially designed to fly suicide missions into Manhattan's skyscrapers.[1] Albert Speer, the Nazi Minister of Armaments, recalled in his diary, "It was almost as if [Hitler] was in a delirium when he described to us how New York would go up in flames. He imagined how the skyscrapers would turn into huge blazing torches. How they would crumble while the reflection of the flames would light the skyline against the dark sky."[2]

The real story of the 9/11 attacks began more than a decade before Atta, al-Shehhi, and their co-conspirators seized control of their doomed flights. The origins of the plot stretch back to November 5, 1990, when El Sayyid Nosair, an Egyptian-born American citizen, shot and killed the radical Brooklyn-born Israeli rabbi Meir Kahane in the lobby of Manhattan's Marriott hotel. After Nosair's arrest, the FBI discovered forty-seven boxes of documents, maps, and diagrams of buildings—including the World Trade Center towers—in his Brooklyn apartment. One of the documents read, "We must thoroughly demoralize the enemies of Allah. This is to be done by means of destroying and blowing up the towers that constitute the pillars of their civilization, such as...the high buildings they are so proud of."[3]

Kahane's assassin belonged to a group of jihadists who were being trained by al Qaeda member Ali Abdelsoud Mohammed. Nicknamed *al-Amriki* ("the American"), Mohammed was a U.S. Army drill sergeant at Fort Bragg who had stolen classified military information later found in Nosair's boxes. Like Nosair, Mohammed was an Egyptian-born American citizen. Despite having been discharged from the Egyptian army for extremism, U.S. authorities allowed him to immigrate to America and gain U.S. citizenship. "The FBI had good reasons to be suspicious of Mohammed—if its agents had been paying attention," writes investigative journalist Rich Miniter in his book *Losing Bin Laden*.[4]

Attending court in Arab attire, Nosair, along with his chanting and screaming supporters outside the courthouse, turned the assassin's trial into a spectacle. In December 1991, the jury acquitted him of murder, convicting Nosair of the lesser charges of assault and possession of an illegal firearm. Nosair's lawyer, William Kunstler, a board member of the American Civil Liberties Union, later revealed he had succeeded in removing "potential jurors who supported Israel and might have been biased against Mr. Nosair because he is an Arab." As a consequence, the jury was almost entirely composed of, as Kunstler described them, "third-world people" and "people who were not yuppies or establishment types." Denouncing the jury's verdict as "devoid of common sense" and accusing Nosair of "conduct[ing] a rape of this country, of our Constitution and of our laws," the judge gave him the maximum sentence of up to twenty-two years in jail.[5]

In February 1993, while Nosair was serving his sentence, Islamic terrorists detonated a car bomb in the parking garage below the World Trade Center's north tower. Although their goal was to bring down both towers by knocking one into the other, the north tower withstood the blast, which killed six people and injured 1,042. The bombing led to the arrest of the blind Islamic scholar Omar Abdel Rahman and several of his followers.[6]

The "blind Sheikh" was a graduate in Koranic studies from Cairo's al-Azhar University. In July 1990, he had been allowed to enter the United States even though his name was on a State Department terrorist watch list. After his arrest, Rahman, too, was defended by Kunstler. On October 1, 1995, Rahman and other members of his gang, including the already-imprisoned Nosair, were convicted of "seditious conspiracy" and sentenced to life imprisonment for plotting to blow up numerous New York landmarks including the Holland Tunnel.

"We know that bin Laden's terrorists had been planning their outrages for years," former British Prime Minister Margaret Thatcher wrote in her book *Statecraft*. "The propagation of their mad, bad ideology—decency forbids calling it a religion—had been taking place before our eyes. We were just too blind to see it. In short, the world had never ceased to be dangerous. But the West had ceased to be vigilant. Surely that is the most important lesson of this tragedy, and we must learn it if our civilisation is to survive."[7]

My favorite American president is Ronald Reagan, the man who saved the West from the Soviet threat and helped liberate Eastern Europe and Russia from communism. Reagan understood the evil nature of totalitarianism but also its fatal weakness: the Soviet regime was bankrupted by decades of stagnation and by its inability to innovate. Unable to compete with the West, the Evil Empire imploded. When I was honored to receive the "Hero of Conscience Award" at the Ronald Reagan Presidential Library in June 2009, I called Reagan "a source of inspiration for many freedom loving people worldwide."

When the captive peoples of Eastern Europe overthrew communism in 1989, they were inspired by dissidents such as Vladimir Bukovsky, Aleksandr Solzhenitsyn, Václav Havel, and others who argued that people have a right and an obligation to "live within the truth"[8]—that is, to reject the lies that justified the regimes of their communist masters. As more and more people overcame their fear and began speaking the truth, the legitimacy and power of the regimes crumbled.

Speaking the truth sounds easy, but it is not always so. Sometimes speaking the truth invites physical threats, persecution, or the loss of money or power. That's why societies must constantly guard against the tendency to replace straightforward truth-telling with more comfortable clichés, euphemisms, and half-truths. "Truth eludes us as soon as our concentration begins to flag, all the while leaving the illusion that we are continuing to pursue it," Solzhenitsyn said. "Also, truth is seldom sweet; it is almost invariably bitter."[9]

The big lie of Marxism, the one rejected by the revolutionaries of 1989, was that the state can make you happy if you sign away your freedom to it. America has always resisted this delusion, in large part thanks to its pioneering past, which encouraged self-sufficiency and individualism. Americans' natural opposition to collectivism and socialism, I believe, is the reason why so many illiberal forces, including some Europeans, despise the United States.

After 1989, in many Eastern European countries, the ruling communists simply renamed themselves "Social Democrats" and were happily welcomed into the international networks of Western Europe's Social

Democratic parties. By continuing to lie, some "former" communists even managed to retain or regain power. The most dramatic example was seen in Hungary in 2006, when Prime Minister Ferenc Gyurcsány, a member of the Hungarian Socialist Party, which is the rebranded Communist Party, was caught on tape admitting that his party had won elections by lying about the magnitude of the problems facing his nation. "We repeated and repeated that you can be richer, fulfill your dreams, and we can give you happiness and fortune as a gift," he told party officials. "This is a real lie."[10]

Vladimir Bukovsky, a former dissident who spent years as a political prisoner in the Soviet Gulag, argues that there should have been a "Nuremberg trial" after the fall of communism. I agree. The purpose of such a trial would not have been to enact revenge on the old "comrades," but to expose the evil committed by the system they served. "Because we didn't win the Cold War, it isn't over," Bukovsky says. "We were given a chance to win in 1991. To do it we needed a Nuremberg trial, but not a trial of people. In a country like the Soviet Union, if you tried to find all the guilty, you would end up with 19 million people, and who needs another Gulag? This isn't about punishing individuals. It's about judging the *system*." Bukovsky claims this crucial "Nuremberg trial" of communism was never held because it would have revealed "that the West was infiltrated by the Soviets much deeper than we ever thought, but also that there was ideological collaboration between left-wing parties in the West and the Soviet Union."[11]

Thus, although defeated Nazi Germany was subject to de-Nazification, there was no de-Marxification after the fall of communism. And without the public accounting of a trial, people tend to forget how evil communism was. Moreover, the hatred of America and of Western civilization, planted by the Soviets in the minds of the Western intelligentsia, has not been rooted out because it was never comprehensively exposed. We failed to reveal the evil of the entire communist system, and we failed to expose those in the West who collaborated with it by advocating policies of détente, improved relations, relaxation of international tension, or peaceful coexistence—in other words, tolerance of evil.

If we fail to understand the nature of evil, we are doomed to become its next victims. We can only learn to understand it by what Bukovsky calls "the power of memory and acknowledgement."[12] As John F. Kennedy said, "Forgive your enemies, but never forget their names."[13]

How is all this relevant to Islam? Simply put, Islam is the communism of today—the worldwide menace that threatens the West and all our rights and freedoms. But our failure to come clean with communism has prevented us from standing up to Islam, trapped as we are in the old communist habit of deceit and doublespeak that used to haunt Eastern Europe and that now haunts all of us.

Because of this failure, we are susceptible to the same old arguments for appeasement, couched in rhetoric about our need to "understand" and "coexist" with Islam. We used to hear that despite all appearances, the Soviets really wanted peace, that if we met them halfway they would reciprocate, that they only asked for a decent measure of respect, and that American "imperialism" was just as bad as Soviet policies, if not worse. Today, we hear the same moral equivalence vis-à-vis Islam. On 9/11, before the jihadists' victims were even buried, we heard the appeasers blaming America for somehow provoking the attack. These arguments serve one purpose: to destroy our willingness to confront evil.

These lies are often grotesque, yet our elected representatives hardly ever call out their purveyors. Former New York City Mayor Rudy Giuliani was a rare exception; a month after the 9/11 attacks, he rejected a $10 million donation for New York disaster relief from Prince Al-Waleed bin Talal, a Saudi hotel and media tycoon, after the prince declared that America "must address some of the issues that led to such a criminal attack. [America] should re-examine its policies in the Middle East and adopt a more balanced stand toward the Palestinian cause.... Our Palestinian brethren continue to be slaughtered at the hands of Israelis."[14] Giuliani responded, "I entirely reject that statement. There is no moral equivalent for this [terrorist] act. There is no justification for it." He continued, "To suggest that there's a justification for [the 9/11 attacks] only invites this happening in the future. It is highly irresponsible and very, very dangerous. And one of the reasons I think this happened is because people were engaged in moral equivalency in not understanding the difference between liberal democracies like the United States, like Israel, and terrorist states and those who condone terrorism. So I think not only are those statements wrong, they're part of the problem."[15]

The Saudis have not forgiven or forgotten Giuliani's extraordinary statement. In a 2003 interview with former U.S. Ambassador to Saudi Arabia Chas Freeman, the Saudi-American Forum cited Giuliani's rejection of bin Talal's money as an example of America's "great...reluctance to examine the roots of terrorism, especially in terms of US foreign policy."[16] Disgracefully, Freeman all but agreed with this malevolent insinuation and even advised the Saudis on how to educate Americans about the wonders of Islam. Freeman replied, "Well, that [Giuliani's rebuff of bin Talal] was of course the classic example of this, but it's far from the only one. Also, I think with better organization, with better funding, with a commitment to a long-term effort in education, some of the slanders that have been put forward about Saudi Arabia or Islam—there are many in the United States—would find a more effective rebuttal."[17]

The false accusation that America is as bad or worse than Islamic terrorists, unsurprisingly, is a popular one within Islam. The aspersion was cast by Imam Feisal Abdul Rauf, who conceived of the project to build a thirteen-story Islamic center and mosque next to Ground Zero in Manhattan—a callous and obnoxious scheme that is overwhelmingly opposed by a majority of Americans.[18] In 2009, once he came under the public spotlight for the Ground Zero mosque project, Rauf spoke like a true American patriot and a life-long moderate. But he sang a different tune in an interview he gave weeks after the 9/11 attacks, when he argued that "United States policies were an accessory to the crime that happened...because we [the United States] have been accessory [sic] to a lot of innocent lives dying in the world. In fact, in the most direct sense, Osama bin Laden is made in the USA."[19]

Similarly, in March 2004, after 191 travellers were killed in the jihadist bombing of four commuter trains in Madrid, Rauf told the congregation at his New York mosque that the United States and the West must acknowledge the harm they have done to Muslims before terrorism can end, and that the U.S. president should give an "America Culpa" speech to the Islamic world.[20] Summing up Rauf's moral equivalence between the United States and the terrorists who attack it, *National Review* observed, "While he cannot quite bring himself to blame the terrorists for being terrorists, he finds it easy to blame the United States for being a victim of terrorism."[21]

I agree, which is why I went to New York on September 11, 2010, to speak at a rally opposing Rauf's Ground Zero mosque project. "His 'Blame the West, Blame America' message is an insult," I told the thousands of demonstrators, including many families of 9/11 victims. "Americans—and by extension, all of us whose civilization was also attacked on 9/11/2001—are not to blame for what happened here nine years ago today. Osama bin Laden is *not* made in the USA. The West never 'harmed' Islam before it harmed us. It was Islam which took the Middle East, Christian Northern Africa and Constantinople by aggressive wars of conquest."[22]

These are simple and obvious facts, yet far too many Westerners refuse to acknowledge them.

The Big Lie is a propaganda technique commonly used by totalitarian regimes. British psychiatrist and cultural commentator Theodore Dalrymple explains how communists employed it to corrupt their own people:

> In my study of communist societies, I came to the conclusion that the purpose of communist propaganda was not to persuade or convince, nor to inform, but to humiliate; and therefore, the less it corresponded to reality the better. When people are forced to remain silent when they are being told the most obvious lies, or even worse when they are forced to repeat the lies themselves, they lose once and for all their sense of probity.

> To assent to obvious lies is to co-operate with evil, and in
> some small way to become evil oneself.... I think if you exam-
> ine political correctness, it has the same effect and is intended
> to.[23]

This is the tried and true tactic Islam has been using against the dhimmis
for fourteen centuries. As stated in the document recovered from Rabbi
Kahane's assassin, the jihadist El Sayyid Nosair, it is for that same purpose—to demoralize the enemy—that jihadists attacked and eventually
destroyed the twin towers.

As Dalrymple notes, in the West today, political correctness pressures
people into assenting to lies. Because those who reject or even question
the dogma of multiculturalism are condemned and ostracized, our discussion of Islam, immigration, and other topics is severely constrained.
Westerners who disdain cultural relativism, who are willing to denounce
barbarism when they see it, and who believe that the West, indeed, is the
centerpoint of civilization today, are dismissed as haters. Denied the right
to ask the most important questions and express even the most self-
evident observations, the West humiliates itself before our enemies and
endangers our own civilization.

We are told we must "respect" the freedom of those who do not
respect ours—and that when necessary, we must limit our own freedom
so as not to "offend" others. By chipping away at our own liberty in this
way, we will eventually lose it. As Karl Popper noted, "Unlimited tolerance [leads] to the disappearance of tolerance. If we extend unlimited
tolerance even to those who are intolerant, if we are not prepared to
defend a tolerant society against the onslaught of the intolerant, then the
tolerant will be destroyed, and tolerance with them."[24]

Those who blame Islamic terrorism on the West and on America
often claim that we invite jihad because we are allegedly responsible for
the poverty of Islamic countries. This comes straight out of the Marxist
playbook, which blames free-market capitalism for all the world's troubles. The argument, however, is undermined by the fact that Islamic
terrorists tend to be relatively well off.[25] Osama bin Laden, of course,

came from a family of Saudi plutocrats. Umar Farouk Abdulmutallab, the "underwear bomber" who tried to blow up a flight over Detroit on Christmas Day 2009, was the son of a wealthy Nigerian banker and lived in a plush London apartment.[26] As the *Economist* notes, a 2008 Princeton University analysis of academic studies "found little evidence that the typical terrorist is unusually poor or badly schooled."[27]

Nevertheless, a July 2011 survey by the Pew Research Center shows that a depressingly large share of Westerners blame the West, at least partially, for our strained relations with the Islamic world. The poll found more than 29 percent of Americans and 26 percent of the French and British place "most of the blame" on Western countries, while 29 percent in Spain and 24 percent in Germany and Britain say that both sides "share responsibility" for the poor state of Islamic-Western relations. Strikingly, the survey showed that moral equivalence and self-blame is far less common in Islamic countries: "Across the Muslim publics included in the survey, fewer than one-in-five believe Muslims are mostly to blame for the poor state of relations."[28]

The Islamic threat has grown so dire largely due to our denial, our apathy, and our fear, as we give in again and again to Islamic demands and mask our capitulations as "tolerance" or "sensitivity." Western politicians simply refuse to see that this "religion" is nothing but a political ideology whose fundamental document, the Koran, exhorts fanatics to violence. Paralyzed, they ignore looming threats to masses of innocent people.

U.S. authorities for some time thought the United States was safe from the threat—on 9/11, we saw they were wrong. As President Woodrow Wilson commented in 1916 as war spread across Europe and beyond, "America cannot be an ostrich with its head in the sand."[29]

The West's appeasers of Islam suffer from a peculiar malady that combines ignorance with Stockholm Syndrome. Some justify their faint-heartedness through hollow theoretical concepts and other phony rationalizations. For example, Richard Nixon's last book, *Seize the Moment*

(1992), written after the fall of the Soviet bloc, shows that the former U.S. president simply could not acknowledge Islam's malevolence and thus rejected the logical and historical conclusions to be drawn from the facts. Nixon writes,

> Some observers warn that Islam will become a monolithic and fanatical geopolitical force, that its growing population and significant financial power will pose a major challenge, and that the West will be forced to form a new alliance with Moscow to confront a hostile and aggressive Muslim world. This view holds that Islam and the West are antithetical and that Muslims view the world as two irreconcilable camps of Dar al-Islam and Dar al-Harb—the house of Islam and the house of war where the forces of Islam have yet to prevail. It foresees the forces of resurgent Muslim fundamentalism orchestrating a region-wide revolution from Iran and other states and prompting the need for a comprehensive...policy of containment.[30]

This was largely correct, but Nixon categorically dismisses "this nightmare scenario" and then repeats the familiar litany of soothing half-truths and flattering lies about Islam. He claims that "Islam has no doctrine of terrorism,"[31] that in the Middle Ages Islam "made enormous contributions to science, medicine, and philosophy,"[32] that for many centuries Islam "led the Christian world in terms of...religious toleration,"[33] that relations between America and Islamic countries are strained because of "the perception that the United States backs Israel uncritically,"[34] that we must show "respect and understanding for peoples who feel that they have been misunderstood, discriminated against, and exploited by Western powers,"[35] and that "our civilization is not inherently superior to theirs."[36]

Based on these false premises, Nixon concludes that the West should "contribute to a renaissance of the Muslim world"[37] and "support the modernists in the Muslim world" who are seeking "to integrate the countries of the Muslim world into the modern world."[38] In order to help the so-called modernist states "become economic and political magnets," Nixon advocates American disengagement from Israel's "extreme demands." He argues, "The Arab-Israeli conflict poisons our relations with the Muslim world and undercuts our ability to cooperate with countries with modernist, pro-Western leaders."[39]

Although Nixon began his career as a stalwart anti-communist, as president he was a classic foreign policy "realist" who advocated détente and appeasement with the Soviet empire. Ronald Reagan vanquished the Soviets by doing the opposite: he rolled back détente and exploited communism's chief weakness—its lack of innovation. Today, most of the Western foreign policy establishment subscribes to a Nixonian policy of appeasing Islam when what we really need is a Reaganite policy of pressuring and challenging it.

That is the only way to stop the *Amerikabombers* once and for all.

CHAPTER NINE

Conquest

In matters of principle, stand like a rock.

—Thomas Jefferson

I knew I was in trouble as soon as I noticed the three Arab youths following me. I wanted to cross the street, but there was another group of them waiting on the other side. Like predators tracking their prey, they had probably been following me for a while, assuming from my suit that I had money. When they caught up with me, they sprayed some sort of gas in my face, causing intense pain and blinding me. I fell on the pavement as they beat me, grabbed my wallet, and ran off.

As I lay on the ground, three young women rushed to me and asked if I was okay. "I can't see anything," I cried out, my throbbing eyes already swelling up. I gave them the address of a friend who lived nearby. They found him, and he took me to get medical attention. It was not the first time I had been robbed, nor would it be the last, but it was the only time I ended up in the hospital.

A few weeks later, a colleague picked me up at my home. "My God, Geert, why the hell do you stay in this neighborhood?" he asked.

"I've been living here longer than they have," I replied. "They won't drive me out." I confess—I am stubborn. The harder people make it for me, the more I persist. That's how I survived in Kanaleneiland for twenty years.

I moved to Kanaleneiland (Canal Island), a borough of Utrecht, in early 1985. From there, it is a short commute to Amsterdam as well as to The Hague, where in 1990 I began working as a staff assistant for the *Volkspartij voor Vrijheid en Democratie* (People's Party for Freedom and Democracy, or VVD) in the Dutch Parliament.

In 1997, I became a VVD member of the Utrecht city council. The following year, I was elected as a VVD representative to the *Tweede Kamer*, the Dutch House of Representatives. I represented my native province of Limburg, so I moved back to Venlo. But I still spent half my time at the Kanaleneiland apartment because it was an easy commute to The Hague. Those were my living circumstances until November 2004, when the police began putting me in safe houses for my own protection.

Kanaleneiland was built up in the 1960s to accommodate 30,000 people in modern and relatively cheap housing. When I first moved to the district, it was predominantly populated by native-born, blue-collar and middle-class Dutch residents. The locals initially welcomed immigrants, and this was expected; Dutchmen, whether lower class or middle class, are famously tolerant of newcomers and of alternative lifestyles. But as they began arriving in greater numbers, it became clear that many Islamic immigrants, unlike previous immigrant groups, adamantly refused to assimilate. Some of the newcomers, mostly of Moroccan origin, demanded that the non-Muslim natives adapt to *their* culture, not the other way around.

As Islam expanded, crime spread throughout the district—cars were vandalized, people were robbed, and eventually Dutch women no longer felt safe in the streets. Marxists claim poverty causes crime, but I noticed the opposite: crime reduced the area to poverty. When I moved to Kanaleneiland, it was a safe and clean lower-middle class neighborhood. As lawlessness spread, Dutch residents began moving out and Dutch shops closed down. The district developed a Middle Eastern feel, with the streets full of Arabic or Turkish shop signs and women wearing headscarves. By 2004, Kanaleneiland had become much poorer and had transformed into one of the most dangerous neighborhoods of Utrecht—at least for non-Muslims. In January 2012, the Dutch authorities revealed that 65 percent of youths of Moroccan origin between twelve and twenty-three years old have been detained at least once by the police.[1]

The indigenous Dutch came to me, as a parliamentarian, for help—but what could I do? I had frequently tried to open a dialogue with the young Moroccans, but to no avail—to them, I was just another *kafir*, an infidel. I was somewhat surprised to learn they still remembered me years later. In 2008, a newspaper reporter asked a group of Kanaleneiland youths about me. "He often came to chat with us," 20-yeard-old Khalid told the journalist. "How are you doing, he used to ask." That was a nice thing to say, unlike what came next: "But since he moved out, he shouts dangerous slogans. He was a nice guy, but now he is filth, a dirty bastard." His friend, 20-year-old Rachid, added, "He must be thrown out of Parliament. If there are riots here, it will be his fault."[2]

Whenever I talked with other parliamentarians about the situation in Kanaleneiland, they looked at me as if I was talking about another planet. The most dramatic sociological change of our lifetime was unfolding before our very eyes, but neither the Dutch media nor the political class wanted to acknowledge it.

Eventually, one man forced the topic into the public realm—Pim Fortuyn, a sociologist, university professor, and former member of the Dutch Labour Party. The flamboyant Fortuyn, an outspoken defender of traditionalist Catholicism but also an open homosexual, was a magazine columnist who audaciously criticized multiculturalism, the Dutch welfare state, and the "backward culture" of Islam. "I have traveled much in the world. And wherever Islam rules, it's just terrible,"[3] he said, confirming my own observations. Advocating a halt to immigration to the Netherlands,[4] Fortuyn warned that "mosques should be seen as front organizations... In the mosques martyrs are bred."[5] He also claimed that Islam is "the main threat to world peace.... Communism has almost finished; it has been replaced by Islam."[6] Therefore, he argued, "I am in favor of a cold war with Islam. I see Islam as an extraordinary threat."[7]

Professor Pim, as some called him, wanted to abolish the first article of the Dutch Constitution, which forbids discrimination. He claimed the clause violates free speech and, more provocatively, that preferential policies should be adopted for Christianity. "Christian inhabitants of the Netherlands...are morally entitled to more rights than Islamic newcomers, because for centuries Christians have contributed to the development of our country," he proclaimed.[8] Along the same lines, he favored banning Islamic schools but not Christian ones, which he considered beneficial to Dutch society.[9] His politically incorrect writings sparked severe criticism from the media and political establishment; after Fortuyn published his book *Tegen de islamisering van onze cultuur* (Against the Islamization of Our Culture) in 1997, a former Labour Party politician and government minister called him "an extremely inferior human being."[10]

In the early 2000s Professor Pim became politically active in his hometown of Rotterdam, the Netherlands' second largest city, which had a growing Islamic community comprising more than 10 percent of its population.[11] In early March 2002, Fortuyn's party *Leefbaar Rotterdam* (Livable Rotterdam) gained 35 percent of the vote in the city's local elections, enough to seize power from the Labour Party, which had governed Rotterdam for thirty years. The Rotterdam victory encouraged Fortuyn to run for Parliament that May. He was predicted to do well, but his life was tragically cut short on May 6, 2002, a week before the elections, when Fortuyn was shot and killed by Volkert van der Graaf, an animal rights activist. The assassin claimed he murdered Fortuyn to "prevent much harm to vulnerable groups such as Muslims and illegal aliens."[12]

Fortuyn's funeral in Rotterdam became a mass event, attended by tens of thousands of mourners stunned by the murder of a fearless man who gave voice to the alienation, desperation, and concern for the future of those who increasingly felt like foreigners in their own land. Despite Fortuyn's death, the *Lijst Pim Fortuyn* (Pim Fortuyn List) went on to win 17 percent of the national vote—the strongest showing ever for a new Dutch party. Gaining twenty-six of the 150 seats in the *Tweede Kamer*, it instantly became the nation's second biggest party, after the Christian Democrats. The death of its leader, however, dealt a mortal blow to the party, which soon disintegrated into quarrelling factions.

My party at the time, the VVD, did poorly in those elections, dropping to twenty-four seats, a loss of fourteen. Clearly, our party leadership was out of touch with the issues that most concerned the Dutch people. During the following two years, I tried to draw my colleagues' attention to the severe problems plaguing our urban neighborhoods, which were rapidly turning into no-go areas for non-Muslims and even for the police.

Upon reentering the *Tweede Kamer* in July 2002, I began to publicly criticize Islam. My warnings were not well received by many of my VVD colleagues; I was denounced for fear-mongering, isolated within the party, and ostracized by party leaders. Since the VVD was part of the governing coalition, some party members were particularly infuriated by my criticism of the government's weak policy toward the threat of Islamic terrorism.

In July 2004, I wrote a memo for VVD members in my constituency listing ten policies I felt the party should adopt, including the expulsion of radical Muslims from the Netherlands and opposition to Turkish membership in the European Union. This sparked a major conflict with outraged VVD leaders. In late August, the party leadership demanded that I endorse the official VVD position supporting Turkey's accession to the EU. I refused, and on September 2 I left the party. In my first speech in the *Tweede Kamer* as an independent parliamentarian, I warned against the "extremist sermons of radical imams in radical mosques."[13]

One month later, when jihadists released an internet video threatening to behead me, my wife and I still slept in our Kanaleneiland apartment or at our home in Venlo, though the police intensified my personal security. After the gruesome ritual murder of Theo van Gogh on November 2, however, the police felt I had to go into hiding. I have lived under police protection at safe houses ever since. It is the price for speaking the truth about Islam.

★ ★ ★

Since I left Kanaleneiland, conditions there have continued to deteriorate for the dwindling non-Muslim population. In fact, by September 2007, crime had become so pervasive in the district that the mayor of Utrecht banned youths from assembling together. Municipal authorities also erected fences around a housing complex for elderly people in order to block the escape routes used by thieves. In August 2009, a van was driven into the fence around the Kanaleneiland police headquarters. The police, fearing the van was filled with explosives, called in the bomb squad. Luckily, the vehicle turned out to be empty.[14]

The press still doesn't like to report on the collapse of towns like Kanaleneiland, and even when journalists want to, they're not always successful. A television crew came to Kanaleneiland to report on the situation but gave up after three failed attempts. On the first occasion, the reporters fled after being assaulted and having their car vandalized. On the second try, they were attacked again and their cameras were stolen. On the third attempt, they had rocks thrown at them.[15]

These problems affect many other parts of the Netherlands as well. In March 2010, an elderly couple who lived for forty years in the Amsterdam borough of Slotervaart described to a journalist how they had endured years of provocations, intimidation, violence, and even arson attempts by Moroccan youths. "The situation we have to live in is worse than during the war," the old man said, bursting into tears. Speaking on condition of anonymity, the couple revealed they were quietly moving out. They kept their move a secret and did not even order a moving truck, fearing their tormentors would follow the truck, discover their new home, and continue terrorizing them there.[16]

The couple, like many other Dutch, were effectively abandoned by the authorities in January 2006, when riots erupted in Slotervaart due to the death of a Moroccan thief who drove his scooter into a pillar while trying to flee from the police. In response to the violence, Amsterdam officials instructed uniformed police to stop entering "sensitive" neighborhoods—that is, areas with a large Islamic presence. "The presence of large numbers of uniformed personnel is often perceived by the youths as a cause for confrontation," stated an internal police memo that was leaked to me by indignant police officers.[17] Trying to justify the new policy, an Amsterdam police spokesman exclaimed, "If you see a bull in the meadow, you do not approach it with red trousers either, do you?" He added, "We were not afraid to enter the neighborhood, but we most certainly did not want to provoke anything."[18] The Dutch press hardly reported on the authorities' abdication of the most basic responsibility of any government—to protect the public.

No wonder the elderly couple felt the police had abandoned them— they had. The couple had no choice but to join the ranks of the thousands of Dutch, including so many of my own former neighbors in Kanale- neiland, who have practically become fugitives in their own country.

Tragically, history is repeating itself. What happened to the native Dutch in Slotervaart, Kanaleneiland, and dozens of other boroughs also happened to the Jewish tribes of Yathrib after 622. By foolishly welcom- ing Muhammad and his Meccan followers into their town, the Yathrib- ians guaranteed their own extinction and the transformation of their land into Medina, the "City of the Prophet," which it has remained ever since. Today, Kanaleneiland is one of many "cities of the prophet" found in the Netherlands.

In August 2011, the Dutch newspaper *De Pers* sent Arnold Karskens, its war correspondent, to the Dutch city of Helmond to investigate reports that Islamic thugs were harassing local residents. Karskens' article details the terrible abuse suffered by the non-Muslim population, including the months-long sexual intimidation of a 9-year-old Dutch girl, a couple whose front door had been attacked with a fireworks bomb, newcomers to the area who already want to leave, and complaints that the police are afraid of the lawless thugs who are terrorizing the peaceful population.[19]

Two weeks after Karskens' article appeared, I went to Helmond to speak with the locals at the neighborhood center. When I left the build- ing, Moroccan schoolchildren shouted curses at me.[20] In light of the serious crimes being perpetrated against so many people in the city, I felt lucky that all I suffered was insults.

★   ★   ★

In March 2007, Ella Vogelaar, the Dutch Minister of Integration and Housing, published a list of forty areas now known as "Vogelaar neighborhoods."[21] Vogelaar, a Labour politician, announced she wanted to address the huge problems in these neighborhoods through poverty-fighting schemes like stimulating economic investment and sending in an army of state-subsidized "community workers." The root cause of the problem—Islam—was not addressed, of course, since Vogelaar, like most of the political establishment, refuses to acknowledge Islam's many pathologies.

The Vogelaar neighborhoods resemble the 751 *zones urbaines sensibles* (sensitive urban areas, or ZUS) listed by the French government.[22] The ZUS, which are dominated by Islamic immigrants and include many suburbs of Paris, were designated as early as 1996, and have since degenerated further into no-go areas where people are advised not to enter, where ambulances and firetrucks do not go without police protection, and where even the police themselves are afraid to venture. The ZUS are the "lost territories" of the French Republic, even though a staggering 5 million people, or 8 percent of the total French population, live in them.

In these parts of France, Shariah law is enforced by street criminals, who especially target women who go on dates, wear makeup, or offend Islam by acting Western in other ways. According to a 2007 CBS report, "It's gotten so bad that, today, most of the young women only feel safe if they are covered up, or if they stay at home. Girls who want to look just like other French girls are considered provocative, asking for trouble." Indeed, the article cites the plight of Samira Bellil, a French woman of Algerian descent who wrote a book revealing she'd been repeatedly gang-raped in a Paris ZUS. Bellil became an advocate for other victims, one of whom was a 13-year-old girl from Lille who was gang-raped by eighty men. In another horrific case, a 17-year-old girl named Sohane Benziane was burned alive by a gang leader in the basement of an apartment complex. CBS reported, "When the young man accused of killing Sohane returned with police to show how he had doused her with gasoline, the highrise he had controlled broke out in cries of support."[23]

Every so often, French politicians talk tough and promise to restore law and order in the lost territories—the "cities of the prophet" on French soil. In April 2010, authorities decided to have the police escort public buses that traverse through the ZUS around Paris. Bus drivers had demanded protection after local youths set several buses ablaze in retaliation for a police swoop on drug dealers—the buses' passengers narrowly escaped being incinerated.[24] French President Nicolas Sarkozy declared that "no part of our territory can remove itself from the rule of the laws of the Republic and that an unabating battle will now be conducted against the drug dealers, wherever they may be."[25] Note how the French president, like most Dutch politicians, refuses to see Islam as part of the problem.

Unfortunately, passengers do not always escape unharmed from torched buses. On October 28, 2006, a public bus was set on fire in a predominantly Muslim area of Marseille. Mama Galledou, a 26-year-old student from Senegal, sustained severe burns over 70 percent of her body.[26] Similarly, as buses were being attacked during the massive riots of November 2005—riots that resulted in the declaration of a state of emergency—a handicapped female bus passenger in Sevran suffered third degree burns over 30 percent of her body.[27]

The French riots of 2005—which was the first event to draw international media attention to the collapse of Europe's urban areas—resulted in the destruction of 10,000 cars and more than 300 buildings, including churches, synagogues, schools, hospitals, and police and fire stations. One hundred thirty police officers and countless civilians were wounded, and two French dhimmis were beaten to death.

Further bouts of French rioting in 2006 and 2007 were hardly covered in the press, indicating the conspiracy of silence that surrounds this issue. Much like the media, France's leadership is uncomfortable discussing these problems, which raise inconvenient questions about Islam and multiculturalism. In some cases, this results in outright censorship. "To discourage more violence, France 3 will no longer publish or present figures on vehicle arson," French state television channel France 3 announced in November 2005.[28] More recently, during yet another riot on July 14, 2009, the Sarkozy administration declared a total news blackout and forbade the police and the firefighters from divulging any information to the press.[29] Even private media outlets find it difficult simply to report the truth; a leading executive of the private television channel TF1 admitted censoring riot coverage "to avoid encouraging the resurgence of extreme rightwing views."[30]

Many European nations with a large Islamic presence have suffered these problems. Take Britain; in January 2008, Michael Nazir-Ali, the Anglican Bishop of Rochester, declared that "the ideology of Islamic extremism" had succeeded in "turn[ing] already separate communities into 'no-go' areas where adherence to this ideology has become a mark of acceptability. Those of a different faith or race may find it difficult to live or work there because of hostility to them and even the risk of violence."[31]

Bishop Nazir-Ali, the son of a Pakistani Christian convert, had the rare courage to name Islam as the cause of the problem. Unsurprisingly, after he published his piece, he received death threats and was placed under police protection. "I do not wish to cause offence to anyone, let alone my Muslim friends," the Bishop explained. "But unless we diagnose the malaise from which we all suffer we shall not be able to discover the remedy."[32] Shiraz Maher, a British journalist with an Islamic background, applauded the bishop's bravery. "Perhaps it had to be someone like Michael Nazir-Ali, the first Asian bishop in the Church of England, who would break with convention and finally point out the elephant in the room," he wrote.[33]

The British military tacitly acknowledges that some areas of Britain are off-limits to the nation's own soldiers. In March 2008, the Royal Air Force advised its personnel not to wear military attire in certain areas of the town of Peterborough in order not to "offend minorities."[34] This kind of deep hostility toward Western militaries pervades many Islamic communities in Britain and throughout the West. In a widely publicized event, in March 2009, a parade in Luton for British soldiers returning from Iraq was disrupted by Islamic youths who waved signs denouncing the soldiers as "butchers," "cowards," and "killers."[35] Five Muslims were prosecuted over the incident and each was fined £500. Since all of them were on welfare, they defiantly declared, "The taxpayer paid for this court case. The taxpayer will pay for the fines too out of benefits." During the trial, the defendants refused to stand when the judge entered and left the court, but the judge said she did not want to "set a precedent" by charging them with contempt of court.[36]

When a state cannot deploy its policemen and soldiers in certain areas or command basic respect for its judicial system, it no longer fully controls its own territory. "Asian Muslims account for about 1 in 50 of British citizens, yet they dominate entire districts in the vicinities of their more than 1,350 mosques: 10 of them in Luton alone," historian John Cornwell observed in a 2008 essay in the *Sunday Times*.[37]

Germany faces similar problems. In July 2008, the newspaper *Die Welt* reported that "in several German cities the police barely dare to enter certain districts because they are immediately attacked." The paper described how police officers in Essen are struggling to prevent the town's predominantly Islamic districts from degenerating, as one police officer said, into "a lawless area" where "narcotics are dealt and stolen goods received with impunity."[38]

In August 2011, Chief Police Commissioner Bernhard Witthaut admitted that no-go zones outside police authority are proliferating in Germany. "Every police commissioner and interior minister will deny it," Witthaut declared, adding, "We know that these areas exist. Even worse: in these areas crimes no longer result in charges.... The power of the state is completely out of the picture."[39]

The population of Brussels, the Belgian capital and seat of NATO and the European Union, is over 25 percent Muslim,[40] and the city has several predominantly Islamic districts. In early 2010, immigrant youths in one such district, Kuregem, shot a policeman in the legs with a Kalashnikov. Following the incident, Jan Schonkeren of the Belgian police union VSOA acknowledged there are boroughs in Brussels "which officers do not dare enter in uniform."[41]

Though Europe has far more Islamic immigrants than the rest of the Western world, Australia, Canada, and the United States have not been entirely spared these sorts of conflicts. Cities of the prophet—where traditional Western freedoms and state authority have been replaced by Sharia law—exist there, too. Consider Dearborn, Michigan, where more than one-third of the city's 100,000 residents are Arab, mostly Muslim. In the 1970s, the Dearborn Mosque was the site of a bitter factional dispute resulting in the ousting of a Wahhabi imam from Yemen who had molested a 12-year-old girl. Today, the mosque uses loudspeakers to broadcast the *azaan*, the Islamic call to prayer, which can be heard blocks away. Annoyed city officials tried to stop the broadcasts but were thwarted by a court ruling that found the *azaan* is the "Muslim equivalent of church bells."[42] Another Dearborn mosque, the Islamic Center of America, is the largest mosque on the American continent, boasting two towering, 10-story minarets. Dearborn's Walmart caters especially to Muslims, featuring an Arabic-speaking staff, *hijab*-clad female employees, and "ethnic-sensitivity" training courses for non-Muslim employees.[43]

As Western cities become more Islamic, authorities tend to bow deeper to Islamic demands—and Dearborn is no exception. This was evident in 2009 at the Dearborn Arab International Festival, an annual street event that is free and open to the public. At that festival, city authorities prevented a group of Arab Christians from proselytizing to passers-by on the street, a ban that was later upheld by a U.S. district court judge. "The police and city officials are cowards," declared Yousif Salem, a Christian activist. "I am an American citizen and my rights were stripped away because they are afraid.... Five times a day through loud speakers from Islamic Mosques, prayers to Allah are freely allowed and tolerated. But you let a Christian hand out literature to a Muslim and they threaten with riot."[44] The following year, police arrested four Christian missionaries for proselytizing at the festival. A jury later acquitted all four of the defendants, who have filed a civil rights claim against the city of Dearborn. The shameful ban against proselytizing at the festival was later overturned on appeal.[45]

In 2009, Frans Timmermans, then-Dutch Minister of European Affairs, visited Dearborn "to discern why Muslims are more accepted in the United States than in the Netherlands." Reporting on the visit, the

Detroit News commented, "Dutch society is plagued with problems of high unemployment and low integration and participation in the society by Moroccan and some Turkish immigrants. There also are ongoing culture wars between Muslims and the Dutch, including the assassination of the filmmaker Theo van Gogh in 2004 and the production of a film 'Fitna,' which Muslims criticized as highly intolerant."[46]

It was a revealing statement, one that suggested a moral equivalence between my movie and a political murder. The paper continued, "Amid the social and religious tensions, the Dutch are trying to negotiate the difficulties sometimes caused by free speech and seeking to reassert their long tradition of tolerance and freedom." *The difficulties sometimes caused by free speech*—what a wonderful euphemism for Islam's tendency to riot and murder whenever it feels offended by a speech, drawing, or film.[47]

The *Detroit News* announced, "While Muslims in Metro Detroit and the United States sometimes struggle with discrimination, religious bigotry, verbal harassment and other forms of intolerance, there is a general sense, backed by public opinion research, that their circumstances here are more tolerable—sometimes considerably so—than in Europe."[48] There is indeed a certain intolerance surrounding Islam in Europe—but it's not Europeans' intolerance for Islam, it is Islam's intolerance for anyone else.

In 2006, Petra Akesson, a Swedish sociologist, conducted a study of Islamic youths in Malmo, a city that has one of the highest crime rates in Sweden along with one of the highest percentages of welfare recipients and one of the largest Islamic communities. Disturbingly, Akesson found that Islamic youths, having been raised in a culture that extols Islamic supremacy, regard their criminal activities as acts of war against non-Muslim infidels. "When we are in the city and robbing, we are waging a war against the Swedes," a typical youth told her. "Power for me means that the Swedes shall look at me, lie down on the ground and kiss my feet. We rob every single day, as often as we want to, whenever we want to."[49]

Few politicians or journalists are willing to admit that significant parts of the West's Islamic communities view their host societies as the enemy. In 2005, a Turkish imam who had been living in Berlin since 1971 was ordered deported after he gave a sermon in which he called Germans "stinking people...doomed to go to hell because they [are] useless creatures and infidels." The shocking statement by the imam, who co-founded an organization responsible for teaching Islam to Muslim students at German schools, did not seem to offend his Muslim congregation. According to a journalist who was there, "There was nobody in the mosque who stood up and demanded that the Imam stop his nasty talk about Germans. Nobody seemed to mind at all. We asked people as they were leaving the mosque to tell us what they thought about the Imam. Everyone was looking daggers at us, and we certainly didn't have the impression that the Imam had voiced an isolated opinion."[50]

Drawing a bitter lesson from the 2005 riots in France, Jewish French philosopher Alain Finkielkraut explained how the basic impetus of Islamic unrest in the West is not poverty, but an urge to attack infidels: "The first targets of those who were violent were their neighbors. And those neighbors are the [non-Muslims] who are demanding that the public order of the Republic be restored.... Here's a charming rap couplet [sung by immigrant youths]: 'France is a slut, don't forget to f*** her till she drops like a bitch, you gotta deal with her, guy! Me, I piss on Napoleon and General de Gaulle.'"[51]

Finkielkraut bemoaned his country's tendency to excuse the violence and its perpetrators. "Instead of being outraged by the scandals of schools being burned, people pontificate about the despair of the arsonists. Instead of listening to what they're saying—'F*** your mother!', 'F*** the police!', 'F*** the State!'—we listen to them, that is, we convert their appeals to hatred as appeals for help and their vandalization of school buildings as demands for education."[52]

In her book *A God Who Hates*, former Muslim Wafa Sultan argues that the behavior of Islamic immigrants is conditioned by Islam, particularly by the Arab desert culture of raiding. "For me," she writes, "understanding the truth about the thought and behavior of Muslims can only be achieved through an in-depth understanding of this philosophy of raiding that has rooted itself firmly in the Muslim mind.... When I immigrated to America I discovered right away that the local inhabitants were not proficient in raiding while the expatriate Muslims could not give it up."[53]

By viewing the world as Islam sees it, we come to understand why some Muslims consider it only natural to extract money out of the infidels, whether by robbing and raiding them or by making them pay *jizya*. The welfare payments they receive in the West are not seen as generosity to the deprived and underprivileged, but as *jizya*, to which they are divinely entitled because Allah himself wrote in the Koran that dhimmis have to pay tribute to Muslims.[54]

Once we find the courage to acknowledge the real problem, the solution becomes clear: we must use the full force of the state to suppress criminal violence and restore law and order in the neighborhoods that are succumbing to jihadist violence.

At the height of the French riots of 2005, Michel Pajon, the Socialist deputy mayor of Noisy-le-Grand, pleaded over the radio for the army to intervene. "Women have been made to stop on the streets of my town," he cried. "They were dragged from their cars by their hair, they were practically stoned and their cars were set ablaze.... My town has a psychiatric hospital which has been attacked with Molotov cocktails. This is beyond comprehension.... For a socialist to say that the army has to intervene is an inconceivable admission of defeat, but what I can say is that one cannot abandon the people like this. At some point we need to know whether this country still has a state."[55]

A similar plea was heard in 2007 when, following another spate of French urban rioting, youths fired shots at the police, causing a well-known French judge to warn of a possible civil war. "The suburbs," Jean de Maillard, Vice-president of the Superior Court of Orléans, declared, "...have been armed for a long time with caches of quality war weapons, lethal weapons, against which the bullet-proof vests will be useless.... The methods become more professional and the police and gendarmes will soon have to confront, if they have not already, experts in urban guerilla warfare.... I hope that the public authorities will become aware of the immence of calamity and especially that they will finally seek solutions.... To shower the [youths] with subsidies to buy armed peace will be the chosen way: it will provide only a short respite."[56]

Seeming to fulfill the judge's grim prediction, in March 2008, four police officers were shot and wounded in Grigny, a suburb of Paris, after being ambushed by around thirty masked youths. According to the BBC, "The armed youths fired cartridges containing lead shot and nails at the police, while others threw stones and Molotov cocktails, setting a car alight."[57]

The huge social problems created by Islam are making Europeans increasingly doubtful that Islam is "enriching" the West, as we're constantly told. A 2011 poll showed that 63 percent of the Dutch are worried by the growing influence of Islam in Western Europe.[58] According to a 2008 poll, 57 percent of the Dutch believe that allowing large-scale immigration was the biggest mistake ever made in Dutch history.[59]

We see similar results throughout Europe when the people themselves, as opposed to the media or the political class, speak out on the issue. On November 29, 2009, 58 percent of Swiss voters approved a ban on the construction of new minarets—the soaring, triumphalist spires that commonly adorn mosques and dominate the surrounding skyline. (The four existing minarets were allowed to remain and the building of new mosques—Switzerland already had some 200—was also permitted.) Turnout for the referendum was unusually high at 53 percent, with the ban passing in twenty-two of Switzerland's twenty-six cantons.

Polls indicate that many other European nations would vote similarly. A 2009 survey showed 46 percent of the French support a ban on minarets, with 40 percent opposed; 41 percent also want to ban construction of new mosques, a substantial rise since 2001, when only 21 percent of the French supported such a ban.[60] A 2009 poll in Belgium found 60 percent support a minaret ban and 57 percent want a ban on mosques.[61] In the Netherlands, my party is currently trying to hold a referendum to ban new minarets.

In some countries, such as France, Belgium, and the Canadian province of Quebec, the *niqab* and the *burka*, two varieties of the full Islamic veil that reveal only a woman's eyes, have been banned from public places. "If you are someone employed by the state and you deliver a service, you will deliver it with your face uncovered," Jean Charest, the Liberal premier of Quebec, says. "And if you are a citizen who receives services, you will receive them with your face uncovered."[62] Quebec's demand is clear: *We want to see your face.* It is a perfectly reasonable demand though, as we saw in chapter seven, it could get you fired if you work in a German post office. In January 2012, the Dutch cabinet submitted a similar bill to ban *niqabs* and *burkas* in public places.

Christian churches are sometimes far too accommodating to Islam and too anxious to find a "common ground" that doesn't really exist—as Thomas Jefferson said, "in matters of principle" one must "stand like a rock."[63] But churches, too, are beginning to draw the line. On March 31, 2010, a fight broke out in the Roman Catholic cathedral of Córdoba, Spain, when guards intervened against Muslims who attempted to pray in the cathedral. One of the Muslims drew a knife and wounded the guards. When the police were called, they too were attacked. Islam claims the cathedral as its own because it was a mosque until the thirteenth century, but Bishop Mgr. Demetrio Fernández, who has forbidden Islamic worship in the church, notes that the location held a church even before the mosque was built in the eighth century. Though the British *Guardian* reported the fight had occurred in "Cordoba's former mosque," the Bishop refuses to see his cathedral as anything but a church.[64]

This begs the question: How would the *Umma* react if Christians or Jews began praying in mosques that had once been churches or synagogues? Consider the prohibition against Jewish prayer on Jerusalem's Temple Mount, formerly the site of the Jewish Temple and now home to Islam's Al-Aqsa Mosque and the Dome of the Rock. Suppose a group of Jewish activists began praying inside the Al-Aqsa Mosque and then attacked its Islamic guards with knives. Would Islam react with as much

restraint as Spanish Catholics showed after the fight in Córdoba's cathedral? History shows the answer: when Israeli politician Ariel Sharon
simply visited the Temple Mount on September 29, 2000, the Palestinians
responded by launching the Second Intifada, which lasted four years and
cost thousands of lives.

CHAPTER TEN

Medina

We are not in politics to ignore people's worries:
we are in politics to deal with them.

—Margaret Thatcher

In his novel *Night*, Holocaust survivor Elie Wiesel conveys an important message: when people say they want to kill you, believe them.[1] In light of the assassination of Theo van Gogh, the attempted killing of Kurt Westergaard, and countless other acts of intimidation against critics of Islam, I believe many people when they say they want to kill me—that's why I have lived under 24-hour police protection for more than seven years. Everywhere I go I am accompanied by armed officers of the *Dienst Koninklijke en Diplomatieke Beveiliging* (The Royalty and Diplomatic Corps Protection Department, or DKDB), the special police force that protects the Dutch royal family, national politicians under threat, diplomats, and high-ranking official visitors to the Netherlands. If I want to go anywhere, even for a simple walk on the beach, I have to inform the DKDB, preferably a day in advance, so the officers can make the necessary arrangements. Sometimes, when it's pouring rain, I go out on my prearranged walks anyway, just so all the planning won't be in vain.

Whenever I travel abroad, DKDB officers come along with me, while a second team of officers goes in advance to liaise with the local police. I recall my first visit to Israel accompanied by the DKDB in January 2005. Upon arriving at Ben Gurion airport in Tel Aviv, I had to wait with a female Israeli border guard while the DKDB officers went to a separate room to register their weapons. The Israeli woman was shouting at me the whole time, "Stay here! Don't move! Sit!" When I stood up to stretch my legs, she snapped, "Come back! Who do you think you are?!"

After my bodyguards reclaimed their guns, we had to show our papers to the same woman. She turned pale when she saw my diplomatic passport. "Oh, I'm so sorry," she pleaded. "I thought you were a prisoner."

Sometimes I do feel like a prisoner; I long for the old days when I could travel by myself, without worrying about someone trying to kill me. Providing permanent protection for critics of Islam is one of the many costs a society has to pay once it allows Islam inside its borders. Britain pays the same price to protect Salman Rushdie, and Denmark and Sweden pay it to protect Muhammad cartoonists Kurt Westergaard and Lars Vilks, respectively. Undoubtedly, the list of threatened public figures will grow much larger as Islam's reach expands throughout the West.

Since I was forced into hiding, one bright spot has been the thousands of letters and emails I've received from everyday Dutch people offering to hide me at their house, let me take walks on their land, or just expressing their support. An elderly lady sent me a €10 bill with a note saying, "I am the last Dutch person on my street. I have no children and my husband passed away. My life is hell. I am afraid to go out. No one speaks Dutch anymore on my street. I have a small pension, and I actually cannot do without it, but here are ten euros to help you establish your new party, because you are the only one speaking on my behalf." I hung her letter on the wall to remind me who I am fighting for.

After I left the VVD party in September 2004, I was on my own for a short period. Then, helped by many volunteers, I founded a new party, the *Partij voor de Vrijheid* (Party for Freedom, or PVV). Our first campaign involved the 2005 referendum on the Constitution of the European

Union—we argued for a "no" vote, opposing a pact that would erode national sovereignty in the Netherlands and throughout Europe. In contrast, most parties, from the governing Christian Democrats and the liberal VVD to the Labour Party, then in opposition, and the far-left Green Left Party, all supported the constitution.

It's not easy to campaign when a whole army of bodyguards has to be mobilized and preparations have to be made weeks in advance just to go for a walk—in a bulletproof vest—among the people. But we campaigned hard despite the challenges, organizing a bus tour through the Netherlands. Everywhere, even in the smallest towns, hundreds of people waited to welcome me. The campaign ended in Rotterdam, where I received a tremendous welcome from members of *Leefbaar*, the late Pim Fortuyn's party.

On June 1, 2005, the EU Constitution was rejected by an overwhelming 62 percent of the vote; only twenty-six of the Netherlands' 467 municipalities approved it. Around the same time, the constitution was rejected in France with 55 percent of the vote. What happened next was a disgrace, though it did not surprise me: refusing to take no for an answer, the EU establishment rewrote the document as the "Treaty of Lisbon." This time the people were not allowed a direct say, as Europe's political class approved the Lisbon Treaty in national parliaments instead of through referenda. In other words, when the people resisted the political class, it retaliated by simply bypassing the people altogether.

By challenging the political consensus that robs Europeans of a meaningful voice on so many issues—especially on Islam, immigration, and multiculturalism—my party later gained some additional victories, but the establishment repeatedly refused to respect the will of the majority. Most notably, in December 2005, a majority in the *Tweede Kamer* supported my motion to demand that the Dutch government ban women from publicly wearing *niqabs* and *burkas*, the full-length Islamic garb covering everything except the eyes.[2] This was a popular proposal that would uphold women's rights (most women who wear these suffocating costumes are pressured or outright forced to do so), public security (it is easier to commit robberies, fraud, and other crimes when people cannot be identified), and our national culture (*burkas* are a total negation of Western norms that hinder Muslim integration in the West). Nevertheless, because the ban challenged the assumptions of multiculturalism, the government refused to implement it. We managed to change that situation in January 2012, when a new Dutch cabinet, which needed the parliamentary support of my party, submitted to Parliament its own bill for a *burka* ban.

Islam claims that Muslims have a legal right to live according to divine Islamic law. "All the law that a Muslim needs is in the Qur'an and Hadith," says Feisal Abdul Rauf, Manhattan's acclaimed "moderate" imam.[3] "What Muslims want is to ensure that their secular laws are not in conflict with the Quran or the Hadith.... What Muslims want is a judiciary that ensures that the laws are not in conflict with the Quran and the Hadith."[4]

In Islam, the political, social, military, commercial, and personal behavior of the faithful is governed by the elaborate legal system of Sharia (Islamic law) and *Fiqh* (the written corpus of Islamic jurisprudence). Experts of Islamic law are called *ulama* (from the singular *alim*, meaning scholar). One of these *ulama* was Sam Solomon, an imam who read the Gospel, converted to Christianity, and then fled the Islamic world for Britain, where he was able to practice his faith openly.

Sam knows the whole Koran and large parts of the Hadith by heart. He has written many books about Islamic doctrine, often together with his friend, Elias Al Maqdisi, a Palestinian *alim* who also converted to Christianity. Al Maqdisi, a native of Jerusalem, was punished for his apostasy by an Islamic gang that ambushed him, beat him up, cut out one of his eyes with a broken bottle, tried to cut out the other eye, and left him for dead. (The attack comported with Muhammad's command that renegades have their eyes branded.)[5] Elias, barely alive, made it to the Palestinian hospital in Jerusalem, where doctors refused to treat the apostate. He was forced to go to a Jewish hospital, where he was attended by Jewish physicians. A few years later, 80 percent blind, Elias fled to Canada.

I gave a copy of Solomon and Al Maqdisi's book *Modern Day Trojan Horse: Al-Hijra: The Islamic Doctrine of Immigration, Accepting Freedom or Imposing Islam?* to all members of the *Tweede Kamer*. In that important tome, the authors note that the Islamic calendar starts with the *hijra*, the migration of Muhammad and his small band of followers from Mecca to Yathrib, which they conquered from within and renamed Medina. Medina is where Islam became a state, and where Muhammad's heretical Judeo-Christian mishmash transformed from a religion into an ideology. "The most important outcome of the *Hijra*," the men write, "was the spread of Islam…not only as a religion but a combined, socio-religious and socio-political system. That is why *Hijra* is considered to be the most important method of spreading Islam…and consolidating it far beyond the Muslim countries. Hence, *Hijra*, as an example set up by the Prophet of Islam must be imitated and emulated by all Muslims as a religious obligation."[6]

Before the *hijra*, when Muhammad was still in Mecca and Islam was but a hodgepodge religious sect, the Muslims had no mosque because there was no Islamic state. But the first thing Muhammad did upon arriving in Yathrib was to build a mosque, erecting it before he even built his own house. The Yathrib mosque, the first ever, was the prototype of all mosques. It was the locus from which the conquest of Yathrib and its transformation into the Islamic state of Medina was planned, organized, and executed. This "mother of all mosques" was Muhammad's propaganda center, the headquarters of his state, the base for all activities political and non-political, and the barracks of his jihad.

Thus, from Islam's very beginning, the mosque was primarily a political institution, not a place of worship. This has grave implications for Europe, which now hosts more than 10,000 mosques.[7] Patrick Sookhdeo, a British Anglican canon who, like Solomon and Al Maqdisi, is a Muslim convert to Christianity, observes that some European mosques "have been used as the bases for insurgency, in particular to store weapons."[8] Solomon and Al Maqdisi explain the bottom line: "Mosques are at the heart of inciting violence and the killing of the enemies of Islam."[9]

Westerners view mosques and minarets as religious symbols, but that is not how Islam sees them. "The mosques are our barracks, the domes our helmets, the minarets our bayonets and the faithful our soldiers," declares Recep Tayyip Erdogan, Turkey's prime minister.[10] Islam also invests immense political value in immigration, viewing it, like Muhammad's *hijra*, as part of a Muslim's duty to spread Islam to foreign lands and ultimately conquer them. "Whoever does not do hijra is ruined," Muhammad told his followers.[11] But of course, once the whole world is Islamic, the need for *hijra* stops. As Muhammad said, "There is no Hijra after the Conquest."[12]

In a 1974 speech at the United Nations, former Algerian President Houari Boumédienne explained the modern *hijra*'s purpose in stark, simple terms. "One day, millions of men will leave the Southern Hemisphere to go to the Northern Hemisphere," he proclaimed. "And they will not go there as friends. Because they will go there to conquer it. And they will conquer it with their sons. The wombs of our women will give us victory."[13]

Solomon and Al Maqdisi note that there are "a variety of reasons for everyday migration: economic, political, religious, social, natural disasters, wars."[14] This should not, however, blind us to the reality that *hijra* is an intrinsic part of Islamic culture established by the Islamic prophet himself. Consequently, some Muslim immigrants refuse to adapt to their new homelands in the West—for them, Islam is meant to dominate, not to assimilate.

Turkey's Erdoğan subscribes to this view. On a 2008 visit to Germany, he told Turkish immigrants that "assimilation is a crime against humanity."[15] In early 2010, he further denounced assimilation at a mass convention of Turks in Paris and at a conference of 1,500 European politicians of Turkish origin in Istanbul. Those 1,500 politicians, whose dual citizenship enables them to be politically active throughout Europe, had been invited to Istanbul by the Turkish government.[16]

Erdoğan is often upheld in the West as a moderate, but he himself rejects that term, claiming it is "very ugly, it is offensive and an insult to our religion. There is no moderate or immoderate Islam, Islam is Islam and that's it."[17] Ironically, Erdoğan's sentiments are close to those of the late Italian writer Oriana Fallaci, a fierce critic of Islam who argued, "A moderate Islam does not exist. It does not exist because there is no difference between Good Islam and Bad Islam. There is Islam and that is the end of it. Islam is the Koran, and nothing other than the Koran. And the Koran is the *Mein Kampf* of a religion that desires to eliminate others—non-Muslims—who are called infidel dogs, and inferior creatures."[18]

Indeed, there are many moderate Muslims, but there is no moderate Islam. "There is, to put it another way, no such beverage as Islam Lite," says David Solway. "One drinks in the real thing or nothing; there is no substitute."[19]

★　★　★

Today, for the third time in history, Islam is waging an offensive to conquer Europe. For the first time, however, it is threatening the continent from within. The doctrine of immigration is Islam's Trojan horse, paving the way for jihad. From the inside, Islam is now eating its way out while many Westerners look on helplessly.

With the arrival of millions of Islamic immigrants over recent decades, Sharia-based Islamic customs have spread throughout Europe. Some of these practices such as honor killings, female genital mutilation, and forced marriages are crimes in our legal system. A second category of Sharia traditions including polygyny and instant divorce for men are unlawful but increasingly open for debate in societies hobbled by moral relativism. A third group of Sharia-imposed practices such as dietary restrictions and Sharia-compliant banking do not violate Western law and are not considered problematic in the pluralistic West.

The spread of Sharia-based crimes is obviously an assault on Western society, but the more innocuous-seeming practices are also dangerous, part of a stealth process of Islamization. Solomon and Al Maqdisi refer to Islamic clothing as an example. "Implementation of the *hijab* [an Islamic female outfit that covers everything except the face and hands] has always been gradual," they write. "It would start as a headscarf and then move to a full garment with a headscarf. Then it would become the wearing of the *hijab* and finally the wearing of the [*burka* or] *neqab*. (*Neqab* is fully covering the face with only two little holes for the eyes). By the time they reach the state of wearing the *neqab*, the society would have become so conditioned by it that no one would give it a second look or thought."[20]

The first thing Islam tells its immigrants to do when they settle in the new Yathribs in the West is to build a mosque—the same thing Muhammad did in Yathrib in 622. Subsequently, the immigrants gradually acquaint the host society with innocent-looking Sharia practices such as *halal* food, special Islamic rules in the workplace and schools, and Islamic family law. "While the *halal* meat is insidious, the *hijab* is overt and an 'in your face' part of Islamic society," write Solomon and Al Maqdisi.[21]

Like the original Yathrib fourteen centuries ago, Europe welcomes Islam and goes to extreme lengths to accommodate it. Windsor Castle, home of the English monarchy since the days of William the Conqueror, created an Islamic prayer room in September 2006, when Queen Elizabeth II set the room aside at the request of Nagina Chaudhry, a 19-year-old employee of the Castle's gift shop who said she needed a place to pray during Ramadan.[22] It was the first time in history that the British monarch set aside a room of the royal castle at the request of a single, non-royal individual. We have to wonder if a Sikh, Buddhist, Shinto, Mormon, Jehovah's Witness, Scientologist, or Wiccan teenager would get her own religious space in Windsor Castle if she asked for it. If not, then we may wonder why Islam is so privileged.

Meanwhile, the West is forced to confront entirely new social problems, such as male Muslims preventing, sometimes violently, male doctors from treating their wives and daughters.[23] This relates to Sharia's maxim that a man may only touch a woman if she is his slave, his wife, or a close blood relative. The Hadith states that Muhammad "never touched the hand of any women."[24]

As Islam constantly challenges Western norms, Western countries have come to tolerate practices that were hitherto unlawful, such as polygyny. Today, municipal authorities in Amsterdam and Rotterdam officially register polygynous marriages.[25] Officials in Antwerp do the same.[26] In Italy, there are an estimated 20,000 polygynous marriages.[27] In France, authorities estimated in 2005 there are 30,000 men in the country who have more than one wife,[28] with estimates of the total number of people in polygynous households reaching as high as 400,000.[29]

We began by accommodating seemingly minor Sharia demands such as women covering their hair, and before we knew it we were tolerating polygyny. Europe is on a slippery slope toward full Islamization and the replacement of our secular legal system by Sharia law. This process of "creeping Sharia" is a non-violent infiltration of our institutions, a stealth jihad. As Solomon and Al Maqdisi warn, Western governments must stop this ever-expanding accommodation of Islam—before it's too late.

Yathrib was a tolerant, pluralist, multicultural oasis where Jewish, Christian, and pagan tribes lived together peacefully. The city's fate was sealed on September 9, 622, the day of the *hijra* and the first day of the Islamic calendar. Will Europe, today's Yathrib, still exist in 2022—the 1,400[th] anniversary of Muhammad's *hijra*—or will it be transformed beyond recognition into a new Medina?

Europe's accommodations of Islam range from the banal to the ludicrous:

- Some Muslims insist their meat be *halal*—that is, the animal is slaughtered according to Islamic law. To accommodate this demand, many European supermarkets and factory and school cafeterias provide *halal* meat to *everyone*. "We have many French customers who don't even know we're totally halal," says the owner of a trendy Paris restaurant. "To us, that is what integration is about."[30]
- Some Muslims refuse to go swimming in the presence of the opposite sex. To accommodate this demand, pools

and beaches across Europe—from Finland in the far north to Italy in the deep south—have introduced gender apartheid, providing separate swimming locations for women where male lifeguards are no longer allowed.[31] Some public pools in Britain require even non-Muslim women to wear so-called *burkinis*—Islamic-style swimwear that covers a woman's entire body.[32]

- Some Muslims refuse to defecate in the direction of Mecca. To accommodate this demand, toilets in some British prisons and bathrooms in public housing blocs, as well as some toilets in London's 2012 Olympic Park, are being built with the bowls facing away from Islam's holy city.[33]

One accommodation that is spreading especially rapidly in the West is Sharia banking, which some Muslims demand due to the Koran's ban on charging interest.[34] (Islamic banks also charge interest, of course, but they undertake various financial machinations to make it look like something else.)[35] Islamic banks are now establishing branches all across Europe, while Western banks are offering Sharia-compliant financial services. Those services are supervised by a board of Islamic scholars tasked with ensuring that the infidel banks properly comply with Islamic law.

Five-hundred thousand Muslims in France and over 75 percent of Britain's 2 million Muslims reportedly want Islamic banking products, while some Westerners are even parroting the Islamic claim that Sharia banking is more ethical than traditional Western banking.[36] Even the Vatican newspaper *L'Osservatore Romano* has expressed approval of Sharia banking. "The ethical principles on which Islamic finance is based may bring banks closer to...the true spirit which should mark every financial service," the paper wrote.[37]

Meanwhile, European governments are trying to out-do each other in encouraging Sharia-compliant banking because of the huge sums it attracts from Sharia-adherent immigrants, "ethically"-driven non-Muslims, and investors from Islamic countries. The British and French governments are competing to make London and Paris, respectively, the hub for Islamic banking.[38] Likewise, former Dutch Finance Minister and Labour leader Wouter Bos argues that "Islamic banking meets a demand from the Muslims living in the Netherlands" and also provides "an opportunity here for the Dutch financial sector."[39] Switzerland also wants a piece of what is, according to one Swiss banker, "the rich prize: which today is worth hundreds of billions, but in the future will be trillions of dollars of Islamic wealth."[40]

Sharia-compliant banking is antithetical to Western norms, but those who want to ban it typically encounter the same objections I did when I tried to prohibit the practice in the Netherlands. "Banning Islamic banking from the perspective of fighting terrorism will have a counter-productive effect," Wouter Bos wrote. "Denial of an actual need can lead to money-flows running via alternative channels out of sight of the government."[41]

Eating *halal*, banking Islamic, and refusing to touch the opposite sex are all examples of Sharia compliance. Fortunately, the Sharia command to kill blasphemers is not followed as widely. However, as far back as 1990, in a poll that coincided with Iran's pronouncement of its death *fatwa* against British author Salman Rushdie, a staggering 42 percent of British Muslims supported the death sentence and only 37 percent opposed it, while 21 percent were undecided.[42] Decades later, the problem remains. A 2006 Pew Research Center survey revealed that around one-third of French Muslims and a quarter of those in Britain and Spain agree that suicide bombings against civilians could be justified in defense of Islam.[43]

Similarly, a survey by the British Centre for Social Cohesion found that one-third of British Islamic students support a worldwide Caliphate, 32 percent find killing in the name of religion justified, and 40 percent favor introducing Sharia law into British law.[44] Another study showed that 48 percent of Dutch Muslims "sympathized with" and 5.6 percent "approved" the 9/11 attacks.[45]

In the Netherlands, only 15 percent of Dutch citizens of Moroccan origin and less than 20 percent of Dutch citizens of Turkish origin feel more connected to the Netherlands than to their country of origin.[46] The Pew Research Center reported that only 13 percent of Germany's 3.5 million Muslims see themselves as more German than Muslim. Seven out of ten Spanish Muslims consider themselves Muslims first, not Spaniards. Fully 81 percent of British Muslims self-identify with their religion rather than their British nationality. France has the best figures for assimilation, but even there, the percentage of French Muslims who consider themselves Muslims first (46 percent) is larger than those who primarily identify themselves as French (42 percent).[47]

Like so much of European life, Europe's cultural and historical exhibits are now circumscribed by the need to avoid offending increasingly assertive Islamic populations. Exhibitions about World War II have been banned for mentioning Arab complicity in Nazi crimes;[48] Islamic organizations have boycotted ceremonies marking the liberation of Auschwitz (because they were supposedly "not racially inclusive" and did not refer to the "Palestinian holocaust");[49] and opera houses have stopped performing Mozart's *Idomeneo* because Muhammad figures in it.[50]

Instead of defending their national identities, Europe's politicians ignore creeping Sharia or even actively facilitate it. These kinds of "leaders" have been around for a long time; they were described by nineteenth-century British Prime Minister Benjamin Disraeli as "cosmopolitan critics, men who are the friends of every country save their own."[51] They do the opposite of what Margaret Thatcher once explained a politician should do: "People are...afraid that this country might be...swamped by people with a different culture.... We are not in politics to ignore peoples' worries: we are in politics to deal with them."[52]

One such cosmopolitan critic is former Dutch Justice Minister Piet Hein Donner. In 2006, he declared that it would be "the ultimate consequence of democracy" if Sharia law became the law of the land, so long as it was supported by a sufficiently large portion of the electorate.[53] In 2008 another well-known Islam accommodationist, the Archbishop of Canterbury Rowan Williams, mused that the adoption of certain aspects of Sharia law in Britain "seems unavoidable."[54] A few months later, the head of the English judiciary, Lord Chief Justice Nicholas Phillips, declared that Sharia law could be used to settle marital and financial disputes.[55]

And local courts in Britain have, in fact, been authorized to adjudicate some cases using Sharia. One of the first British Sharia rulings settled an inheritance dispute involving a man whose estate had to be divided between his three daughters and two sons. The Sharia court gave the sons twice as much as the daughters,[56] in accordance with the Koranic pronouncement that a woman is only worth half a man.[57]

As Islam insists on accommodations in every aspect of life, it also demands that its Western host societies provide cash payments in the form of welfare benefits. In France, authorities tend to ignore how Islamic immigrants abuse the welfare system by collecting state benefits for several wives,[58] a problem also found in Britain, where a 2009 government review found that an Islamic man with several wives can claim state support of more than £10,000 ($15,000) a year.[59]

This wealth transfer from Western taxpayers to Islamic immigrants is consistent with Islam's history of raiding (*ghazwa*, or *razzia*), which resulted, as former Muslim Patrick Sookhdeo observes, in "a redistribution of wealth (e.g. livestock) or women from the losing tribe to the winning tribe."[60] Indeed, some imams in Germany, the Netherlands, and Britain have instructed the faithful to live on welfare and to refuse to work or pay taxes specifically as a means of harming the Western host state.[61]

These exhortations indicate that some Islamic activists regard welfare fraud as part of their deliberate campaign to undermine Western governments. Here's another indication: in 2005, an undercover reporter from Britain's *Sunday Times* posed as a follower of a Sharia-adherent Islamic group. He revealed how these groups "are so opposed to the British state that they see it as their duty to make no economic contribution to the nation." His Islamic "brothers" warned him "against getting a job because it would be contributing to the kuffar (non-Muslim) system. Instead, the young follower, Nasser, who receives £44 job seekers' allowance a week, said it was permissible to 'live off benefits,' just as the prophet Muhammad had lived off the state while attacking it at the same time. Even paying car insurance was seen as supporting the system. 'All the brothers drive without insurance,' he said."[62]

Similarly, a Pakistani immigrant in Norway admitted in a Norwegian newspaper that he worked in a Pakistani shop, but "neither the boss nor I pay taxes to the Norwegian authorities. In addition to this, I receive 100 percent disability benefits and welfare. I have to be cunning to make as much money as possible, since this is my only objective with being in Norway."[63]

In the Netherlands, non-Western immigrants comprise 11 percent of the population but nearly 44 percent of welfare recipients.[64] In light of these types of findings, in 2009 I asked the Dutch government to conduct a cost-benefit analysis of the effects of immigration. The cabinet refused—as a matter of principle, said Integration Minister Eberhard van der Laan. "We are not interested in what an individual costs, whether he be a Frisian, someone with blue eyes or a handicapped person," he declared. Immigrants' "presence cannot be reduced to a simple profit-loss calculation measured in euros."[65]

With the government unwilling to even acknowledge, much less measure, the costs of immigration, I asked Nyfer, a prestigious, independent economic research institute, to calculate the net cost of the 25,000 non-Western immigrants and 25,000 children that settle in the Netherlands each year. Nyfer calculated the annual cost at €7.2 billion, or $9.5 billion.[66]

Estimates of the number of Islamic immigrants in Europe vary widely. The think tank Network of European Foundations estimates the number of Muslims in Western Europe at just over 16.5 million.[67] The British magazine the *Economist* says the EU has "no more than 20m Muslims, or 4% of the union's inhabitants."[68] The German Islamic organization Zentralinstitut Islam-Archiv Deutschland puts the number of Muslims in Europe at 53.7 million, including 15.9 million in the EU, 5.9 million in the European part of Turkey, and 25 million in Russia. According to the Zentralinstitut, of the 680 million Europeans, 7.9 percent are Muslims, including about 3.2 percent in the EU.[69] In my native Netherlands, 6 percent of the 16.5 million inhabitants are Muslims, which is the highest percentage in Western Europe aside from France, whose 5.5 million Muslims comprise 8 percent of its population.[70]

Regardless of what the precise figures may be, Europe is undeniably Islamizing. This process is accelerating every year—and nearly everyone is afraid to talk about the implications.

On October 31, 2006, in the same monastery in Erfurt, Germany, where Martin Luther took his monastic vows in 1505, Roland Weisselberg, a 73-year-old Lutheran vicar, doused himself with gasoline and set himself on fire. "Jesus!" and "Oskar!" the burning Weisselberg cried out before he died. "Oskar" referred to Oskar Brüsewitz, a German Lutheran pastor who fatally immolated himself in 1976 to protest East Germany's communist regime. Before Weisselberg committed suicide, he had regularly warned the Lutheran authorities in Germany about Islam. In a farewell letter, he wrote that he was sacrificing his life in protest against the Islamization of Europe.[71]

Weisselberg hoped his gruesome sacrifice would awaken his compatriots, but it did not. And sadly, his desperation seems to be spreading across the continent. A 2007 British survey shows that British adults have so little faith in the future that 15 percent of them are reluctant to have children and 27 percent are less inclined to make future plans. Asked what troubled them, 70 percent cited the rise of terrorism, 58 percent immigration, 38 percent climate change, and 23 percent the threat of natural disaster.[72] Politicians are supposed to address people's worries, as Thatcher noted, but Europe's political establishment ignores the two major causes of unease because they don't fit the political agenda of the cosmopolitan Left.

Ignored by the political class, the people are voting with their feet. Emigration has reached levels not seen since before World War I, with 200,000 British citizens leaving their native country every year. In 2007, a record 250,000 middle-class residents quit the British capital London, either for the countryside or to move abroad. This exodus, the *Daily*

Mail wrote, was caused mainly by high immigration rates of foreigners into London.[73] In his book *Time to Emigrate?*, George Walden, Thatcher's Education Minister, leaves no doubt about the cause of Britain's malaise: immigration has created unacceptable terrorist and crime risks, he says.[74] As the *Daily Telegraph* explains simply, "Unchecked immigration over the past decade is creating a country many Britons no longer feel comfortable in."[75]

This phenomenon is evident across Europe. In 2005, for the first time in recent history, more emigrants left Germany than immigrants moved in.[76] Most of the emigrants were foreigners (primarily Poles and Romanians) returning home, but a considerable number of indigenous Germans also left.[77] In the Netherlands, the murder of Pim Fortuyn in 2002 triggered what the *New York Times* called "a quickening flight of the white middle class."[78] The Dutch emigrants, mostly highly motivated and well-educated, are being replaced by immigrants who are mostly unskilled.[79]

Amidst this population shift, the sophisticates deny that the emergence of Eurabia is anything to worry about, accusing anyone who voices misgivings of spreading fear and hate. "Eurabian Follies" declares *Foreign Policy*.[80] "Fears of a Muslim takeover are all wrong," *Newsweek* exclaims.[81] "Scaremongering," sniffs the *Economist*, adding that "for every depressing statistic about integration...there are several reassuring ones.... In 50 years' time, Americans may be praising this generation of European Muslims for leading the enlightenment that Islam needed."[82]

I believe it's more likely that Americans will ruefully be recalling Benjamin Franklin's warning that "he that lives upon Hope will die fasting."[83] The discomforting truth is that the U.S. political establishment, blinded by the same unquestionable multicultural assumptions as its European counterparts, simply does not comprehend the drastic implications of what is happening in Europe and the world with regard to Islam.

In its 2009 report on human rights, the U.S. State Department wrote that Europe's "discrimination" against Muslims is "an increasing concern" for the U.S. government. The report criticized the Netherlands for widespread "hatred of Muslims," who allegedly "faced societal resentment,...intimidation, brawls, vandalism, and graffiti with abusive language." There was not a word about the living conditions of my former neighbors, the native Dutch, in places like Slotervaart or Kanaleneiland. The report condemned France because President Sarkozy had uttered that *burkas* are "not welcome in France" and because a woman wearing a *burkini* was denied entry into a public pool. Switzerland was denounced because its citizens approved a referendum to ban the construction of new minarets.[84]

Unsurprisingly, the U.S. State Department does not have a high opinion of me either, having criticized me especially for my opposition to Turkey's admission to the European Union. In a July 2009 briefing document for President Obama published by Wikileaks, the U.S. embassy called me a "golden-pompadoured, maverick parliamentarian" who is "no friend of the U.S." and who "forments [sic] fear and hatred of immigrants."[85]

This is quite an attack on me, considering I proudly regard myself as one of the most pro-American political figures in the Netherlands and one of the biggest Dutch admirers of the American spirit. However, I do believe that the U.S. political establishment, both Democrats and Republicans, severely underestimates the threat Islam poses to the West. This is evident in America's solid support for Turkish membership in the EU. In my opinion, Turkey can be a good neighbor with close economic ties to Europe, but it cannot be a member of the family. If the 72.5 million Turks join the EU, Turkey will be the second most populous EU state after Germany and will probably be the most populous by 2020. Turkey will then have the most seats in the European Parliament and will profoundly influence the EU's agenda from within, including through the new flood of Turkish immigration that EU membership will make possible.

This is intolerable. Europe, like America, is a community of values rooted in Judeo-Christian and humanist principles. Islamic Turkey, now led by the man who denounces Turkish assimilation in Europe and who declared mosques, domes, minarets, and Muslims to be an advance Islamic army, is simply not compatible with these values. Turkey's inclusion in the EU will hasten the Islamization and fall of Europe, the culture and tradition from which America sprang. Europe is an integral part of the Western heritage, and its transformation into Eurabia will have the most profound effects on the world's balance of power. I fear that those Americans who think the United States will not be affected by Europe's demise live upon hope—and they will die fasting.

CHAPTER ELEVEN

The Facilitators

The time is now near at hand which must...determine whether Americans are to be freemen or slaves.

—George Washington

The party I founded, the Party for Freedom (PVV), competed in its first general elections on November 22, 2006. We won 6 percent of the vote, earning us nine of the 150 seats in the *Tweede Kamer*. Our parliamentarians included Martin Bosma, a journalist who joined me after Theo van Gogh had been murdered; Fleur Agema, a provincial councilor in North Holland; and Barry Madlener, a municipal councilor in Rotterdam and former spokesman for the late Pim Fortuyn. On June 4, 2009, we participated in our first European elections and won 17 percent of the vote, good for four of the Netherlands' twenty-five seats in the European Parliament.

An anti-establishment party like the PVV that questions the ruling paradigms of cultural and moral relativism will face a lot of difficulties. For one thing, it takes courage to join our party. Civil servants jeopardize their careers by supporting me, teachers risk their jobs, and professionals risk losing customers and contacts.[1]

This is no exaggeration. Politically incorrect citizens who challenge the tenets of multiculturalism are harassed from the top down by state authorities, media figures, and employers, and from the bottom up by leftists and Islamic activists. I've even heard from people whose families disowned them for supporting the PVV.

PVV supporters have been subjected to physical intimidation and attacks. People who distribute PVV flyers or election posters have had stones thrown through their windows, had their cars vandalized, and have been beaten up and pelted with eggs. The threats and attacks have succeeded, to a certain extent, in dissuading some people from openly supporting me and my party. I fully understand their hesitation; I do not expect anyone to jeopardize his family, career, or personal safety for me.

Throughout its entire history, Islam has intimidated and attacked its critics, often with the assistance of groups of infidels. When Muhammad and his followers settled in Yathrib, they were helped by a group of Yathribians who became their allies. The *ansar* ("helpers"), as the Muslims called them, facilitated the fall of Yathrib and its transformation into the Islamic city of Medina.

Today, Islam finds its *ansar* in Western leftists and other fellow travelers who ferociously attack Islam's critics and other defenders of Western civilization. For example, in October 2007, I advocated that criminals with dual nationality be stripped of their Dutch nationality and expelled from the Netherlands. My proposal became the topic of a debate on Dutch television during which former Amsterdam Police Chief Joop van Riessen said about me, "Basically one would feel inclined to say: let's kill him, just get rid of him now and he will never surface again."[2] In reference to PVV voters, van Riessen declared, "There are thousands of people who do not fit into the world of the new society which we are all creating; of whom in fact one should say: kick them out of the country, they no longer belong here."[3]

Van Riessen's exhortation to banish those who do not "fit into the new society" eerily resembles the musings of German communist Bertolt Brecht. Commenting on the 1953 East German uprising, Brecht asked,

"Would it not be easier … for the government to dissolve the people and elect another?"[4]

Totalitarian movements, whether communism or Islam, always seem to find their *ansar*.

Why have Europe's elites acted as *ansar* by abetting Islam's thrust into Europe over the past three decades? One explanation is the Eurabia hypothesis put forward by Bat Ye'or in her 2005 book *Eurabia: The Euro-Arab Axis*. Bat Ye'or posits that after the 1973 oil crisis, when Arab countries used oil as a weapon to punish European nations that had allied with Israel, European Union leaders began building an alliance with the Islamic world to ensure Europe's oil supply. As part of this arrangement, Bat Ye'or contends, European leaders agreed not to hinder the spread of Islam in Europe, not to pressure Islamic immigrants to assimilate, and to ensure that European schools and media outlets would portray Islam positively.[5]

In order to implement these agreements, Bat Ye'or argues, the EU seized power over many immigration issues from Europe's national governments. For example, in 2008, the European Court of Justice (ECJ), the EU's highest court, annulled separate Irish and Danish immigration legislation and proclaimed that national law is subordinate to EU-level laws.[6] I personally saw the effect of this usurpation of national sovereignty in March 2010, when the ECJ annulled Dutch legislation restricting family reunification for immigrants on welfare.[7] Similarly, citing EU rules, a Dutch court in August 2011 annulled Dutch legislation that obliged Turkish immigrants to the Netherlands to take classes on integration.[8]

Bat Ye'or makes a strong argument, but in my view, Europe's Islamization stems from cultural relativism rather than a reliance on Arab oil. Cultural relativism dictates that all cultures are equally moral and valuable—though in practice, Western culture is often presented as inferior to all others, stained as it supposedly is by racism and imperialism. If all cultures are equal, it follows that the state cannot promote any specific cultural values, even those of its own native people. Thus, cultural relativists deny that immigrants should assimilate, since that would champion European culture over the immigrants' native cultures.

Cultural relativism, the ruling ethos of Europe's political establishment, is gradually destroying our traditions and cultural identity. The so-called multicultural society tells newcomers who settle in our cities and villages: you are free to violate our norms and values, since your culture is just as good, and perhaps even better, than ours.

Cultural relativists realize their views are widely unpopular among everyday Europeans, which is why they often hide their real agenda. Consider, for example, Britain's mass immigration policy. In October 2009, Andrew Neather, former advisor to British Prime Minister Tony Blair, revealed that the governing Labour Party had organized mass immigration into Britain as part of a hidden social engineering project "to make the UK truly multicultural." Neather recalled, "I remember coming away from some discussions with the clear sense that the policy was intended—even if this wasn't its main purpose—to rub the Right's nose in diversity and render their arguments out of date."[9]

Neather emphasized that the mass immigration policy was shrouded in secrecy: drafts of the policy were only distributed "with extreme reluctance" and "there was a paranoia about it reaching the media"; the final report was "innocuously labelled"; "there was a reluctance" in government to discuss the true implications of mass immigration, so the published report only discussed the impact on immigrants themselves, not on the native British; and "ministers wouldn't talk about" the policy. Neather explained why the ministers insisted on so much secrecy: "In part they probably realised the conservatism of their core voters: while ministers might have been passionately in favour of a more diverse society, it wasn't necessarily a debate they wanted to have in working men's clubs."[10]

In other words, the ministers wanted to hide their mass immigration policy because they knew the British people wouldn't support it.

Thanks to this policy, Britain took in three million immigrants between 1997 and 2010, permanently altering the country's social and demographic composition. This led to growing social tensions, especially between native Brits and rapidly expanding Islamic communities. This was unavoidable; contrary to the beliefs of government social engineers, most everyday people do not want to be subject to population replacement. People feel attached to the civilization their ancestors created, and they don't want it exchanged for a society in which they are forced to adapt to immigrants' cultures. It is not xenophobic for Westerners to favor our own culture over others—it is plain common sense.

Belatedly, European politicians are beginning to realize their folly— at least up to a point. In February 2011, Tony Blair's successor, British Prime Minister David Cameron, passionately denounced cultural relativism:

> We have allowed the weakening of our collective identity. Under the doctrine of state multiculturalism, we have encouraged different cultures to live separate lives, apart from each other and apart from the mainstream.... We've even tolerated these segregated communities behaving in ways that run completely counter to our values. So, when a white person holds objectionable views, racist views for instance, we rightly condemn them. But when equally unacceptable views or practices come from someone who isn't white, we've been too cautious frankly—frankly, even fearful—to stand up to them. The failure, for instance, of some to confront the horrors of forced marriage, the practice where some young girls are bullied and sometimes taken abroad to marry someone when they don't want to, is a case in point.[11]

Cameron further argued that Britain's tolerance of anti-Western behavior has led to the radicalization of some young Muslims who, "feeling rootless," have turned to "Islamist extremism." However, in truly politically correct fashion, the British prime minister added that "the ideology of extremism is the problem; Islam emphatically is not."[12] *The ideology of extremism*, of course, is meaningless nonsense, a cowardly euphemism that leaders employ when they want to absolve Islam of all the violence perpetuated in its name.

Still, Cameron deserves respect for denouncing cultural relativism. And he is not alone. In early 2011 French President Nicolas Sarkozy made similar remarks, declaring, "We have been too concerned about the identity of the immigrant and not enough about the identity of the country that was receiving him." Asked whether the policy of multiculturalism had been a failure, Sarkozy replied, "My answer is clearly yes, it is a failure."[13]

These comments echoed those made a few months earlier, in October 2010, by German Chancellor Angela Merkel, who called multiculturalism "an absolute failure."[14] However, that same month, her fellow Christian Democrat party member, then-German President Christian Wulff, emphasized that "Islam is a part of Germany."[15]

Europe's leaders still make a false distinction between peaceful, mainstream Islam and dangerous, extremist Islamism. This is symptomatic of their refusal to acknowledge the intrinsic problems of Muhammad's ideology. Nevertheless, their new willingness to acknowledge the failure of multiculturalism is a promising sign. They may not really believe it, but they now realize that, at the very least, they need to pay lip service to their voters' widespread dissatisfaction with mass immigration and other policies based on cultural relativism.

Everyday Europeans have been victimized by a cynical, condescending cultural elite that loathe their own people's supposed illiberalism, intolerance, lack of sophistication, and inexplicable attachment to their traditional values. These ruling cosmopolitans do not see European culture as a tradition worth defending, but as a constantly evolving political project. In this utopian scheme, everyday people are reviled for their cultural conservatism, while immigrants are lionized precisely because they are not attached to those traditions.

It's hard to say which is worse: Bat Ye'or's accusation that the ruling elites have sold out Europe to Islam in return for a steady supply of oil, or the prospect that these elites are betraying their own people because the elites despise the people's values and traditions. Either way, the result has been the same: the gradual Islamization of Europe.

Even democracy and human rights are sometimes made subservient to the elites' cultural relativism

In November 2009, the Swiss people approved the referendum banning the construction of new minarets. Daniel Cohn-Bendit, leader of the Green group in the European Parliament, responded in the Swiss newspaper *Le Temps* by declaring that the Swiss would "have to vote again." "But the Swiss people have spoken," the paper objected. Cohn-Bendit replied succinctly: "So what?"[16]

A similar attitude is found in the Council of Europe (CoE), a supranational human rights institution. CoE Resolution 1605, accepted in 2008 by the CoE Parliamentary Assembly, states that the forty-seven CoE member states must "condemn and combat Islamophobia" and ensure "that school textbooks do not portray Islam as a hostile or threatening religion."[17] Demonstrating the CoE's determination to re-engineer people to think correctly, at a September 2009 human rights conference in Paris, Catherine Lalumière, a former French Cabinet Minister and former CoE Secretary General, said that "there really is a problem at the level of the mass of the population. Ordinary citizens do not really support human rights. It is here that we really need to go on the attack."[18]

The overwhelming pressure to accommodate and appease Islam has eroded not just democracy, but freedom of speech as well. There are two main threats to free speech. First, there is censorship and self-censorship stemming from the constant threat of violence against those who criticize or offend Islam. One example is the decision by Random House publishing group not to publish *The Jewel of Medina*, a novel about Muhammad's wife Aisha.[19] Another case is the refusal by Yale University Press to publish the Danish Muhammad cartoons, or any other depictions of Muhammad, in a book about the cartoon controversy. As Yale University

Press Director John Donatich said, he had published other controversial books and "I've never blinked." However, "when it came between that and blood on my hands, there was no question"—and so the Muhammad images were censored. [20]

The second threat to free speech is "legal jihad" or "lawfare"—a process in which litigants, particularly Islamic sympathizers, exploit Western laws and legal systems to attack their critics and threaten them with suppression or other forms of retribution. Lawfare, says Brooke Goldstein, an American human rights attorney, is "the use of the law as a weapon of war" and "the wrongful manipulation of the legal system."[21] Shockingly, our Western legal apparatus, which used to guarantee and defend our basic liberties, is now being manipulated to erode these very liberties.

One type of lawfare, sometimes called "libel lawfare" or "libel tourism,"[22] consists of intimidating people into silence through malicious lawsuits. A favorite weapon used by Arab plutocrats against Western authors and publishers, these suits can impose huge costs on their targets even if courts ultimately dismiss the complaints. "The cumulative effect of these lawsuits is a culture of fear, and a detrimental chilling effect" on the expression of opinions, says Goldstein.[23]

In recent years, Islamic apologists in Canada have turned quasi-judicial bodies called Human Rights Commissions into weapons of lawfare. One case involved complaints submitted by various Islamic apologists against conservative commentator Ezra Levant and his defunct magazine, the *Western Standard*, for having the audacity to publish the Danish Muhammad cartoons. The complaints were eventually dropped or dismissed, but not before Levant had been put through a 900-day investigation and racked up more than $100,000 in legal fees. Levant observed, "The process I was put through was a punishment in itself—and a warning to any other journalists who would defy radical Islam."[24]

In a similar case, Canadian weekly news magazine *Maclean's* faced a long legal ordeal when it was sued by proponents of Islam in numerous jurisdictions for publishing an excerpt from Mark Steyn's book *America Alone*. Characterizing Steyn's writing as "flagrantly Islamophobic," these charges, too, were eventually dismissed, but Steyn noted that poorer defendants surely could not have withstood the legal onslaught. "If you have the wherewithal to stand up to these totalitarian bullies, they stampede for the exits," he noted. "But, if you're just an obscure Alberta pastor or a guy with a widely unread website or a fellow who writes a letter to his local newspaper, they'll destroy your life."[25]

British courts, known for their strict libel laws and for awarding high libel damages, are a common venue for these suits—so common that a 2010 British parliamentary report found that "the reputation of the UK is being damaged" by the embarrassing parade of such cases.[26]

A case in point: in 2004, Dr. Rachel Ehrenfeld, an American academic and terrorism expert, published the book *Funding Evil: How Terrorism Is Financed and How to Stop It*.[27] Ehrenfeld was sued in London by a Saudi tycoon whom Ehrenfeld had accused of supporting terrorist organizations. Though Ehrenfeld's book had not even been published in Britain, the Saudi billionaire turned to a British court ostensibly because twenty-three copies of the book had been sold there.[28] A British judge ordered Ehrenfeld to apologize, destroy all copies of her book, and pay the sheikh $230,000 in damages.[29]

Ehrenfeld countersued in a New York court to keep the judgment from being enforced in the United States, but the court dismissed the case. Fortunately, action was taken by the New York state senate, which in 2008 unanimously approved the "Libel Terrorism Reform Act," dubbed "Rachel's Law"—a bill that protects New York citizens and publishers from abusive libel judgments in foreign countries. "New Yorkers must be able to speak out on issues of public concern without living in fear that they will be sued outside the United States, under legal standards inconsistent with our First Amendment rights," then-New York Governor David Paterson declared.[30] In 2010, the U.S. Congress passed, and President Obama signed, the Speech Act, which granted similar protections on the federal level.

In his address to the Continental Army before the 1776 Battle of Long Island, George Washington told his men, "The time is now near at hand which must probably determine whether Americans are to be freemen or slaves.... Our cruel and unrelenting enemy leaves us only the choice of brave resistance, or the most abject submission."[31] Indeed, in light of the steady diminution of national sovereignty in Europe, America seems to stand alone in safeguarding its dominion over its own laws.

In the controversy over libel tourism, New Yorkers used the political process to resist Islam's encroachments. In Europe, this kind of resistance is becoming more difficult as Islam becomes an increasingly powerful political force.

In Britain, for example, the Labour Party not only enabled mass Islamic immigration, but also allowed Islamic radicals to infiltrate the party itself. In 2010, Labour Party member and then-Environment Minister Jim Fitzpatrick warned that a fundamentalist Islamic group had wormed its way into the Labour Party and secretly taken over local Labour groups.[32] "They are acting almost as an entryist organisation, placing people within the political parties, recruiting members to those political parties, trying to get individuals selected and elected so they can exercise political influence and power, whether it's at local government level or national level," Fitzpatrick said.[33]

In her book *Londonistan*, journalist Melanie Phillips explains how some Labour members have helped to empower Islam. For example, the Pakistani-born Bishop of Rochester, Dr. Michael Nazir-Ali, told Phillips that numerous Labour politicians with large Islamic constituencies have become electorally dependent on Islamic leaders in Pakistan who tell their followers in Britain how to vote. One such leader, an Islamic fundamentalist, was welcomed to Britain by the Labour government. When the Bishop asked the Foreign Office why this extremist was given the red carpet treatment, he was simply told that "he had a very strong following in Britain."[34]

Throughout Europe, the Islamic electorate is pushing European politics to the Left. In the 2002 general elections in Germany, the Socialist Gerhard Schröder beat the conservatives by less than 9,000 votes. At the time, Germany had 700,000 Turkish-Germans who voted overwhelmingly for Schröder, providing him with the margin of victory.[35] Likewise, in the Netherlands' 2010 local elections in Amsterdam,

Labour got 59 percent of the Turkish vote, the Green Left Party got 15 percent, and Democrats 66, a progressive-liberal party, got 14 percent. Turks voted along ethnic lines, overwhelmingly supporting the Turkish candidates from these three leftist parties. The Moroccans voted in a similar way, giving 74 percent of their vote to Labour and 10 percent to the progressive liberals.[36]

Labour politicians in the Dutch town of Helmond were surprised when that same election produced a municipal council in which five of the six Labour councilors were Islamic.[37] "When you see this you begin to wonder whether Wilders isn't right after all," a Labour candidate in Rotterdam exclaimed after Turkish candidates secured superior positions on the party list for municipal elections.[38] Some Labour members in Rotterdam's Feijenoord district even complain that district councilors are speaking Turkish with each other and are intimidating their native Dutch colleagues.[39]

As Islam has spread in the Netherlands, Dutch political culture has begun to Islamize. "We are bound to run into trouble with our new immigrant councilors," Labour leader Wouter Bos remarked in 2006, adding that they "conduct politics according to the culture of their home countries, where clientelism is the norm."[40] Nevertheless, Bos' party continues to court the Islamic vote; for the European Left, Islam has become its electoral life insurance.

Islam has also created an avenue for foreign influence in Europe. During the Dutch 2006 general elections, for example, emails were sent directly from the Turkish government's offices in Ankara to Turkish organizations and individuals in the Netherlands, instructing Turkish-born Dutch citizens to vote for Democrats 66 and its Turkish-born candidate Fatma Koşer Kaya.[41] As a result of her large number of pref-erential votes, Koşer-Kaya became one of the party's three representatives in the *Tweede Kamer*.

When the Dutch secret service AIVD investigated Islamic interference in the Dutch democratic process, it found that in 2006 some Islamic lead-ers advised Muslims to vote for the non-Muslim leader of Democrats 66, arguing that he was the "least hostile towards Islam" of all the native Dutch politicians.[42]

In the 2010 British general elections, the British Muslim Initiative (BMI) emailed its supporters a list of recommended candidates, emphasizing that "Muslims need to vote responsibly and tactically, which may require supporting a candidate with whom we may not agree on every political view." In some constituencies where the BMI considered an Islamic candidate too Westernized, the organization recommended voting for a non-Muslim *ansar*.[43] The president of the BMI, incidentally, is Mohammed Sawalha, a man described by the BBC's John Ware as a "fugitive Hamas commander" who "is said to have master minded much of Hamas' political and military strategy" from London.[44]

In America, too, Islamic activists are organizing themselves in lobbying groups in order to enhance Islam's political influence. Unsurprisingly, some of the leading Islamic organizations were named by the U.S. Justice Department as unindicted co-conspirators in the Holy Land Foundation trial, a landmark terrorism funding case.[45] For now, America's Islamic lobby remains small and marginalized. But Europe offers a cautionary tale, as it often does in matters related to Islam, of what the future could hold if America's vigilance falters.

CHAPTER TWELVE

Fitna

*That's all a man can hope for during his lifetime—to set
an example—and when he is dead, to be an inspiration
for history.*

—William McKinley

In late 2007, I decided to make *Fitna*, a 15-minute documentary film about the Islamic threat. The most common translation of the Arabic word *fitna* is "ordeal" or "trial." The title of the film symbolizes my view that Islam is an ordeal currently confronting the West. I was assisted in making the film by Koran experts who, to protect their personal safety, remained anonymous.

Featuring an exquisite copy of a Koran I bought in East Jerusalem, *Fitna* juxtaposes Koranic verses calling for violence, particularly against non-Muslims, with footage of terrorist attacks and other violent deeds these verses have inspired, along with clips of Islamic leaders inciting violence for the sake of Allah.[1] *Fitna* also reveals the ongoing Islamization process in the Netherlands. My movie shows real-life images from real-life Islam. Actually, one could say that I did not really make the movie; Islam made it for me.

Fitna is not just *about* the Koran; it unfolds *inside* the Koran, as the edges of the book remain visible throughout the whole film. Inside these edges I show images of what the Koran prescribes. Viewers shocked by the violent images should not get angry with me, but with the people who perpetrate these acts and with the book that commands them.

The film ends with a hand gripping a page of the Koran. The image fades out amidst the sound of a page being ripped from a book. Then the following message appears: "The sound you heard was a page being removed from the phonebook. For it is not up to me, but to Muslims themselves to tear out the hateful verses from the Quran."

The reaction to *Fitna* proved the film's entire point: outraged at my film's suggestion that the Koran advocates violence, furious Islamic activists unleashed wild threats of violence. In an immigrant neighborhood of Gouda, swastikas and the slogan "Wilders must die" appeared on the walls of a school. A Moroccan youth group posted a video clip on the internet showing hooded youths beating up what appeared to be two Dutch skinheads on a train. The clip ends with the warning: "F*** all those who support Wilders because you had better realize: one will reap the consequences of one's actions!!!!"[2]

People with the last name Wilders, though unrelated to me, received letters threatening that if they failed to prevent me from releasing *Fitna*, "The first deadly victim will be you, one of your children or grandchildren."[3] The Dutch Muslim Council labeled me a "racist, fascist, and authoritarian" and a "threat to Dutch society."[4] A spokesman for the Dutch branch of *Hizb ut-Tahrir* (Party of Liberation), a radical Muslim group aiming to impose a worldwide Caliphate, declared that the Netherlands was due for a terror attack.[5]

All this came in reaction to news reports about *Fitna*—the film had not even been released yet, and none of my hysterical critics had actually seen it. Nevertheless, several Dutch Islamic and leftist organizations and individuals lodged criminal complaints against me for inciting hatred, discrimination, and "group insult." Gerard Spong, a leading Dutch lawyer, offered to represent some of my accusers free of charge.[6]

Threats against me and my entire country poured in from across the Islamic world. Iran warned that it would "react to the Dutch insult."[7] Pakistan banned access to YouTube until it removed a "blasphemous" video of me announcing the making of *Fitna*.[8] An al Qaeda-linked website proclaimed that I should be killed.[9] NATO Secretary General Jaap de Hoop Scheffer, a Dutchman, told the BBC that he feared my movie would affect NATO troops in Afghanistan—and indeed, the Taliban threatened to attack Dutch troops, while demonstrators in Afghan cities demanded the troops' expulsion.[10] On January 15, 2008, the Grand Mufti of Syria, Ahmad Badr Al-Din Hassoun, told the European Parliament in Strasbourg that if I tore up or burned a Koran (as some reports falsely claimed I was about to do in *Fitna*), "this will simply mean he is inciting wars and bloodshed. And he will be responsible."[11] Interestingly, the official press release issued by the European Parliament after the Grand Mufti's address did not mention these words, but applauded his statement that "war can never be holy; peace is holy."[12]

Dutch businessmen, too, reacted angrily, fearing my film would provoke a worldwide boycott of Dutch products. AkzoNobel CEO Hans Wijers called me a "rude clown."[13] VNO-NCW, the organization of Dutch enterprises and employers, announced that it would investigate whether I could be held personally responsible for their losses in the event of an Arab boycott.[14] "Geert Wilders is evil, and evil must be stopped," Doekle Terpstra, a former trade union leader, declared. "It is important that the indigenous Dutch, too, rise in order to stop Wilders," he added, announcing the establishment of a "resistance movement against Wilders."[15]

The Dutch police provided pre-printed forms that people could use to press criminal charges against me.[16] Authorities sent letters to all Dutch municipalities warning that the release of my film could provoke tension.[17]

In one notable attack, Henk Hofland, the former editor of *NRC Handelsblad*, the Netherlands' leading liberal newspaper, called for the lifting of my police protection. "Then he will be able to contemplate the fate of those whom he puts at risk," he said.[18] Hofland, who had been named "Journalist of the century" by his colleagues in 1999, apparently believed that people who warn that Islam is dangerous should be punished by exposing them to that very danger. Note that Hofland did not

deny the existence of the danger—otherwise he would not advocate
making me experience it.

Due to the seething reaction to reports about *Fitna*, releasing the
movie became my own ordeal. I repeatedly had to postpone the film's
release because no network, public or private, would air it, even though
40 percent of the Dutch population indicated they wanted to see it. Networks would normally be scrambling to reel in such a huge audience, but
of course, airing a movie doesn't normally place networks at risk of attack
by Muslim fundamentalists. Non-Dutch networks were equally afraid to
show the film, so I decided to launch *Fitna* over the internet. YouTube,
however, refused to host it, as did Network Solutions. Fortunately, Live-
Leak, a British-based video sharing website, courageously accepted the
film.

Two days before *Fitna*'s scheduled debut, Islamic organizations took
me to court in order to block the release. Unsure how the court would
decide, I released the movie twelve hours before it was to rule on the case.
(In the end, the court permitted the release of my film.) On March 27,
2008, *Fitna* was released on LiveLeak in both English and Dutch. Seen
by three million people within its first three hours, the film became one
of the most widely viewed Dutch movies ever. It is now available in dozens of languages.

The Dutch Islamic community reacted relatively calmly to the film's
release. There were some minor riots and a few cars were set on fire, but
even Dutch Islamic organizations said the movie was within the boundaries of the law.[19]

Not everyone showed restraint, however. Within an hour of *Fitna*'s
release, Prime Minister Balkenende issued a statement denouncing me,
declaring that the movie "equates Islam with committing atrocities. We
reject this interpretation. The vast majority of Muslims reject extremism
and violence. In fact, the victims are often also Muslims. Hence, we
deplore that Mr. Wilders has released this movie. We do not see what
purpose this movie serves but to offend the feelings of others."[20]

In fact, though Balkenende implied otherwise, I never said that "the vast majority of Muslims" condone extremism and violence. I simply warned that the existence of peaceful Muslims should not blind us to the fact that Islam is a violent ideology that should be rejected by Muslims and non-Muslims alike. That, and that alone, is the message of *Fitna*.

United Nations Secretary General Ban Ki-moon also blasted *Fitna*, suggesting I had no right to make a film this offensive to Muslims. "I condemn, in the strongest terms, the airing of Geert Wilders' offensively anti-Islamic film," the UN boss said. "There is no justification for hate speech or incitement to violence. The right of free expression is not at stake here. I acknowledge the efforts of the Government of the Netherlands to stop the broadcast of this film, and appeal for calm to those understandably offended by it. Freedom must always be accompanied by social responsibility."[21]

The European Union issued a similar statement, warning that freedom of speech "should be exercised in a spirit of respect for religious and other beliefs and convictions.... We believe that acts such as the above-mentioned film serve no other purpose than inflaming hatred."[22]

Indonesian President Susilo Bambang Yudhoyono banned me from ever visiting his country again for the rest of my life, while his government warned that it would block YouTube in Indonesia if *Fitna* appeared on it.[23] In a particularly pathetic display of groveling, the Dutch ambassador in Jakarta, Nikolaos van Dam, received Ismail Yusanto, leader of the Indonesian branch of the Islamic fundamentalist group *Hizb ut-Tahrir*, which was demonstrating in front of the Dutch embassy. Van Dam explained to Yusanto that my views "do not represent the official opinion of the Dutch government and the majority of the Dutch citizens," and that protests should be directed at me instead of the Dutch government. Yusanto rejected the argument and demanded that the Dutch government ban *Fitna* and punish me.[24]

One of the most extreme responses came out of Jordan, where a court threatened to issue an international arrest warrant against me for "discrimination, insulting religion/the prophet and inciting hatred."[25] In an op-ed piece, I asked the Dutch government to protest Jordan's threats to prosecute a member of the Dutch Parliament for his political views.

I pointed out that Jordan is not a democracy and has no independent judiciary. "Nothing happens in the Hashemite Kingdom without the acquiescence of the King," I wrote. "King Abdullah II is a direct descendant of the barbaric prophet Muhammad. That explains a lot."[26]

Back in the Netherlands, I faced a litany of legal cases over *Fitna*. One of these complaints, seeking €55,000 ($72,700) in damages, was filed by Sheikh Fawaz Jneid.[27] He is the imam who had cursed Theo van Gogh and implored Allah to make him suffer in a sermon given a few weeks before van Gogh was murdered.[28] He had also cursed Ayaan Hirsi Ali, imploring Allah to give her brain and tongue cancer.[29]

On June 30, 2008, the public prosecutor's office in Amsterdam declared that it would not prosecute me for *Fitna* or for other statements I made about Islam and the Koran. "The fact that statements are hurtful and offensive to a large number of Muslims does not necessarily mean that such statements are punishable," it stated. "It is true that some statements insult Muslims, but these were made in the context of public debate, which means that the statements are no longer of a punishable nature. The Public Prosecutor has also concluded that there is no liability to punishment for inciting hatred or discrimination."[30]

The prosecutor's decision was roundly criticized by the multiculturalist establishment. "Some say [*Fitna*] was not as bad as expected. I disagree," Amsterdam police chief Bernard Welten said at the annual police *Iftar* dinner marking the end of Muslims' daily fasts during Ramadan. "The movie incorrectly suggests that violence and even terror are rooted in Islam."[31]

People even demanded my prosecution during ceremonies honoring victims of Nazi Germany. "*Fitna* stigmatizes and incites hatred," former Labour Party leader, Minister of the Interior, and Mayor of Amsterdam Ed van Thijn declared during a commemoration of the anniversary of *Kristallnacht*. He bemoaned that "expressions of Muslim hatred are a frequent phenomenon in Parliament," adding that "exactly because *Fitna* is part of a political debate it has to be combated."[32]

Another speaker at that ceremony was Moroccan-born former parliamentarian Mohamed Rabbae of the far-left Green Left Party, who compared my attitude toward Muslims in the Netherlands to the Nazis' persecution of Jews. Rabbae further demanded that I be prosecuted over *Fitna*. That was unsurprising, since he'd previously demanded a ban on Salman Rushdie's novel *The Satanic Verses* for supposedly insulting Islam.[33]

A ceremony for Jewish victims of Nazism was hijacked by activists demanding censorship and decrying free expression—that was a chilling sight. Sadly, it seemed to characterize the overwrought reaction my short movie provoked both in the West and in the Middle East. Still, I took some comfort from the thousands of supportive emails I received from people all over the world, including Muslims in Islamic countries. They showed that, although we're not supposed to talk about the problems of Islam, people everywhere are intimately familiar with them.

"If history teaches anything, it teaches self-delusion in the face of unpleasant facts is folly," Ronald Reagan declared in his 1982 speech to the British Parliament in Westminster.[34]

I was going to use Reagan's quote in a speech I had prepared for a meeting with British parliamentarians slated for February 12, 2009. The meeting had been arranged by Baron Malcolm Pearson of Rannoch and Baroness Caroline Cox of Queensbury, who had both invited me to show *Fitna* in a conference room of the parliament building.

I had met Malcolm and Caroline in November 2008, when they hosted me at lunch in the restaurant of the House of Lords. (Before I flew to London, the Dutch government asked their British counterparts to guarantee that I would not be arrested during my trip and extradited to Jordan.) I found that I had much in common with Caroline and Malcolm, who are both Eurosceptics, supporters of Israel, and long-standing human rights activists. Caroline also heads a charity that supports Christian minorities in Islamic countries, and she has worked with organizations that raise money to free slaves. We agreed that I would return to London in early February to show *Fitna* in the Palace of Westminster and to discuss my movie and my policy proposals with British MPs.

The following January, however, when Malcolm and Caroline sent out invitations to British parliamentarians to attend the *Fitna* screening, Lord Nazir Ahmed went into a rage. The Pakistan-born Ahmed, Britain's first Islamic peer, was made a baron in 1998 and took his oath on the Koran. In 2005, he hosted a book launch in the Palace of Westminster for Isreal Shamir, who used the opportunity to call on the Islamic community in England to "turn the tide" of "Zionist infiltration" of Britain's political parties and mass media.[35] In 2007, Ahmed protested the knighting of Salman Rushdie, accusing the author of having "blood on his hands" because he had "provoked violence" by writing *The Satanic Verses*, among other things.[36]

Ahmed told Malcolm he did not want me visiting the Palace of Westminster. He wrote to the British Home Office, the speaker of the House of Lords, and Black Rod, the head of security at the Palace of Westminster, to warn that my presence "would lead to the incitement of religious and racial hatred, which constitutes a public order offence." He advocated banning me not just from Parliament, but from Britain altogether.[37] Malcolm stood firm and went to see Black Rod, who assured him that he would draft extra police to deal with any threats. Due to security concerns, however, we had to postpone the screening of *Fitna* from January 29 to February 12.

I was in the *Tweede Kamer* on the afternoon of February 10 when the British embassy in The Hague delivered an official letter informing me that Jacqui Smith, the British Home Secretary, had declared me *persona non grata* and barred me from entering the United Kingdom. "The purpose of this letter," the document read, "is to inform you that the Secretary of State is of the view that your presence in the UK would pose a genuine, present and sufficiently serious threat to one of the fundamental interests of society. The Secretary of State is satisfied that your statements about Muslims and their beliefs, as expressed in your film *Fitna* and elsewhere, would threaten community harmony and therefore public security in the UK."

This was too much—I had been banned from Britain for showing how the Koran advocates violence. The faithful who teach and recite these violent injunctions in mosques across the world are left alone, and I didn't see why I should be singled out merely for showing what they are saying and doing. So I decided to challenge the ban by flying to London as scheduled—at the very least, I'd make a public stand for free expression. As William McKinley said, "That's all a man can hope for during his lifetime—to set an example—and when he is dead, to be an inspiration for history."[38]

I landed in Heathrow on February 12 with dozens of Dutch and British journalists in tow. Upon arrival, I was met by two immigration officials who told me that I was being refused entry to the country. Despite being accompanied by the Dutch ambassador, I was locked up for three hours in a Heathrow detention room and then put on a flight back to Amsterdam.

The Dutch Prime Minister and Foreign Minister lodged formal protests with Britain over my treatment.[39] Also supporting me were Lord Pearson and Lady Cox—who accused the British government of "appeasing violent Islam"—as well as the British National Secular Society, which wrote a letter to Home Secretary Smith defending my right to free expression.[40]

Much of the British establishment supported my expulsion, however. British Foreign Secretary David Miliband defended my deportation on the grounds that *Fitna* is "a hate-filled film which is designed to stir up religious and racial hate"—though he admitted he had not actually seen the movie.[41] Britain's Liberal Democrats also backed the ban, with party spokesman Chris Huhne declaring, "There is a line to be drawn even with freedom of speech, and that is where it is likely to incite violence or hatred." The "revolting" *Fitna* movie, he said, crossed that line.[42]

Unfortunately for Huhne, the ban on me was overturned when I challenged it before the British Asylum and Immigration Tribunal. On October 16, 2009, three days after the ruling, I returned to London to meet with Malcolm Pearson in Westminster and plan our showing of *Fitna*. About forty men from the organization Islam4UK demonstrated in front of the building. Dressed in Middle Eastern garb, they demanded that Sharia law be introduced in Britain and chanted slogans ranging from "Freedom go to hell" to "Wilders go to hell."[43]

On March 5, 2010, at the invitation of Caroline Cox and Malcolm Pearson, I was finally able to show *Fitna* at the Palace of Westminster and discuss the issue of Islamization with my British colleagues. There were no incidents and no disturbances of Britain's "fundamental interests," "community harmony," or "public security."

My visit to London followed an international campaign I organized to show and discuss *Fitna* with politicians and citizens. In some places, such as the Danish Parliament, I spoke without trouble. I was, however, banned from screening *Fitna* at the European Parliament (EP) despite an invitation from EP member Gerard Batten. In fact, even before *Fitna* had been released, the EP's Conference of Presidents prohibited showing the "movie on caricatures of Islam by Mr Wilders" in "any space in the European Parliament." I visited the EP building in Strasbourg, but the EP president told me that screening *Fitna* anywhere on the EP premises, including in the private offices of parliamentarians, was forbidden. So Gerard and I had to limit ourselves to holding a press conference.[44]

America behaved as befits a free country. On February 26, 2009, I showed *Fitna* at the U.S. Capitol at the invitation of Arizona Senator Jon Kyl. I also screened the movie without incident in several other U.S. cities, though the Marriott Hotel in Delray Beach, Florida, and the Loews Vanderbilt Hotel in Nashville, Tennessee, both cancelled conferences when they learned I was involved.[45]

One of the most memorable events was my February 2009 visit to Rome, where I received the Oriana Fallaci Free Speech Award. Italian authorities provided intense security, organizing an escort of ten police cars that halted traffic during morning rush hour to take me from the airport to my hotel. All the parked cars in front of the hotel were towed away, while an army of heavily armed policemen and soldiers guarded the hotel. They even posted snipers on the surrounding rooftops. When I went to the bathroom in the hotel lobby, thirty-five policemen—my colleague actually counted them—guarded the door.

It was the best-protected pee of my life.

★ ★ ★

Islam's leftist fan club in the West has proven time and again that it will go to extraordinary lengths to protect Islam from criticism. In my case, after failing to prevent me from releasing *Fitna* in the first place, they dragged me to court to shut me up.

As previously mentioned, in June 2008, the Amsterdam public prosecutor ruled that he would not prosecute me for producing *Fitna* or for my statements about the Koran and Islam. The Netherlands, however, is one of the few countries in the world where individuals who claim to have a direct interest in the prosecution of a crime can appeal against the prosecutor's decision not to pursue a certain case.[46] If the Court of Appeal subsequently rules that the suspect should be prosecuted, the prosecutor is obliged to do so.

This is what happened after leftist groups, Islamic organizations, and various other parties appealed against the prosecutor's ruling on my case. On January 21, 2009, the Court of Appeal in Amsterdam ordered the prosecutor to try me in an Amsterdam court. The court argued that, based on the standards set by the European Court of Human Rights, criminal prosecution is appropriate for "insulting Muslim worshippers" by making "comparisons between Islam and Nazism."[47]

Ultimately, I faced five charges: group insult of people, i.e. Muslims based on their religion; the two charges of incitement of hatred and incitement of discrimination against people, i.e. Muslims because of their religion; and the two charges of incitement of hatred and incitement of discrimination against people, i.e. non-Western foreigners and/or Moroccans because of their race.

"This is my finest hour," exulted Gerard Spong, the lawyer who had encouraged my supposed victims.[48] "This is a happy day for all followers of Islam who do not want to be tossed on the garbage dump of Nazism."[49]

I could hardly believe I was being prosecuted for merely stating my opinion about a dangerous political ideology that had marked me for death. But there I was, on January 20, 2010, sitting on the bench of the

Criminal Court in Amsterdam, being referred to as "the suspect," looking at a possible sentence of up to sixteen months in prison.

With the Dutch multiculturalists, European leaders, and the entire Islamic world determined to silence me, the proceedings reeked of bias from the beginning. My lawyer, Abraham Moszkowicz, argued that my right to a fair trial had been breached because the Amsterdam Court of Appeal had ordered my prosecution in a way that expressed a premature guilty verdict—essentially, he was saying that I had been convicted before I was even tried. The court rejected the argument.[50]

We asked the court to hear eighteen expert witnesses who, we argued, could either demonstrate that my statements were protected free speech or show that what I said about Islam was entirely true. The witnesses included legal experts on free speech, experts on Islam, former Muslims, and Theo van Gogh's assassin Mohammed Bouyeri. We also listed national and international Islamic leaders such as Imam Jneid, two Iranian ayatollahs, and the influential mufti Yusuf al-Qaradawi, the spiritual leader of the Muslim Brotherhood. The court rejected fifteen of the eighteen proposed witnesses, agreeing to hear only the former Muslim Wafa Sultan and Dutch Arabists Hans Jansen and Simon Admiraal.[51]

As the trial dragged on month after month, the court occasionally slipped and indicated a semblance of bias against me. For example, Judge Jan Moors, President of the Court, criticized me when I invoked my right to remain silent. More damning still, when one of the complainants left the courtroom as *Fitna* was about to be shown, Moors commented that he could well imagine why she did not want to see the film.

The trial was a farce from beginning to end, an anti-democratic exercise to suppress my freedom at the behest of the Islamic world. The Amsterdam Court of Appeal ordered an unwilling prosecutor to move forward with the prosecution, a course of action that would never happen in many Western states but is allowed in the Netherlands.

The true extent of this travesty of justice was revealed by the newspaper *De Pers* on October 22, 2010, the last day of the court hearing. The paper reported that Tom Schalken, one of the three judges of the

Amsterdam Court of Appeal that had ordered the prosecutor to try me, had had dinner with Professor Hans Jansen, one of the three expert witnesses I had been allowed, three days before Jansen testified in court. According to Jansen, he had arrived at a dinner in Amsterdam hosted by the Vertigo Club and discovered that Judge Schalken was also there. Since the dinner was meant to double as a discussion forum about Islam, Jansen immediately announced he would go home; it would be inappropriate to speak to the judge just before giving testimony at my trial, and besides, he feared that he, too, might end up on the docket just like me for expressing his opinion.[52]

Vertigo chairman Bertus Hendriks, however, persuaded Jansen to stay after Schalken guaranteed that he would not have Jansen prosecuted for whatever he said. According to Jansen, Judge Schalken then tried to convince him "of the correctness of the Court of Appeal's decision to take Wilders to court."[53]

After we learned about this incident, my lawyer Moszkowicz requested that the court hear Jansen to ascertain whether Judge Schalken had tried to influence his testimony. Despite Jansen's presence in the courtroom that morning, the court refused to hear him. After that, Moszkowicz asked for the court's dismissal due to its semblance of bias against me. An oversight panel of judges granted our request, calling their colleagues' refusal to hear Jansen "incomprehensible."[54]

With the trial judges disqualified, the case against me collapsed—it would have to be retried with a new set of judges. "It's time to drop the charges against Mr. Wilders before [this trial] further undermines the credibility of the Dutch legal system and the country's tradition of free political discourse," a *Wall Street Journal* editorial commented.[55]

But the case continued, with round two beginning on February 7, 2011. In order to assess whether Judge Schalken had attempted to influence Jansen, the new judges heard testimony from Schalken, Jansen, and Vertigo chairman Bertus Hendriks. According to Jansen, after being invited to the club to participate in a debate on Islam, he was confronted by Schalken, who had a few sheets of paper with him that he called "an important and thoroughly written piece." Realizing this was the Court of Appeal's decision ordering my prosecution, Jansen believed Schalken was seeking his approval for the decision.

When Judge Schalken testified, he initially denied he had brought the decision along to the dinner party. Cross-examined by Moszkowicz, however, he admitted otherwise. At one point Schalken also claimed he had not known before the dinner that Jansen was to testify in court a few days later. But under Moszkowicz's questioning, he said he did not remember whether he had known it before the dinner party or not, and indeed, that he did not remember much of what had happened that evening.

The date for my verdict was set for June 23. I wrote an op-ed piece in advance that the *Wall Street Journal* agreed to publish the day after the verdict was announced. I prepared two versions—one in case I was convicted and another if I was acquitted. The former version ended with this passage: "This is a sad day for the Netherlands. However, this will not discourage me. On the contrary, it will stimulate me to fight even harder for the preservation of liberty. I spoke, I speak, and I shall continue to speak."

To my relief, the verdict ultimately called for the other version, which began as follows: "Yesterday was a beautiful day for freedom of speech in the Netherlands. An Amsterdam court acquitted me of all charges of hate speech after a legal ordeal that lasted almost two years."[56]

Given the international interest in my case, the court had its verdict translated (very poorly) into English. The court stated,

> As a politician, the suspect has expressed his utterances during the period of indictment in the public debate, as a fanatic fighter of the—evil in his view—Islam. Thereto, he has expressed himself in an offending and shocking manner, and he uses images and texts in the movie Fitna as well which are shocking and provocative. In this debate, he has repeatedly proposed measures which have to limit the influence of the Islam in the Netherlands. In this respect, he has stressed on more occasions that he does not have anything against Muslims, and, for example, he has stated that Muslims who

assimilate are just as good as any other person. The main message of the suspect about the Islam is a message which he simply should be able to express in the Netherlands.[57]

The court acquitted me because I had criticized Islam, not Muslims, and because, as an elected politician participating in a public debate, I was entitled to greater freedom of speech than everyday citizens.

CHAPTER THIRTEEN

How to Turn the Tide

*Let not the defeatists tell us that it is too late. It will never
be earlier. Tomorrow will be later than today.*

—Franklin Roosevelt

In the Dutch general elections of June 9, 2010, the political party I
lead, the Party for Freedom (PVV), won 15.5 percent of the vote,
giving us twenty-four of the 150 seats in the *Tweede Kamer*. Having
gained fifteen seats, the PVV surpassed the Christian Democrats to
become the Netherlands' third biggest party, after the center-right VVD
and the left-wing Labour Party.

Our electoral victory shows that many Dutch people will no longer
tolerate being shut out of the discussion about Islam, multiculturalism,
and immigration. These are topics that impact our democracy, our liberties, and the very fabric of our society, and the people are demanding to
be heard even if the political establishment believes such topics should
be off-limits to popular debate.

Despite our successes, my party frequently encounters the same
obstacle: some people believe the Islamic threat is so immense that they
lose heart, thinking the battle has already been lost. However, I am no
defeatist—I know in my heart we can still turn the tide if we act now.

In fact, I have written this book not just to warn against Islam, but to show how Islamization can actually be stopped. As Franklin Roosevelt declared, "Let not the defeatists tell us that it is too late. It will never be earlier. Tomorrow will be later than today."[1]

After the June 2010 elections, when it became clear that the left-wing parties could not form a coalition government, I entered into negotiations with the leaders of the VVD and the Christian Democrats (CDA). Since neither party agreed with the PVV view of Islam as a dangerous ideology, it was impossible for these three parties to form a governing coalition. The PVV, however, agreed to support a minority VVD-CDA coalition in return for numerous concessions. On July 30, 2010, the three parties signed a protocol announcing, "The VVD, PVV and CDA differ in their opinions on the nature and character of Islam. The differences lie in whether they consider Islam a religion or a (political) ideology. The three parties respect each others' different perspectives and will each act according to their own principles."

So we agreed to disagree about Islam—that was fine with me. The crux of the matter was that the VVD and CDA needed our support for the government's austerity plan, and we wanted them to commit to restrict immigration, roll back crime, counter cultural relativism, and insist on the integration of immigrants. Eventually, all three parties signed a historic agreement ushering in a VVD-CDA government supported by the PVV.

In 2010, 52,000 non-Western immigrants entered the Netherlands, of whom more than 19,000 hailed from Islamic countries.[2] I agreed with the VVD and CDA leaders that the cabinet would aim to reduce the number of non-Western immigrants by "a very substantial" number by 2014. This could lead to a decrease of 50 percent. Islam is not specifically mentioned in the agreement, but the text states that Dutch immigration policy will henceforward be "focuse[d] on restricting and reducing the number of migrants with few future prospects coming to the Netherlands."[3]

The new government also agreed to restrict the "family formation" and "family reunification" policies through which many non-Western immigrants are brought to the Netherlands by family members who are already legal residents.[4] The coalition agreement stipulates that future immigrants will only be allowed to bring in their spouses, registered partners, and young children. Moreover, spouses and partners must be at least twenty-four years old, only one can be brought in every ten years, and no family members can be admitted unless the applicant in the Netherlands earns at least 120 percent of the Dutch minimum wage. Furthermore, labor immigration from outside Europe is no longer allowed, unless the employer can prove that it was impossible to fill a specific vacancy with Dutch or European employees.

Our agreement also stipulated the implementation of measures to restore law and order. These included making it a criminal offense to remain in the Netherlands as an illegal immigrant, and expelling foreigners who are lawful residents if they are convicted of a crime.

Those who settle in the Netherlands are now obliged to integrate. "We are entitled to expect this of newcomers. They themselves are responsible for their integration," our agreement with the VVD and CDA says. "Those who fail their civic integration examination will, with some exceptions, have their temporary residence permits revoked."[5]

Overall, the government now makes it clear that the Dutch people no longer want immigrants to live at our expense; immigrants must benefit the Netherlands, not the other way around. Our guiding principle is based on John F. Kennedy's famous quote: "Ask not what your country can do for you—ask what you can do for your country."

This is why the agreement not only states that immigrants are required to "abide by the rules that apply here," but also that they must "play an active part in society by acquiring a sufficient command of the Dutch language, and through education and employment.... It is therefore important to impose stricter language and educational requirements on those who wish to be admitted to and settle in our country."[6]

While the Netherlands continues to admit and protect victims of persecution, asylum seekers—like all immigrants—are now responsible for their own integration into Dutch society. For those who do not have sufficient resources of their own, the government will introduce a system of loans that will have to be repaid.

The government also agreed to attempt to amend the Association Agreement between the European Union and Turkey in order to ensure that Turks, too, are obliged to take integration classes when they settle in the Netherlands.

The government further pledged to ban *burkas* and other face-covering garments as well as the wearing of headscarves by police officers and members of the judiciary. Unemployed workers who behave or dress in ways that lower their chances of finding a job will have their welfare payments refused, reduced, or revoked. The government also agreed to abolish affirmative-action and diversity policies based on gender and ethnic origin; integration will no longer be tailored to specific groups.

Moreover, the government expanded the requirements for naturalization by adding criteria related to educational qualifications, financial resources, and good behavior. For example, people who want to become Dutch citizens must prove they can speak Dutch and must renounce any other nationalities insofar as they can be renounced. The government will also present a bill to revoke Dutch nationality from those who, within five years of being granted Dutch nationality, are convicted of a crime carrying a sentence of twelve years or more.

In a June 2011 letter outlining the Dutch cabinet's new integration policies, Dutch Interior Minister Piet Hein Donner wrote, "The government distances itself explicitly from the relativism contained in the concept of a multicultural society and envisions a society which may change, also through the influence of immigrants who settle here, but is not interchangeable with any other society. The fundamental elements which determine Dutch society are rooted in its history and constitute reference points which many Dutchmen share and which cannot be discarded."[7]

The changes to be implemented by the new cabinet represent a sea change in the Dutch political establishment, reversing decades of multiculturalist rot. By securing these changes, the PVV ended the policies that had led to the creation of a parallel Islamic society. More important, we brought hope to millions of Dutch men and women who were finally assured that their government would no longer abandon them.

★   ★   ★

Indicative of its new outlook, in July 2011, the Dutch government did something that no other nation has dared to do—it denounced the Organization of Islamic Cooperation (OIC), the tyrannical organization of fifty-seven Islamic countries, most of them barbaric dictatorships, that tries to bully Western nations into submitting to Islam's diktats.

A week after I was acquitted in my Amsterdam trial, Ekmeleddin Ihsanoglu, the OIC Secretary General, issued a statement urging the Dutch government "to take necessary appropriate action to contain the campaign of hatred and incitement by Wilders who is a coalition partner of the Dutch government."[8] According to Ihsanoglu, "Mr. Wilders has taken upon him a dangerous path of derailing inter-civilizational harmony and peace by spreading and fanning hatred against Islam and Muslims in his country as well as in other European countries." Speaking on behalf of the OIC Council of Foreign Ministers, he condemned "the continued attacks on Islam and insult and vilification of the Prophet Muhammad (PBUH) [Peace Be Upon Him] and his wives by the extremist Dutch right wing politician Geert Wilders." In a thinly veiled threat, Ihsanoglu declared that "the silence of the Dutch Government in this respect may undermine the existing good bilateral relations between the OIC Member States and the Netherlands."[9]

A previous Dutch government would have cowered before a politically correct organization that forms one of the largest voting blocs in the United Nations. It would have immediately dissociated itself from me and sent apologetic officials throughout the Islamic world to explain that my views are not those of the government. But the OIC did not take into account the Netherlands' new cultural self-confidence vis-à-vis Islam. In place of the usual groveling, Dutch Minister of Foreign Affairs Uri Rosenthal issued a statement condemning the OIC's attempt to silence an elected representative of the Dutch people. "The Dutch government dissociates itself fully from the request to silence a politician," he exclaimed, adding, "The Netherlands has a very high regard of freedom of speech."[10]

The OIC's attempt to intimidate the Netherlands backfired badly. Never before has a Western government had the audacity to speak out so firmly against these Islamic bullies. The Dutch essentially told them: We will never submit! Don't tread on us!

The Dutch government has also stood up to Islamic intimidation by strengthening its political and economic relations with Israel and by expressing outspoken support for the Jewish state. While anti-Israel groups demand divestment from Israel, we are following the opposite course, even cutting government funding from so-called humanitarian organizations that support anti-Israel boycotts, divestment, and sanctions or that deny Israel's right to exist. "The financing of activities such as calling for boycotts, the retracting of investments and the call for sanctions against Israel do not fit within the Dutch government's policy," Minister Rosenthal wrote to the *Tweede Kamer* on August 23, 2011, adding that tax-funded organizations are not permitted to nurture or support activities that are "contradictory to Dutch foreign policy."[11]

The Dutch government also joined Israel, the United States, and other Western nations in boycotting the United Nations' anti-racism conference of September 2011, widely known as Durban III.[12] Since the first Durban conference in 2001, these meetings have served as a shameful tribunal for Islamic nations and other anti-Western elements to hurl outrageous accusations against Israel, the United States, and the entire Western world, and to demand a galaxy of compensatory programs that typically involve the West handing over vast sums of money to non-western countries.

The Dutch example shows that when people overcome their fear, David can defeat Goliath. For decades, the multicultural elite suppressed dissent by denouncing as racists anyone who questioned their pro-Islam, pro-mass immigration dogma. But finally, after silently watching for years the immense damage done to our nation by the elite's policies, the Dutch people had enough. In the face of all the threats and intimidation levelled against my supporters, enough people had the courage to vote for the PVV that we fundamentally altered our country's politics.

All it takes is courage—that has been true throughout history. The Soviet Empire was defeated by a handful of brave dissidents who lived by the motto "Be not afraid." When people are no longer afraid to speak the truth, seemingly invincible evil empires begin to crumble.

Islam is one of those evil empires, and it too will collapse once people begin telling the truth. Indeed, 2011 may have marked a turning point that exposed Islam's inherent weakness. I am not referring to the so-called "Arab Spring"—as explained earlier in this book, all that's happening in the Arab Spring is that one set of Islamic tyrants is replacing another. What is needed in Islamic countries is not a change in leadership, but for Muslims themselves to renounce Islam and liberate themselves from the ideology's mental prison. And this may have begun to happen.

My hope is based on the courage shown by a few women in Saudi Arabia, the heartland of Islam. The Saudi regime is famously misogynistic, ruthlessly enforcing laws that force women to dress in stifling costumes and refrain from publicly associating with men. These laws generally reduce women to an infantile state of dependence on male family members, but in August 2006, Wajeha al-Huwaider had enough of this injustice. She staged a one-woman demonstration by holding a placard proclaiming "Give Women Their Rights!" She was promptly arrested by the Mutaween, the religious police.

Her activism, she explained to an American journalist, is meant to "defend her existence as a person." It began as a young girl at home, "to prove to my parents that I am no less than my brothers." But she was most affected by her brief stay in the United States. "Before that, I knew that I'm a human being," she said. "However, in the United States I felt it, because I was treated as one. I learned life means nothing without freedom."[13]

Al-Huwaider posted articles on the internet (since she is not allowed to publish in Saudi Arabia) condemning the abuse of women in Arab countries. "Among the Arabs, the cycle of discrimination against the woman usually begins at home. From a young age, the son receives the lion's share (the share of two women), in love, in outlay, in status, and even in education," she writes. "The young man has opportunities, while the young girl has obligations."[14]

In one article she argues that prisoners in Guantanamo Bay in some respects are better off than some Arab women who are kept as prisoners in their own homes. While the Guantanamo prisoners "wear practical, light-colored clothing suitable for the climate...some Arab women are forced to wear impractical and suffocating garments.... A prisoner in Guantanamo [can] see the sun, feel its rays and enjoy the caress of fresh air on his face, even when he is physically in chains, whereas the women in some Arab states are shackled [both] physically and spiritually.... The minute the girl enters her teens, she no longer sees the light of day, and she cannot breathe fresh air except through a veil, since she is covered from head to toe in black garments."[15]

Unfortunately, al-Huwaider laments, the world does not seem to notice or care. "Nobody has lifted a finger for the Arab women who have been kept prisoner for hundreds of years. No organization, local or international, official or unofficial, has bothered to expose what is happening to them in the dungeons incorrectly referred to as 'their homes.'... Why do the human rights activists ignore their suffering as though they do not even exist? Why isn't the cry of these millions of women heard, and why isn't it answered by anyone, anywhere? Why? Why? Why?"[16]

Since 2006, Wajeha al-Huwaider's campaign has slowly gained support from other women who, like al-Huwaider, long to live in a country where they can sleep freely, knowing "there won't be a knock at my door and they will say, 'You are arrested.'"[17] In May 2011, as part of an initiative called Women2Drive, al-Huwaider filmed a video, later posted on YouTube and Facebook, of her fellow activist Manal al-Sharif driving a car.[18] This seemingly routine action was in fact a bold challenge to one of the Saudi regime's iconic misogynistic policies: its ban on women drivers. The initiative followed up on al-Huwaider's protest from 2008, when she posted a video clip on YouTube of herself driving a car.[19]

For al-Sharif, the knock on the door came shortly after midnight on May 22, 2011. She was detained in Dammam prison on charges of disturbing public order and inciting public opinion. But al-Sharif's brave act quickly drew popular support. Her Facebook page attracted more than 12,000 supporters before the authorities blocked it, and more than 3,300 Saudis, men and women alike, signed an online petition asking King Abdullah to release her.[20] As France's AFP reported, "A Facebook page titled 'We are all Manal al-Sharif: a call for solidarity with Saudi women's rights,' on Sunday had over 24,000 supporters. However, another Facebook page called on men to use 'iqals'—the cords used with traditional headdresses by many Gulf men—to beat Saudi women who drive their cars in a planned June 17 protest against the kingdom's ban on women taking the wheel."[21]

The Saudi authorities, uneasy with the international attention the case was drawing, released al-Sharif on bail nine days after her arrest, on condition that she refrain from driving or talking to the media. But al-Sharif had already inspired other Saudi women. During the following weeks, up to forty women publicly defied the driving ban, while al-Sharif began campaigning on Twitter for the release of female prisoners in Dammam prison. Many of these women are Filipino or Indonesian domestic workers imprisoned over some small debt. Abandoned by their employers, they cannot afford to pay for a flight home.[22]

On September 26, 2011, Women2Drive again made international headlines when a Saudi court sentenced Shaima Jastaina to be whipped with ten lashes for driving a car. King Abdullah quickly overturned the sentence, most likely due to the publicity Women2Drive had brought to the case.[23]

These events may seem insignificant, but they prove that just a few brave people can achieve great things. A despotic monarch ruling an Islamic dictatorship of 27 million inhabitants can be forced to give in to the pressure of barely forty courageous women. As Andrew Jackson said, "One man with courage makes a majority."[24]

It is our responsibility as Westerners to oppose the expansion of Islam, but it should be the Muslims' responsibility to *outgrow* Islam. The fact that Islam forbids Muslims from leaving the fold does not mean Muslims don't have the option to do so.

The American Declaration of Independence states that "all men are created equal, that they are endowed by their Creator with certain unalienable Rights, that among these are Life, Liberty and the pursuit of Happiness." *All men*—that includes Muslims. And just as Americans liberated themselves from their British oppressors, Muslims must free themselves from Islam because they, too, have an unalienable right to freedom. In liberating themselves from Islam, they will ensure a happier life for themselves and their children, and a safer, more peaceful world for the rest of us.

Muslims must break the asphyxiating rules that Muhammad imposed on their societies. They must liberate themselves from the mental prison that traps them. In short, Muslims must defeat Islam.

Brave women such as Wajeha al-Huwaider and Manal al-Sharif are beginning to liberate themselves. They reject the "outdated chauvinistic interpretations" of Islam which, as al-Huwaider writes, are "no longer right for an era in which dogs and cats in the developed world have more rights than Arab women—or even Arab men."[25] Of course, the reason why these "chauvinistic interpretations" dominate the Islamic world is because these interpretations are true to the Koran and to Muhammad's life. These interpretations *are* Islam. People who reject Islam's violent, intolerant, and misogynistic commandments may be moderates, but they are not practicing "moderate Islam"—they are not practicing Islam at all.

I wholeheartedly support those who struggle for freedom in the Islamic world. The Arab, Turkish, Iranian, Pakistani, and Indonesian peoples have tremendous potential. If they could liberate themselves from the yoke of Islam, if they would stop taking Muhammad as a role model, and if they got rid of the hateful Koran, they would be able to achieve amazing things.

As I wrote in a dispatch to Muslims in July 2010, "My message...is clear: 'Fatalism is no option; *Inch' Allah* is a curse; Submission is a disgrace. Free yourselves. It is up to you.'"[26]

While brave women such as Wajeha al-Huwaider and Manal al-Sharif in Saudi Arabia, and countless other men and women in Egypt, Iran, Pakistan, and elsewhere in the Islamic world, are risking their lives, we— the men and women of the free world—must do our duty as well. Islam has marked us, collectively, for death, but we remain free individuals. We should never give in to fear.

To preserve our freedoms from the encroachments of Islam, we must do four things: defend freedom of speech, reject cultural relativism, counter Islamization, and cherish our national identity. Let's discuss each of these actions in turn.

First, we must defend freedom of speech, which is the most important of our liberties. So long as we are free to speak, we can tell people the truth and make them realize what's at stake. The truth is our only weapon—we must use it. The West's political, academic, and media establishment are concealing the true scope of the Islamic threat. But the people sense they are not getting the whole story, and they are eager to know more. We must spread the message.

We must also repeal all hate speech laws, which are used to silence Islam's critics. Europe, where hate speech laws strictly circumscribe the bounds of free speech, should adopt some sort of "European First Amendment" that will abolish the current restrictions and allow the people to fully debate Islam just like any other public issue. Free speech is a fragile thing that must be vigilantly defended, for it is the cornerstone of a free society. As George Orwell said, "If liberty means anything at all, it means the right to tell people what they do not want to hear."[27]

Second, we must reject all forms of cultural relativism. Let's say it frankly: our civilized Western culture is far superior to the barbaric culture of Islam. Once we acknowledge this and stop being afraid of saying it, we will be better prepared to defend our civilization. Western nations should add an amendment to our constitutions stating that our societies are based on Judeo-Christian and humanist values. In other words, we owe nothing to Islam. We should also stop the political indoctrination of our children and begin proudly teaching them the real history of the West instead of multiculturalist lies designed to instill shame in our own heritage. We must also prepare the coming generation for the difficult times ahead by explaining Islam's true, bloody history.

Third, we must stop the Islamization of the West. We begin by recognizing two politically incorrect facts: that migration, or *hijra*, is one of the most important instruments of Islamization, and that throughout history, more Islam has meant less freedom. Once we acknowledge these facts, our course of action is clear: we must close the floodgates of Islamic immigration to the West by stopping *all* immigration from Islamic countries. Having accepted millions of Islamic immigrants in recent decades, the West has already been welcoming enough to Islam. Instead of admitting even more Islamic immigrants, it's time to focus on integrating the immigrants who are already here and preventing the appearance of any new "cities of the prophet" on Western soil.

We must also demand that immigrants who are already here assimilate to our societies, adapt to our values, and abide by our laws. We must oppose the introduction of Sharia, or Islamic law, anywhere in our countries. As for immigrants who insist on Sharia, we should recall British Prime Minister William Gladstone's statement about the Ottomans: "Let the Turks now carry away their abuses in the only possible manner, namely by carrying off themselves."[28]

Criminals with dual nationality should automatically be stripped of their Western nationality and sent back to the country of their other nationality. We should not allow people with dual nationality to assume political office.

The message to all newcomers in our societies should be clear: if you subscribe to our laws and values, you are welcome to stay and enjoy all the rights our society guarantees; we will even help you to assimilate. But if you commit crimes, act against our laws, or wage jihad, you will be expelled.

We have to stop pretending that Islam is merely a religion—it is primarily a totalitarian ideology that aims to conquer the West. A free society should not grant freedom to those who want to destroy it. Every *halal* shop, every mosque, every Islamic school, and every *burka* is regarded by Islam as a step toward the ultimate goal of our submission. As such, we must close down all Islamic schools, for they are totalitarian institutions where young children are indoctrinated into an ideology of violence and hatred. We must also close down all radical mosques and forbid the construction of new mosques, which Islam regards as symbols of its triumph. And we must ban the *burka*—people's faces should not be hidden in society, for it is our faces that give us our identity and our fundamental means of communication with others.

The West must also stand up to intolerant Islamic regimes. They should recognize that human rights exist to protect individuals, not religions and ideologies. Member states of the Organization of Islamic Cooperation that do not renounce the Cairo Declaration, which elevates Sharia law over human rights, should be expelled from the United Nations. Until this happens, Western nations should refuse to make any financial contributions to the UN. As I have argued since 2007, Western countries should cut all development aid to OIC members that adhere to the Cairo Declaration and minimize bilateral relations with them.[29]

Since Islam has global ambitions, we are all in danger, and we should stand with every nation and every people that is threatened by jihad. This includes Israel, the only democracy in the Middle East. We should recognize that the Israelis' conflict with the Palestinians is not about land; it is an ideological conflict between freedom and tyranny. We must also stand with all the oppressed non-Muslim groups suffering in silence throughout the Islamic world—the Christians, Zoroastrians, animists, and secularists in nations like Egypt, Iran, the Sudan, Nigeria, Indonesia, and elsewhere.

Fourth, we must cherish our national identity. In Europe, this means we have to restore the supremacy and sovereignty of the nation-state and reverse the intrusions of the European Union. Our nation-states embody our democratic liberties and safeguard our national political freedom. That is why multiculturalists are hostile to the nation-state; they want to dissolve our sovereignty in a giant, Europe-wide bureaucracy that they control. People cannot attain security or preserve their collective identity without a nation-state, which enables self-government and self-determination. This insight led the Zionists to re-establish the state of Israel, with Theodor Herzl arguing that a Jewish state would facilitate "a new blossoming of the Jewish spirit."[30] Today, we need our respective nation-states to preside over a new blossoming of the *Western* spirit.

The peoples of the free world can defend their liberties only if they can rally around a flag with which they identify. This flag, symbolizing ancient loyalties, can only be the flag of our nation. We love our nations because they are our home, because they are the legacy our fathers bestowed on us and which we want to bestow on our children.

Uniformity is not characteristic of the West; it is a feature of Islam, which eradicated the national identities of the peoples it conquered. The Coptic identity of Egypt, the Indian identity of Pakistan, the Assyrian identity of Iraq, the Persian identity of Iran—they were all suppressed, if not totally wiped away. Islam wants all nations replaced by the *Umma*, the collective identity of the Islamic nation to which all must be subservient and into which all national identities must vanish.

Resistance against Islamization is a patriotic duty. There is no Dutch flag in the Dutch Parliament, but a copy of the Koran lies on the Speaker's desk. Let's get rid of the Koran and bring in the national flag—in the Netherlands and in all free nations.

Striving to create a supranational Caliphate, Islam threatens the survival of all free peoples. Dutchmen, Americans, Canadians, Australians, Indians, Germans, Brits, Russians, Irishmen, Frenchmen, Italians, Danes, Swiss, Israelis, and others should unite against our common adversary. We must stand together to counter Islamization. The Islamic tide is strong, but the West has repulsed it before, and we can do it again.

The political elite reject my proposed solutions to Islamization and mass immigration, believing that the problems can be solved largely by accommodating Islam. They can call their policies "tolerance," "coexistence," or some other pleasant-sounding euphemism, but in fact they are all tantamount to surrender. And as Winston Churchill said, "Never give in, never, never, never, never—in nothing, great or small, large or petty—never give in except to convictions of honour and good sense. Never yield to force; never yield to the apparently overwhelming might of the enemy."[31]

If we do not oppose Islamization, we will lose everything: our freedom, our identity, our democracy, our rule of law, and all our liberties. It is our duty to defend the legacy of Rome, Athens, and Jerusalem.

In 1862, during the Civil War, Abraham Lincoln proclaimed, "The dogmas of the quiet past are inadequate to the stormy present. The occasion is piled high with difficulty, and we must rise with the occasion. As our case is new, so we must think anew and act anew. We must disenthrall ourselves, and then we shall save our country."[32]

Just so. The West is in danger, but we can still prevail. We begin the struggle by standing up for our values and telling the truth about Islam. Even when we are insulted, even when we are harassed and intimidated, even when we are marked for death just for stating an opinion—we must never be silenced.

Notes

CHAPTER 1

1. Thomas Landen, "Heeere's Muhammed!" Stonegate Institute, January 4, 2010, http://www.stonegateinstitute.org/980/heeeres-muhammed.
2. Flemming Rose, "Why I Published Those Cartoons," *Washington Post*, February 19, 2006, http://www.washingtonpost.com/wp-dyn/content/article/2006/02/17/AR2006021702499.html.
3. Adrian Humphreys, "The Most Hated Man in Mecca: Meet the Cartoonist Who Set the World on Fire," *National Post* (Toronto), October 3, 2009.
4. Patricia Cohen, "Yale Press Bans Images of Muhammad in New Book," *New York Times*, August 12, 2009, http://www.nytimes.com/2009/08/13/books/13book.html.
5. Matthew Campbell, "Panic Room Saved Artist Kurt Westergaard from Islamist Assassin," *Sunday Times* (London), January 3, 2010, http://www.timesonline.co.uk/tol/news/world/article6973966.ece.
6. "Muhammad Cartoonist 'Full of Angst,'" AFP (Paris), November 15, 2010, available at News24.com, http://www.news24.com/World/News/Muhammad-cartoonist-full-of-angst-20101115.

7. "Norwegian Held over Cartoonist Plot," AFP (Paris), September 17, 2011, available at News24.com, http://www.news24.com/World/News/Norwegian-held-over-cartoonist-plot-20110917.

8. Kurt Westergaard, "Why I Drew the Cartoon: The 'Muhammad Affair' in Retrospect," *Daily Princetonian*, October 1, 2009, http://www.dailyprincetonian.com/2009/10/01/23967/.

9. "Somali Man Charged in Attack on Danish Cartoonist," Associated Press, available on *USA Today*, January 2, 2010, http://www.usatoday.com/news/world/2010-01-01-danish-cartoonist-attack_N.htm.

10. "Westergaard Is Best Forgotten: Revenge Attack on Danish Cartoonist Highlights Insult Wrought by Danish Media," Gulf News, January 3, 2010, http://gulfnews.com/opinions/editorials/westergaard-is-best-forgotten-1.561259.

11. Leviticus 24:20. Also: Exodus 21:24; Deuteronomy 19:21.

12. Landen, "Heeere's Muhammed!"

13. Ronald Reagan, "The Future Doesn't Belong to the Fainthearted," Oval Office of the White House, January 28, 1986, in Brian MacArthur, ed., *The Penguin Book of Twentieth-Century Speeches* (Penguin, 1999), p. 455.

CHAPTER 2

1. *Fitna* is available for viewing at: http://www.liveleak.com/view?i=216_1207467783.

2. "US Media Pins Europe as Training Ground for Terror," *Economic Times* (New Delhi), April 17, 2003, http://articles.economictimes.indiatimes.com/2003-04-17/news/27540826_1_al-qaeda-militants-jammu-and-kashmir-german-intelligence-officials.

3. "'Geitenneuker zeggen mag. Allah beledigen niet,'" *Elsevier* (Amsterdam), December 27, 2004, http://www.elsevier.nl/web/Nieuws/Nederland/09156/Geitenneuker-zeggen-mag.-Allah-beledigen-niet.htm. "Theo van Gogh: 'Wat is er mis met geitenneuker?'" *HP/De Tijd* (Amsterdam), October 28, 2009, http://www.hpdetijd.nl/2009-10-28/theo-van-gogh-wat-is-er-mis-met-geitenneuker.

4. Statement of Theo van Gogh to the Amsterdam police, "Proces-Verbaal 99023171," Politie Amsterdam-Amstelland, District 3, November 11, 1999, http://www.theovangogh.nl/proverb1.html.

5. Frank van Hoorn, "73 jaar 'vrijheid,'" *Elsevier Magazine* (Amsterdam), May 15, 2007, http://www.elsevier.nl/web/Artikel/175175/Vrijheid-Dat-mag-je-niet-zeggen.htm.

6. Leon de Winter, "Fatal Detraction: A Provocative, and Offensive, Film-maker and Columnist Attacks Islam and Pays with His Life," *Wall Street Journal*, November 5, 2004.

7. Hans Jansen, "In negentig seconden, graag," *HP/De Tijd* (Amsterdam), December 19, 2008.

8. "'Syriër die Hofstadgroep inspireerde al lang weg,'" *Trouw* (Amsterdam), December 27, 2004, http://www.trouw.nl/tr/nl/4324/nieuws/archief/article/detail/1738560/2004/12/27/Syrier-die-Hofstadgroep-inspireerde-al-lang-weg.dhtml.

9. "Moslimorganizaties spreken afschuw uit," *De Telegraaf* (Amsterdam), November 3, 2004.

10. The NCTV website says "The authorities avoid using the terms 'Islamic terrorism' or 'Muslim terrorism' or 'Islamist terrorism' as much as possible. The large majority of Muslims consider terrorism to be un-Islamic and resent their religion being in any way connected with terrorism. For similar reasons the term 'religiously inspired terrorism' cannot be used. This encourages the notion that a religion as such could be a foundation for violence." "Jihadism and Jihadist Terrorism," Nationaal Coördinator Terrorismebestrijding en Veiligheid website, http://www.nctb.nl/onderwerpen/terrorismebestrijding/wat_is_terrorisme/jihadisme_en_jihadistisch_terrorisme.aspx.

11. James Slack, "Government Renames Islamic Terrorism as 'Anti-Islamic Activity' to Woo Muslims," *Daily Mail* (London), January 17, 2008, http://www.dailymail.co.uk/news/article-508901/Government-renames-Islamic-terrorism-anti-Islamic-activity-woo-Muslims.html.

12. "Aan de Voorzitter van de Tweede Kamer der Staten-Generaal—Onderwerp: Van Gogh," letter of the Minister of Justice and the Minister of the Interior to the Speaker of the Dutch House of Representatives, *Tweede Kamer*, November 10, 2004, available on the Buro Jansen & Janssen website, http://www.burojansen.nl/documenten/brief10nov2004terrorisme.doc.

13. Both letters are available on Militant Islam Monitor, "Articles," "English Translation—Letter Left on Theo Van Gogh's Body by the Militant Islamist Killer was 'Jihad Manifesto'—A Call to Destroy America and All 'Unbelievers,'" November 5, 2004, http://www.militantislammonitor.org/article/id/312.

14. Anthony Browne, "Anti-Muslim Dutch Politicians in Hiding after Death Threats," *Times* (London), November 5, 2004, http://www.timesonline.co.uk/tol/news/world/article503307.ece.

15.   Barack Obama, "Remarks by the President on A New Beginning," White-house.gov, June 4, 2009, http://www.whitehouse.gov/the_press_office/Remarks-by-the-President-at-Cairo-University-6-04-09/.

16.   "A Fear of Ideas: *3:AM* Columnist David Thompson Talks about Islam, Freedom and Denial with the Muslim Novelist and Exile Tahir Aslam Gora," *3:AM Magazine* (Paris), September 11, 2007, http://www.3ammagazine.com/3am/a-fear-of-ideas/.

17.   "Al-Azhar's Response to the US on Religious Freedom: The Islamic Research Academy of Al-Azhar Response to the US State Department's 2010 Report on Religious Freedom in Egypt," Islamic Research Academy of Al-Azhar, OnIslam.net, December 19, 2010, http://www.onislam.net/english/shariah/contemporary-issues/interfaith-intercivilizational-and-intercultural/450186-al-azhars-response-to-the-us-on-religious-freedom.html?Intercultural=.

18.   "Egypt Blogger Jailed for 'Insult': An Egyptian Court Has Sentenced a Blogger to Four Years' [sic] Prison for Insulting Islam and the President," BBC News (London), February 22, 2007, http://news.bbc.co.uk/2/hi/middle_east/6385849.stm.

19.   Having served his sentence, Amer was released in November 2010, but not before he was beaten up by an Egyptian security officer. "Prior to His Release after Spending Four Years in Prison State Security Officer Beat Kareem Amer and Held Him Illegally," Arabic Network for Human Rights Information, November 10, 2010, http://www.anhri.net/en/?p=1636.

20.   Wafa Sultan, "Who Should We Believe?" Stonegate Institute, June 12, 2009, http://www.stonegateinstitute.org/579/who-should-we-believe.

21.   "The Future of the Global Muslim Population: Projections for 2010–2030," Pew Research Center, January 27, 2011, http://pewforum.org/The-Future-of-the-Global-Muslim-Population.aspx.

22.   J. B. Duroselle and Ian J. Bickerton, "Treaties—Creating a Framework for Making Treaties," *Encyclopedia of the American Foreign Relations*, ed. The Gale Group, 2002, http://www.americanforeignrelations.com/O-W/Treaties-Creating-a-framework-for-making-treaties.html.

23.   In 1786 Thomas Jefferson, then-U.S. Ambassador to France, and John Adams, then-U.S. Ambassador to Britain, met in London with Sidi Haji Abdul Rahman Adja, the Dey of Algiers' Ambassador to Britain, to negotiate a peace treaty. To the U.S. Congress, these two future presidents later reported the reasons for the Muslims' hostility toward America, a nation

with which they had no previous contacts. Jefferson wrote in his report to Secretary of State John Jay that upon inquiring "concerning the ground of the pretensions to make war upon nations who had done them no injury," the ambassador replied "that [this right] was founded on the Laws of the Prophet, that it was written in their Koran, that all nations who should not have answered their authority were sinners, that it was their right and duty to make war upon them wherever they could be found, and to make slaves of all they could take as prisoners, and that every mussulman who should be slain in battle was sure to go to Paradise. He said, also, that the man who was the first to board a vessel had one slave over and above his share, and that when they sprang to the deck of an enemy's ship, every sailor held a dagger in each hand and a third in his mouth; which usually struck such terror into the foe that they cried out for quarter at once." "American Peace Commissioners to John Jay," March 28, 1786, in the Thomas Jefferson Papers, Series 1: General Correspondence. 1651–1827 (Library of Congress: Washington, D.C.).

24. William J. Federer, "Obama—Student of History? (Part 5)—Treaty of Tripoli," *Worldview Times*, September 22, 2009, http://www.worldview weekend.com/worldview-times/article.php?articleid=5420.

25. John Quincy Adams in Joseph Blunt, *The American Annual Register; for the Years 1827–8–9* (E. & G. W. Blunt, 1830), 29:269, http://www. archive.org/stream/p1americanannual29blunuoft.

26. Ibid.

27. George W. Bush, "Islam Is Peace Says President: Remarks by the President at Islamic Center of Washington, D.C.," the White House: President George W. Bush website, September 17, 2001, http://georgewbush-white-house.archives.gov/news/releases/2001/09/20010917-11.html.

28. Obama, "Remarks by the President on A New Beginning."

29. "Treaty of Peace and Friendship between the United States of America and the Bey and Subjects of Tripoli of Barbary," signed at Tripoli, Barbary (contemporary Libya), November 4, 1796. The text can be found at the website of the Avalon Project: Documents in Law, History and Diplomacy, Yale Law School: Lillian Goldman Law Library, http://avalon.law.yale. edu/18th_century/bar1796t.asp.

30. Andrew Walden, "The Colonial War against Islam," *FrontPage Magazine*, January 5, 2007, http://archive.frontpagemag.com/readArticle. aspx?ARTID=758.

31. John Quincy Adams in *The American Annual Register*, 29:274, http://www.archive.org/stream/p1americanannual29blunuoft.

32. *Bey* is the Turkish word for "chieftain." *Dey*, which literally means "maternal uncle," was the title given to the Regent of Algiers.

33. John Quincy Adams in *The American Annual Register*, 29:274–75, http://www.archive.org/stream/p1americanannual29blunuoft.

34. Ibid., 29:299–300.

35. Ibid., 29:274.

36. The correct Arabic plural for *sura* (verse) is *suwar*; the plural for *kafir* (unbeliever) is *kuffar*. I use the normal English plural for the Arabic word in its singular form.

37. Koran 24:27. The sura translations are from *The Koran*, trans. with notes by N. J. Dawood (Penguin Books, 1956).

38. Alfred Guillaume, *Life of Muhammad: A Translation of Ibn Ishaq's Sirat Rasul Allah* (Oxford University Press, 1955), pp. 482–84.

39. Koran 4:89.

40. Ali Sina, M. A. Khan, Abul Kasem, M. A. Hussain, Sher Khan, Syed Kamran Mirza, Mumin Salih, "Who are We?" Islam Watch, http://www.islam-watch.org/IW/aboutus.htm.

41. "'Draw Muhammad' Cartoonist Goes into Hiding at FBI's Insistence after Assassination Threat," Fox News, September 16, 2010, http://www.foxnews.com/us/2010/09/16/draw-muhammad-cartoonist-goes-hiding/.

42. Dutch Penal Code, articles 137c and 137d.

43. Ayaan Hirsi Ali, "In Holland, Free Speech on Trial," *Wall Street Journal*, October 11, 2010, http://online.wsj.com/article/SB10001424052748704657304575539872944767984.html?mod=WSJ_newsreel_opinion.

44. Thomas Jefferson, "Notes on the State of Virginia," 1781, in *Thomas Jefferson: Writings: Autobiography, Notes on the State of Virginia, Public and Private Papers, Addresses, Letters*, ed. Merrill D. Peterson (Library of America, 1984).

45. Thomas Jefferson, *Notes on Religion*, 1776, Papers 1:548. This quote is originally from John Locke.

46. Abraham Lincoln, "Letter to Henry L. Pierce & Others," April 6, 1859, in *The Collected Works of Abraham Lincoln, Vol. III*, ed. Roy P. Basler (Rutgers University Press, 1953), p. 376.

47. Robert Spencer, *The Truth About Muhammad: Founder of the World's Most Intolerant Religion* (Regnery, 2006), p. 153.

CHAPTER 3

1. Theodore Roosevelt, "The Great Adventure," *Metropolitan Magazine*, October 1918, quoted in "'Great Adventure' Roosevelt's Topic: Fate of His Son the Basis for a Moving Tribute to Our Soldier Dead," *New York Times*, September 17, 1918, http://query.nytimes.com/gst/abstract.html?res=9C04EEDC1531E433A25754C1A96F9C946996D6CF.

2. F. A. Hayek, *The Fatal Conceit: The Errors of Socialism*, ed. W. W. Bartley III (University of Chicago Press, 1988), pp. 139–40.

3. Patt Morrison, "Feminism's Freedom Fighter: Ayaan Hirsi Ali Has Put Her Life on the Line to Defend Women against Radical Islam," *Los Angeles Times*, October 17, 2009, http://articles.latimes.com/2009/oct/17/opinion/oe-morrison17.

4. The Pledge of Allegiance is as follows: "I pledge allegiance to the flag of the United States of America, and to the republic for which it stands, one nation under God, indivisible, with liberty and justice for all."

5. Thomas Jefferson to Martin Van Buren, 1824, ME 16:55, http://etext.virginia.edu/jefferson/quotations/jeff0200.htm.

6. Leszek Kolakowski, "Politics & the Devil," *Encounter* (London), December 1987, http://www.unz.org/Pub/Encounter-1987dec-00059?View=PDF.

7. Ibid.

8. Ronald Reagan, California Gubernatorial Inauguration Speech, Sacramento, CA, January 5, 1967, http://www.reagan.utexas.edu/archives/speeches/govspeech/01051967a.htm.

9. Some Muslims claim that the exact date was August 10, 610, see "Basic Knowledge about the Life of Holy Prophet Muhammad (PBUH). Questions and Answers," HubPages, http://knowledgebox.hubpages.com/hub/Holy-Prophet-PBUH-Life-and-Achievements-a-brief-History-Question-and-Answers.

10. The word *Muslim*, like the word *Islam*, is derived from the Arabic verbal root SLM, "submit."

11. *Qadr* is the Arabic word for "power"; *Al-Ilah* is the Arabic word for "the god"; and *Qu'ran* is the Arabic word for "recitation."

12. Koran 96:1–5.

13. Koran 68:1.

14. Alfred Guillaume, *Life of Muhammad: A Translation of Ibn Ishaq's Sirat Rasul Allah* (Oxford University Press, 1955), p. 107.

15. Paul Johnson, *A History of the Jews* (Weidenfeld and Nicolson, 1987), p. 166.
16. Karen Armstrong, *Islam: A Short History* (Weidenfeld and Nicolson, 2000), p. 11.
17. Guillaume, *Life of Muhammad*, p. 107.
18. Koran 21:5, 36:69, 37:36, 52:30.
19. Koran 15:6, 23:70, 34:8, 34:46, 37:36, 44:14, 52:29, 68:2, 68:51, 81:22.
20. Koran 53:19–23.
21. Guillaume, *Life of Muhammad*, p. 131.
22. Koran 2:61, 3:110, 4:160–61, 5:12, 5:51, 5:57, 5:63–66, 9:30, etc.
23. Koran 3:110, 5:14, 5:51, 5:57–60, 5:66, 5:75, etc.
24. Koran 2:256.
25. Benedict XVI, "Faith, Reason and the University: Memories and Reflections," lecture of the Holy Father given at Regensburg University, Regensburg, Germany, September 12, 2006, http://www.vatican.va/holy_father/benedict_xvi/speeches/2006/september/documents/hf_ben-xvi_spe_20060912_university-regensburg_en.html.
26. Johnson, *A History of the Jews*, pp. 166–67.
27. Koran 33:37–38.
28. Koran 8:12.
29. Koran 2:216. Other bellicose verses are suras 2:191–93, 3:157–58, 3:169–71, 4:74, 4:76, 8:15–16, 8:39–42, 8:65, 9:5–6, 9:14, 9:29–30, 9:39, 9:41, 9:73, 9:111, 9:123, 10:4–15, 25:52, 46:9, 47:4–15, etc.
30. Kolakowski, "Politics & the Devil."
31. Koran 8:1.
32. Koran 8:67.
33. Guillaume, *Life of Muhammad*, pp. 675–76.
34. Koran 3:152.
35. Guillaume, *Life of Muhammad*, p. 327.
36. Ibid., p. 515. Hadith Sahih Bukhari 5:59:512.
37. Koran 69:30–35.
38. Koran 5:33.
39. Guillaume, *Life of Muhammad*, pp. 461–64.
40. Theodore Roosevelt, "A Confession of Faith," speech delivered at Chicago, IL, August 6, 1912, http://www.cooperativeindividualism.org/roosevelt-theodore_on-the-land-question.html.
41. Theodore Roosevelt, *Fear God and Take Your Own Part* (George H. Doran Company, 1916).

42. Ibid.
43. Adolf Hitler, August 28, 1942. Quoted in *Hitler's Table Talk; 1941–1944*, trans. N. Cameron and R. H. Stevens (Enigma Books, 1953), p. 667.
44. Albert Speer, *Inside the Third Reich* (Simon & Schuster, 1997), chapter 6.
45. Himmler to Kersten, December 1, 1942, in Felix Kersten, *Totenkopf und Treue: Heinrich Himmler ohne Uniform* (Robert Mölich Verlag, 1952), pp. 206–8.
46. Koran 44:54, 52:20.
47. Felix Kersten, *Totenkopf und Treue: Heinrich Himmler ohne Uniform*, p. 203.
48. Peter Longerich, *Heinrich Himmler: Biographie* (Siedler Verlag, 2008), p. 277. The original document of November 26, 1944 is available in the Federal Archives in Berlin (Bundesarchiv Berlin, BAB), file NS 19/4013.
49. Koran 2:223.
50. Mervyn Hiskett, *Some to Mecca Turn to Pray: Islamic Values in the Modern World* (Claridge Press, 1993), p. 117.
51. Felix Kersten, *Totenkopf und Treue: Heinrich Himmler ohne Uniform*, p. 226.
52. Koran 7:166.
53. Koran 2:65.
54. Koran 5:60.
55. Quoted in David G. Dalin, "Hitler's Mufti," *First Things; A Journal of Religion, Culture, and Public Life*, August/September 2005, http://www.firstthings.com/article/2007/01/hitler8217s-mufti-29.
56. Quoted in Jeffrey Herf, *The Jewish Enemy: Nazi Propaganda During World War II and the Holocaust* (Harvard University Press, 2006), p. 181.
57. Johann von Leers in a letter to the American Nazi H. Keith Thompson, November 1957. Quoted in Andrew Bostom, "Tariq Ramadan's Appointment at Leiden Uni: An Insult to Huizinga's Anti-Nazi Legacy," Islam Watch, November 8, 2007, http://www.islam-watch.org/Bostom/Tariq-Ramadan-at-Leiden-University.htm.
58. Koran 5:51; also Koran 3:28.
59. Koran 9:5.
60. Hadith Sahih Bukhari 4:52:177; also Hadith Sahih Muslim 41:6985.
61. Ali Sina, "Muslims Pooh Pooh the Golden Rule," Faith Freedom International, October 8, 2005, http://www.faithfreedom.org/oped/sina51007.htm.
62. See, for example, Koran 3:18, 5:72, 8:13–14, 8:55, 9:7, 9:23, 9:28, 9:101, 25:55, 58:23, 60:4, etc.

CHAPTER 4

1. "Schoolgirls die in Mecca stampede," BBC News (London), March 11, 2002, http://news.bbc.co.uk/2/hi/middle_east/1867039.stm.

2. *Mutaween* is the Arabic word for "volunteers."

3. "Saudi police 'stopped' fire rescue," BBC News (London), March 15, 2002, http://news.bbc.co.uk/2/hi/1874471.stm.

4. Hadith Sahih Bukhari 1:9:490.

5. Dahlia Mogahed, "The Battle for Hearts and Minds; Moderate vs. Extremist Views in the Muslim World. A Gallup World Poll Special Report," Gallup Organization, 2006, http://media.gallup.com/WorldPoll/PDF/ExtremismInMuslimWorld.pdf.

6. "Muslim leader blames women for sex attacks," *Australian* (Sydney), October 26, 2006, http://www.theaustralian.com.au/news/nation/muslim-leader-blames-women-for-sex-attacks/story-e6frg6nf-1111112419114.

7. Ibid.

8. Winston Churchill, *The River War* (Longmans, Green & Co., 1899), vol. 2, p. 248.

9. Koran 4:3, 23:1,5,6, 33:49–51.

10. Koran 2:282.

11. Koran 4:11.

12. Koran 4:34.

13. Koran 24:31.

14. Koran 24:30.

15. Koran 4:15.

16. Josh Wingrove, Jim Wilkes and Bob Mitchell, "Teen died of strangulation,"*Toronto Star* (Toronto), December 12, 2007, http://www.thestar.com/News/GTA/article/284823.

17. Tanya Eiserer, "Slain Lewisville sisters mourned at Christian, Muslim services," *Dallas Morning News*, January 6, 2008, formerly available at http://www.dallasnews.com/sharedcontent/dws/dn/latestnews/stories/010 608dnmetfunerals.216ceab.html; article is available at http://www.scribd.com/doc/63791943/Slain-Lewisville-Sisters-Mourned-at-Christian-Muslim-Services-By-TANYA-EISERER.

18. Stine Jensen, "Eerwraak is een Nederlands fenomeen," *NRC Handelsblad* (Rotterdam), June 6, 2008, http://www.nrcboeken.nl/column/eerwraak-is-een-nederlands-fenomeen.

19. "Antwerpse 'imam' in cel voor doodslag en marteling," *Gazet van Antwerpen* (Belgium), October 28, 2009, http://www.gva.be/antwerpen/

antwerpen/antwerpse-imam-in-de-cel-voor-marteling-en-dood-18-jarige-laila.aspx.

20. "The Death of a Muslim Woman. 'The Whore Lived Like a German,'" *Der Spiegel* (Berlin), March 2, 2005, http://www.spiegel.de/international/0,1518,344374,00.html.

21. "'Honour killing' father begins sentence," BBC News (London), September 30, 2003, http://news.bbc.co.uk/2/hi/uk_news/england/london/3149030.stm.

22. Alistair MacDonald, "Afghan Immigrants in Canada Found Guilty of Honor Killing," *Wall Street Journal*, January 30, 2012, http://online.wsj.com/article/SB10001424052970203920204577191321206664022.html.

23. Joe Warmington, "Shafia Called Girls 'Filthy Rotten Children,' Wife Testifies," *Ottawa Sun* (Ottawa), January 10, 2012, http://www.ottawasun.com/2012/01/10/shafia-mom-said-she-lied-to-protect-son.

24. Christie Blatchford, "A Dozen Officials Didn't Know How to Help Desperate 'Honour Killing' Shafia Sisters," *National Post* (Toronto), November 24, 2011, http://fullcomment.nationalpost.com/2011/11/24/christie-blatchford-officials-help-never-enough-to-save-desperate-shafia-girls/.

25. Robert Fulford, "Robert Fulford: Too Much Sensitivity Doomed the Shafia Girls," *National Post* (Toronto), November 26, 2011, http://fullcomment.nationalpost.com/2011/11/26 robert-fulford-too-much-sensitivity-doomed-the-shafia-girls/.

26. P. J. Gladnick, "NBC, AP Avoid 'M-word' in Report About 'Honor Killings,'" NewsBusters, January 30, 2012, http://newsbusters.org/blogs/pj-gladnick/2012/01/30/nbc-ap-avoid-m-word-report-about-honor-kill ings.

27. Birgit Schwarz, "Der Koran ist überflüssig," interview with Taslima Nasrin, *Der Spiegel* (Hamburg), June 13, 1994.

28. Koran 8:12, 8:60, 33:26, and 59:2.

29. Churchill, *The River War*, vol. 2, pp. 248–50.

30. Ibid.

31. Koran 6:99.

32. Fanous, "Who Burned the Historic Bibliotheca Alexandrina?" *Independent Copt*, October 5, 2006, http://english.freecopts.net/english//index.php?option=com_content&task=view&id=343; and http://www.faithfreedom.org/articles/op-ed/did-omar-order-the-burning-of-alexandria-library/.

33. Paul Johnson, *A History of the Jews* (Weidenfeld and Nicolson, 1987), p. 188.

34. Moses Maimonides, Epistle to the Jews of Yemen, written in 1172. Quoted in Andrew Bostom, *The Legacy of Islamic Antisemitism: From Sacred Texts to Solemn History* (Prometheus Books, 2008), p. 11.

35. Barack Obama, "Remarks by the President on A New Beginning," Cairo University, Egypt, June 4, 2009, http://www.whitehouse.gov/the_press_office/Remarks-by-the-President-at-Cairo-University-6-04-09/.

36. "NASA Chief: Next Frontier Better Relations with Muslim World," Fox News, July 5, 2010, http://www.foxnews.com/politics/2010/07/05/nasa-chief-frontier-better-relations-muslims/.

37. Thomas Cahill, *How the Irish Saved Civilization: The Untold Story of Ireland's Heroic Role from the Fall of Rome to the Rise of Medieval Europe* (Hodder and Stoughton, 1995), pp. 208–9.

38. Sylvain Gouguenheim, *Aristote au mont Saint-Michel: Les racines grecques de l'Europe chrétienne* (Editions du Seuil, 2008).

39. Sylvain Gouguenheim, quoted in John Vinocur, "Europe's debt to Islam given a skeptical look," *New York Times*, April 28, 2008, http://www.nytimes.com/2008/04/28/world/europe/28iht-politicus.2.12398698.html?_r=1.

40. Horst Junginger, "Sigrid Hunke: Europe's New Religion and its Old Stereotypes," manuscript of a paper given at a workshop at the international workshop "Neo-Paganism, 'voelkische Religion' and Antisemitism II: The Religious Roots of Stereotypes," Tübingen University, Tübingen, Germany, October 1997, http://homepages.uni-tuebingen.de/gerd.simon/hunke.htm.

41. Sigrid Hunke, *Allahs Sonne über dem Abendland: Unser arabisches Erbe* [Allah's Sun Over the Occident: Our Arab Heritage] (Deutsche Verlaganstalt, Stuttgart, Germany, 1960).

42. Colin Wells, *Sailing from Byzantium: How a lost Empire shaped the world* (Delta Press, 2006).

43. "Algebra" is derived from the Arabic *al-jabr*, which means "transposition," i.e., the transposition of subtracted terms to the other side of an equation. The term was used in the title of the book *Kitab al-Jabr wa-l-Muqabala* [The Compendious Book on Calculation by Completion and Balancing] by the Persian mathematician Muhammad al-Khwarizmi. The book is indebted to earlier works of Indian Hindu mathematicians and astronomers, such as *Brahmagupta* (598–668). As for "algorithm," the word is derived from the name of the Persian mathematician Muhammad al-Khwarizmi, known in the West as Algoritmi (c.780–c.850).

44. Deuteronomy 22:22; Leviticus 20:10.

45. John 8:7.

46. Alfred Guillaume, *Life of Muhammad: A translation of Ibn Ishaq's Sirat Rasul Allah* (Oxford University Press, 1955), p. 267.

47. Hadith Sahih Bukhari 4:56:829. Also in Guillaume, *Life of Muhammad: A Translation of Ibn Ishaq's Sirat Rasul Allah*, p. 267.

48. "Abolish Stoning and Barbaric Punishment Worldwide," International Society for Human Rights (ISHR), Frankfurt-am-Main, Germany, http://www.ishr.org/index.php?id=857. And "Human Rights in the United Arab Emirates," Amnesty International Report, 2007, London, UK, 2007, http://www.amnesty.org/en/region/uae/report-2007.

49. "Aceh passes adultery stoning law," BBC News (London), September 14, 2009, http://news.bbc.co.uk/2/hi/8254631.stm. And "Malaysian state passes Islamic law," BBC News (London), July 8, 2002, http://news.bbc.co.uk/2/hi/asia-pacific/2116032.stm.

50. "Rape Victim Stoned to Death in Somalia Was 13, U.N. Says," *New York Times*, November 4, 2008, http://www.nytimes.com/2008/11/05/world/africa/05somalia.html.

51. Koran 24:13.

52. Hannah Block Kohat, "Blaming the Victim," *Time*, May 20, 2002, http://www.time.com/time/magazine/article/0,9171,238673,00.html.

53. Ibn Warraq, "Islam, Middle East and Fascism," *New English Review*, August 15, 2006, http://www.newenglishreview.org/custpage.cfm?frm=3766&sec_id=3766.

54. Koran 5:6.

55. Koran 33:40.

56. Koran 33:21.

57. Koran 16:74, 42:11.

58. Koran 3:31, 4:80, 24:62, 48:10, 57:28.

59. Koran 112:1–4.

60. Koran 2:213.

61. *Fitra* is the Arabic word for "instinct" or "intuition."

62. Hadith Sahih Bukhari 2:23:441.

63. Koran 5:56.

64. Soeren Kern, "France Bans Muslim Street Prayers," Stonegate Institute, September 20, 2011, http://www.stonegateinstitute.org/2435/france-bans-muslim-street-prayers.

65. Yusuf Al-Qaradawi, "Spending Zakah Money on Jihad," OnIslam.net, March 9, 2011, http://www.onislam.net/english/ask-the-scholar/

international-relations-and-jihad/jihad-rulings-and-regulations/174504-spending-zakah-money-on-jihad.html?Regulations.

66. Hadith Sunan Abu Dawud 13:2381.
67. Hadith Sunan Abu Dawud 13:2380.
68. Koran 57:21.
69. Koran 9:51.
70. Koran 54:49.
71. Koran 3:145.
72. Koran 14:4.
73. Ibn Warraq, "Islam, Middle East and Fascism," *New English Review*, August 15, 2006, http://www.newenglishreview.org/custpage.cfm?frm=3766&sec_id=3766.
74. Mervyn Hiskett, *Some to Mecca Turn to Pray: Islamic Values in the Modern World* (Claridge Press, 1993), p. 294.
75. Aldous Huxley, "In a Tunisian Oasis," *The Christmas Bookman* (George H. Donan Company, December 1925).
76. Koran 9:111.
77. Salman Rushdie, *The Satanic Verses* (Viking Press, 1988), p. 213.
78. Rania Abouzeid, "Bouazizi: The Man Who Set Himself and Tunisia on Fire," *Time*, January 21, 2011, http://www.time.com/time/magazine/article/0,9171,2044723,00.html.
79. "Update on the Size of Protests in Cairo," Pacific Rim Trading, February 1, 2011, http://www.pacificrimcoins.com/pacrim/content/update-size-protests-cairo.
80. "Muslim Publics Divided on Hamas and Hezbollah," Pew Research Center, December 2, 2010, http://www.pewglobal.org/2010/12/02/muslims-around-the-world-divided-on-hamas-and-hezbollah/. The Koranic command for punishing thieves is found in Koran 5:38.
81. "Egypt revolution unfinished, Qaradawi tells Tahrir masses," *Christian Science Monitor*, February 18, 2011, http://www.csmonitor.com/World/Middle-East/2011/0218/Egypt-revolution-unfinished-Qaradawi-tells-Tahrir-masses.
82. "In Egypt's Tahrir Square, women attacked at rally on International Women's Day," *Christian Science Monitor*, March 8, 2011, http://www.csmonitor.com/World/Middle-East/2011/0308/In-Egypt-s-Tahrir-Square-women-attacked-at-rally-on-International-Women-s-Day.
83. "9 Christians Killed, 150 Injured in Attack By 15,000 Muslims and Egyptian Army," Assyrian International News Agency, March 9, 2011,

http://www.aina.org/news/20110308211907.htm. And "Muslims Attack Christians in Egypt, 12 Killed, 232 Injured," Assyrian International News Agency, May 8, 2011, http://www.aina.org/news/20110508144114.htm. And "Egypt forces clash with Copt protesters, 24 dead," AFP (Paris), October 10, 2011, http://www.hurriyetdailynews.com/n.php?n=egypt-forces-clash-with-copt-protesters-24-dead-2011-10-10.

84. "100,000 Christians Have Left Egypt Since March: Report," Assyrian International News Agency, September 27, 2011, http://www.aina.org/news/20110926194822.htm.

85. "Libya protests: EU condemns violence and fears influx," BBC News (London), February 21, 2011, http://www.bbc.co.uk/news/mobile/world-europe-12525155.

86. "Libyan rebel commander admits his fighters have al-Qaeda links," *Daily Telegraph* (London), March 25, 2011, http://www.telegraph.co.uk/news/worldnews/africaandindianocean/libya/8407047/Libyan-rebel-commander-admits-his-fighters-have-al-Qaeda-links.html.

87. "European authorities aware of need for vigilance," *Irish Times* (Dublin), September 6, 2011, http://www.irishtimes.com/newspaper/world/2011/0906/1224303592648.html.

88. Christopher Dickey, "Intelligence Test," *Daily Beast*, June 12, 2011, http://www.thedailybeast.com/newsweek/2011/06/12/how-the-arab-spring-has-weakened-u-s-intelligence.html.

89. Boaz Ganor, "The Arab Spring from a Counter-Terrorism Perspective," *Jerusalem Issue Briefs*, Vol. 11, No. 1, Jerusalem Center for Public Affairs, May 27, 2011, http://www.jcpa.org/JCPA/Templates/ShowPage.asp?DBID=1&LNGID=1&TMID=111&FID=442&PID=0&IID=7209.

90. J. M. (John Morris) Roberts, *The Triumph of the West* (Guild Publishing/BBC, 1985), p. 388.

91. Hugh Fitzgerald, "Twenty-Five (Out Of One Hundred) Things We All Should Know About Islam," *New English Review*, December 2009, http://www.newenglishreview.org/custpage.cfm/frm/52705/sec_id/52705.

92. Nonie Darwish, *Cruel and Usual Punishment: The terrifying global implications of Islamic Law* (Thomas Nelson, 2008), p. 198.

93. Ibid.

94. Howard Kainz, "Islam and the Definition of Religion," *Catholic Thing*, Faith & Reason Institute, July 13, 2010, http://www.thecatholicthing.org/columns/2010/islam-and-the-definition-of-religion.html.

95. Mark Alexander, "Stop the Islamization of Europe! Stop the Islamization of the West!" Librabunda, May 27, 2007, http://librabunda.blogspot. com/2007/05/stop-islamization-of-europe-stop.html.

96. Urbain Vermeulen, *Islam en Christendom: Het onmogelijke gesprek?* [Islam and Christianity: The Impossible Dialogue] (Davidsfonds, 1999), p. 18.

97. Union Euripéenne des Arabisants ed Islamisants webpage, http://www.ueai. eu/index.htm.

98. Urbain Vermeulen, "De Koran wil geen integratie," *Katholiek Nieuwsblad*, March 25, 2005. Urbain Vermeulen, "Moderniteit relativeert alles, behalve zichzelf," *Katholiek Nieuwsblad*, April 27, 2007. And Urbain Vermeulen, "Een boek verbied je niet," *Katholiek Nieuwsblad*, August 17, 2007.

99. Urbain Vermeulen, "Urbain Vermeulen over de islamisering van onze samenleving," *Het Laatste Nieuws*, October 27, 2004.

100. Mark Durie, "A Double Bind upon the Copts of Egypt: Dhimmitude in Action," markdurie.com blog, October 10, 2011, http://markdurie. blogspot.com/2011/10/double-bind-upon-copts-dhimmitude-in.html.

101. Abul Ala Maududi, "Islam is an ideology," lecture under the auspices of Islami Jamiat-e-Talaba, Karachi, Pakistan, December 10, 1963, http://www.sa.niu.edu/msa/articles/ideology.htm.

102. Ibid.

103. Vermeulen, *Islam en Christendom: Het onmogelijke gesprek?*, p. 19.

104. Daniel Pipes, *The Hidden Hand: Middle East Fears of Conspiracy* (St. Martin's Press, 1996), p. 292.

CHAPTER 5

1. Hadith Sahih Muslim 20:4543.

2. Mustafa Kemal Atatürk, quoted in H. C. (Harold Courtenay) Armstrong, *Grey Wolf, Mustafa Kemal: An Intimate Study of a Dictator* (Arthur Barker, 1935), p. 205.

3. *Mahdi* is the Arabic word for "the righteous one."

4. Mervyn Hiskett, *Some to Mecca Turn to Pray: Islamic Values in the Modern World* (Claridge Press, 1993), p. 200.

5. Hadith Sahih Muslim 20:4568.

6. Abu Bakr quoted in "The Khulafa-ur-Rashiduun," Islamic-World.net, http://islamic-world.net/khalifah/khulafa_ur_rashiduun1.htm.

7. Saba Imtiaz, "Tablighi Cleric's Political Meetings Raise Eyebrows," *Express Tribune* (Karachi), August 22, 2011, http://tribune.com.pk/ story/236730/tablighi-clerics-political-meetings-raise-eyebrows/.

8. Oren Kessler, "Muslim Brotherhood Text Reveals Scope of Radical Creed," *Jerusalem Post* (Jerusalem), February 9, 2011, http://www.jpost.com/MiddleEast/Article.aspx?id=207415.

9. Ed West, "Extremists Call for Caliphate in London(istan)," *Telegraph* (London), July 28, 2009, http://blogs.telegraph.co.uk/news/edwest/100004840/extremists-call-for-caliphate-in-londonistan/.

10. Jamie Doward, "Battle to Block Massive Mosque: Project for 40,000 Worshippers 'Has Links with Radical Islam,'" *Observer* (London), September 23, 2006, http://www.guardian.co.uk/society/2006/sep/24/communities.religion; Lorenzo Vidino, "The Muslim Brotherhood's Conquest of Europe," *Middle East Quarterly* 12, no. 1 (Winter 2005): pp. 25–34, http://www.meforum.org/687/the-muslim-brotherhoods-conquest-of-europe.

11. Karl Vick, "Reunified Islam: Unlikely but Not Entirely Radical: Restoration of Caliphate, Attacked by Bush, Resonates With Mainstream Muslims," *Washington Post*, January 14, 2006, http://www.washingtonpost.com/wp-dyn/content/article/2006/01/13/AR2006011301816.html.

12. *Dawa* is the Arabic word for "issuing a summons" or "making an invitation."

13. Majid Khadduri, *War and Peace in the Law of Islam* (Johns Hopkins University Press, 1955), p. 64.

14. Speech given at the Town Hall in Lahore, British India, April 13, 1939. Abul Ala Maududi, "Jihad in Islam;" Muhammadanism.org, March 27, 2006, p. 26, www.muhammadanism.org/Terrorism/jihah_in_islam/jihad_in_islam.pdf.

15. Abul Ala Maududi, *The Faithful Struggle*, vol 2., no 1 in the section entitled "Permanent Jihad." As quoted by Tanveer, "Abul Ala Maududi," Islamic lab blog, July 14, 2011, http://islamiclab.blogspot.com/2011/07/abul-ala-maududi.html.

16. Ed Koch, interviewed by Neil Cavuto, Fox News, January 7, 2010. Available on YouTube, "Koch: Not Every Muslim Is a Terrorist 'But There Are Hundreds of Millions Who Are,'" http://www.youtube.com/watch?v=SSA10qKwNuA.

17. Andrew Jackson, "Farewell Address," Washington, D.C., March 4, 1837. Available on Wikisource, "Andrew Jackson's Farewell Address," http://en.wikisource.org/wiki/Andrew_Jackson%27s_Farewell_Address.

18. Karl Barth, *The Church and the Political Problem of Our Day* (Scribner, 1939), p. 43.

19. Bernard Lewis, "Communism and Islam," *International Affairs* (London) 30, no. 1 (January 1954): pp. 1–12.

20. Muhammad Sayyid Tantawi, "The Children of Israel in the Koran and the Sunna," doctoral dissertation, published in Cairo, 1986, quoted in Andrew Bostom, *The Legacy of Islamic Antisemitism: From Sacred Texts to Solemn History* (Prometheus Books, 2008), p. 11.

21. William F. Zeman, "World Leaders Praise Tantawi's Legacy," *Daily News Egypt*, March 12, 2010, http://www.thedailynewsegypt.com/world-lead ers-praise-tantawis-legacy.html.

22. "Leading Egyptian Government Cleric Calls for: 'Martydrom Attacks that Strike Horror into the Hearts of the Enemies of Allah,'" Middle East Media Research Institute (MEMRI), April 7, 2002, http://www.memri.org/report/ en/0/0/0/0/0/0/641.htm.

23. Bostom, *The Legacy of Islamic Antisemitism*, p. 90.

24. "History of Jews in Arab Countries: Before and after 1948," Historical Society of Jews from Egypt, 1999–2000, http://middleeastfacts.com/ Articles/history-of-jews-in-arab-countries.php.

25. Lisa Palmieri-Billig, "Following Calls for Deportation, Gerbi to Return to Rome: Angry Protesters Gather in Tripoli to Demand Deportation of Libyan Jew David Gerbi, Who Has Been Trying to Reopen a Sealed Syna-gogue," *Jerusalem Post* (Jerusalem), October 10, 2011, http://www.jpost. com/MiddleEast/Article.aspx?id=241109.

26. "History Of Jews In Arab Countries: Before and after 1948." See also Bostom, *The Legacy of Islamic Antisemitism*, pp. 154, 157–59, 470, 472, 474–75, 477, 663–67.

27. "Jewish Refugees from Arab Countries: The Historical Narrative," Justice for Jews from Arab Countries, 2002, http://www.justiceforjews.com/ resource_and_reference.pdf.

28. "UNRWA in Figures as of 1 January 2011," Public Information Office, United Nations Relief and Works Agency for Palestine Refugees (UNRWA) Headquarters, July 2011, http://www.unrwa.org/userfiles/ 2011092751539.pdf.

29. Thomas Jefferson, "A Summary View of the Rights of British America," 1774, text available on the Library of Congress website, http://www.loc. gov/rr/rarebook/guide/ra008001.html.

30. Koran 3:110.

31. Bruce Lawrence, ed., *Messages to the World: The Statements of Osama Bin Laden* (Verso, 2005), p. 14.

32. Alfred Guillaume, *Life of Muhammad: A Translation of Ibn Ishaq's Sirat Rasul Allah* (Oxford University Press, 1955), p. 228.

33. "Jews Arrested for Praying on Temple Mount," JTA (Jewish Telegraphic Agency), December 9, 2009, http://jta.org/news/article/2009/12/09/1009624/jews-arrested-for-praying-on-temple-mount.

34. Roee Nahmias, "Geert Wilders: Change Jordan's Name to Palestine: Rightist Dutch Leader Wants to End Mideast Conflict by Finding Palestinians 'Alternate Homeland,'" Ynetnews, June 20, 2010, http://www.ynetnews.com/articles/0,7340,L-3907722,00.html; Geert Wilders, "Jordan is Palestine" speech in Tel Aviv, Israel, December 5, 2010, available at "Speech Geert Wilders, Tel Aviv, 5 December 2010," Partij Voor De Vrijheid, http://www.pvv.nl/index.php/component/content/article/36-geert-wilders/3752-speech-geert-wilders-tel-aviv-5-december-2010.html.

35. Abdul Jalil Mustafa, "[Jordanian] Parliament Blasts Dutch Politician for Calling Jordan Palestine," Arab News, June 22, 2010, http://arabnews.com/middleeast/article70500.ece.

36. Daniel Pipes and Adam Garfinkle, "Is Jordan Palestine?" *Commentary*, October 1988, author submission version available on DanielPipes.org, http://www.danielpipes.org/298/is-jordan-palestine.

37. Andrew G. Bostom, ed., *The Legacy of Jihad: Islamic Holy War and the Fate of Non-Muslims* (Prometheus Books, 2005).

38. *Taqiyya* is the Arabic word for "concealment."

39. Koran 16:105.

40. Hadith Sahih Bukhari 7:67:427.

41. Hadith Sahih Bukhari 6:60:138.

42. *Hudna* is the Arabic word for "truce."

43. Daniel Pipes, "Terrorism: The Syrian Connection," *National Interest*, (Spring 1989), author submission version available on DanielPipes.org, http://www.danielpipes.org/1064/terrorism-the-syrian-connection.

44. Mervyn Hiskett, *Some to Mecca Turn to Pray: Islamic Values in the Modern World* (Claridge Press, 1993), p. 157.

45. Mohammed Bouyeri, quoted in "LJN BC2576, Gerechthof 's-Gravenhage, 2200189706," Court of Appeal, The Hague, January 23, 2008. Available at Jure: Rechterlijke Uitspraken Online, http://jure.nl/bc2576.

46. Emerson Vermaat, "Hofstad Group—Wrong decision by Dutch appeals court," Militant Islam Monitor.org, January 31, 2008, http://www.militantislammonitor.org/article/id/3341.

47. Hadith Sahih Muslim 8:3371, 8:3374.

48. Will Durant, *The Story of Civilization: Our Oriental Heritage* (Simon & Schuster, 1935), p. 459.
49. K. S. (Kishori Saran) Lal, *Growth of Muslim Population in Medieval India* (Research, 1973).
50. Henry Miers Elliot and John Dowson, *The History of India as Told by Its Own Historians: The Muhammadan Period*, vol. 2 (Trübner & Co., 1869), pp. 28, 30–31.
51. Bostom, *The Legacy of Jihad*, p. 641.
52. Ibid., p. 644.
53. Ibid., p. 645.
54. Steven Runciman, *A History of the Crusades*, vol. 1 (Cambridge University Press, 1951), p. 15.
55. Bostom, *The Legacy of Jihad*, p. 161.
56. Bostom, *The Legacy of Islamic Antisemitism*, p. 84.
57. Vincent Arthur Smith, *The Oxford Student's History of India* (Clarendon Press, 1921), p. 200, available on Internet Archive, http://www.archive.org/stream/oxfordstudentshi00smituoft/oxfordstudentshi00smituoft_djvu.txt.
58. Hugh Collett, "The Last of the Perkeniers of Banda," *Jakarta Post* (Jakarta), October 26, 2008, http://www.thejakartapost.com/news/2008/10/26/the-last-perkeniers-banda.html.

CHAPTER 6

1. John W. Whitehead, "Eurabia: The Euro-Arab Axis An Interview with Bat Ye'or," *OldSpeak*, The Rutherford Institute, June 9, 2005, https://www.rutherford.org/publications_resources/oldspeak/eurabia_the_euro_arab_axis_an_interview_with_bat_yeor.
2. Bat Ye'or, *Islam and Dhimmitude: Where Civilizations Collide* (Fairleigh Dickinson University Press, 2002), pp. 414–17.
3. Koran 48:29.
4. Koenraad Elst, *De islam voor ongelovigen* (Stichting Deltapers, 1997), pp. 35–44.
5. Bat Ye'or and David Maisel, *The Dhimmi: Jews and Christians under Islam* (Fairleigh Dickinson University Press, 1985).
6. Andrew G. Bostom, *The Legacy of Jihad: Islamic Holy War and the Fate of Non-Muslims* (Prometheus Books, 2005), p. 26.
7. Koran 9:29.
8. Paul Johnson, *A History of the Jews* (Weidenfeld and Nicolson, 1987), pp. 175, 178–79.

9. Ye'or, *Islam and Dhimmitude*, p. 65.

10. *Chronique de Denys de Tell-Mahre*, quoted in Bat Ye'or, *The Decline of Eastern Christianity under Islam: From Jihad to Dhimmitude: Seventh-Twentieth Century* (Fairleigh Dickinson University Press, 1996), p. 74.

11. "What Does Marriage to a Muslim Involve?" Christian Broadcasting Network (CBN), February 19, 2011, http://www.cbn.com/spirituallife/OnlineDiscipleship/UnderstandingIslam/What_does_marriage_to_a_Muslim_involve.aspx.

12. Bernard Lewis, *What Went Wrong?: Western Impact and Middle Eastern Response* (Oxford University Press, 2002), p. 158.

13. Jean-Claude Barreau, *De l'islam en général et du monde moderne en particulier* (Le Pré-aux-Clercs, 1991).

14. Samuel Shahid, "Rights of Non-Muslims in an Islamic State," Answering Islam.org, http://answering-islam.org/NonMuslims/rights.htm.

15. "Egypt's Endangered Christians," Center for Religious Freedom, Freedom House, 1999, pp. 34–37, http://crf.hudson.org/files/publications/egypt%20report%20w-cover.pdf.

16. Isabelle Mandraud, "Expulsés pour prosélytisme," *Le Monde* (Paris), April 6, 2010.

17. Gert van Langendonck, "Children Abandoned as Morocco Deports Adoptive Parents," *NRC Handelsblad* (Rotterdam), March 16, 2010, http://www.nrc.nl/international/article2504728.ece/Children_abandoned_as_Morocco_deports_adoptive_parents.

18. Ibid.

19. Andrew Bostom, *The Legacy of Islamic Antisemitism: From Sacred Texts to Solemn History* (Prometheus Books, 2008), p. 113.

20. Ye'or, *Islam and Dhimmitude*, pp. 76–77.

21. Johnson, *A History of the Jews*, pp. 204–205.

22. William Shaler, 1826, quoted in David Littman and Bat Ye'or, *Protected Peoples Under Islam* (Centre d'Information et de Documentation sur le Moyen-Orient, 1976), p. 10.

23. Karl Marx, "Declaration of War.—On the History of the Eastern Question," *New-York Daily Tribune*, April 15, 1854, text available at Marxists.org, http://www.marxists.org/archive/marx/works/1854/03/28.htm.

24. H. E. Wilkie Young, 1909, quoted in Ye'or, *Islam and Dhimmitude*, p. 107.

25. "Medieval Sourcebook: Pact of Umar, 7th Century?: the Status of Non-Muslims under Muslim Rule," Paul Halsall, ed., *Internet Medieval Sourcebook*, Internet History Sourcebooks Project, Fordham University, November 4, 2011, http://www.fordham.edu/halsall/source/pact-umar.asp.

26. "Paying Jizyah is a Sign of Kufr and Disgrace," Q Tafsir.com, http://www.qtafsir.com/index2.php?option=com_content&task=view&id=2566&pop=1&page=0&Itemid=64.

27. Mark Durie, "A Double-Bind upon the Copts: Dhimmitude in Action," markdurie.com, October 10, 2011, http://markdurie.blogspot.com/2011/10/double-bind-upon-copts-dhimmitude-in.html.

28. Sidney H. Griffith, *The Church in the Shadow of the Mosque: Christians and Muslims in the World of Islam* (Princeton University Press, 2007).

29. Alice Fordham, "Fear of Jihad Driving Christians from Iraq," *USA TODAY*, November 11, 2010, http://www.usatoday.com/news/world/2010-11-12-iraqchristians12_ST_N.htm.

30. Jason Goodwin, *Lords of the Horizons: A History of the Ottoman Empire* (Vintage, 1999), p. 59.

31. John Dunn, "Africa Invades the New World: Egypt's Mexican Adventure, 1863–1867," *War in History* (London) 4, no. 1 (1997): pp. 27–34.

32. Paul E. Lovejoy and Jan S. Hogendorn, "Slave Marketing in West Africa," in Henry A. Gemery and Jan S. Hogendorn, eds., *The Uncommon Market: Essays in the Economic History of the Atlantic Slave Trade* (Academic Press Inc., 1979), pp. 217–21.

33. Louis Bertrand, *The History of Spain: From the Visigoths to the death of Philip II* (Dawsons, 1952), p. 160.

34. Thomas Sowell, *Conquests and Cultures: An International History* (Basic Books, 1998), p. 111.

35. "Iraq's Blacks Demand Recognition," Islam Online, September 29, 2009.

36. Raheem Salman and Tina Susman, "Iraq: Black Iraqis Hoping for a Barack Obama Win," *Los Angeles Times*, August 14, 2008, http://latimesblogs.latimes.com/babylonbeyond/2008/08/baghdad-black-i.html.

37. Ibid.

38. Sowell, *Conquests and Cultures*, p. 153, 157.

39. Bernard Lewis, *Race and Slavery in the Middle East: An Historical Enquiry* (Oxford University Press, 1990), pp. 10, 56, 59, 65, 74.

40. Mariyah Saalih, *Harem Girl: A Harem Girl's Journal* (iUniverse, 2004), p. 63.

41. Hadith Sunan Abu Dawud 41:5251.

42. Lewis, *Race and Slavery in the Middle East*, p. 59.

43. Akbar Muhammad, "The Image of Africans in Arabic Literature: Some Unpublished Manuscripts," pp. 47–74, in John Ralph Willis, ed., *Slaves*

& *Slavery in Muslim Africa, Volume I: Islam and the Ideology of Slavery* (Frank Cass, 1985), p. 68.

44. Lewis, *Race and Slavery in the Middle East*, p. 46.

45. Ibid., p. 53.

46. Robert C. Davis, *Christian Slaves, Muslim Masters: White Slavery in the Mediterranean, the Barbary Coast and Italy, 1500–1800* (Palgrave Macmillan, 2003). See also Jeff Grabmeier, "When Europeans Were Slaves: Research Suggests White Slavery Was Much More Common than Previously Believed," Ohio State Research News, March 8, 2004, http://researchnews.osu.edu/archive/whtslav.htm.

47. Barb Karg and Arjean Spaite, *The Everything Pirates Book: A Swashbuckling History of Adventure on the High Seas* (F+W Publications, 2007), pp. 36–38.

48. Peter Lamborn Wilson, *Pirate Utopias: Moorish Corsairs & European Renegadoes* (Autonomedia, 2003), pp. 95–101.

49. Thomas Osborne Davis, "The Sack of Baltimore," in Edmund Clarence Stedman, ed., *A Victorian Anthology; 1837–1895* (Riverside Press, 1895). This book is available on Bartleby.com, 2003, http://www.bartleby.com/246/207.html. Reis' son, Anthoni Jansen van Salee, emigrated from Morocco to New Amsterdam, the Dutch colony on Manhattan, in the early 1630s. Some speculate that his buccaneering father had given him a fortune, because he became one of the largest landholders in Manhattan and Long Island. Literate in Arabic but not in Dutch, Jansen was the first Muslim to live in New York. He had brought a Koran along from Morocco, probably the first in the New World, which was passed down in the Van Sicklen and Gulick families, his descendants. Later in life, Jansen seems to have converted to Christianity before dying in New York in 1676. His four daughters all married into respectable New Amsterdam families. See Michael A. Gomez, *Black Crescent: The Experience and Legacy of African Muslims in the Americas* (Cambridge University Press, 2005), pp. 131–33, and Peter Lamborn Wilson, *Pirate Utopias: Moorish Corsairs & European Renegadoes* (Autonomedia, 2003), pp. 205–12.

50. Harry Crocker, *The Politically Incorrect Guide to the British Empire* (Regnery, 2011), 28.

51. Ehud R. Toledano, *The Ottoman Slave Trade and Its Suppression: 1840–1890* (Princeton University Press, 1982), p. 51.

52. "Slavery and Slave Redemption in the Sudan," Human Rights Watch, March 2002, http://www.hrw.org/legacy/backgrounder/africa/sudanupdate.htm.

53. Sean O'Callaghan, *The Slave Trade Today* (Crown Publishers, 1961), p. 75.

54. Ibid., p. 83.

55. Ibid., pp. 92–93.

56. Ibid., p. 76.

57. Pascale Harter, "Slavery: Mauritania's Best Kept Secret," BBC News (London), December 13, 2004, http://news.bbc.co.uk/2/hi/africa/4091579.stm.

58. "Chad: Children Sold into Slavery for the Price of a Calf," Integrated Regional Information Networks (IRIN), December 21, 2004, http://www.irinnews.org/report.aspx?reportid=52490.

59. Hilary Andersson, "Born To Be a Slave in Niger," BBC News (London), February 11, 2005, http://news.bbc.co.uk/2/hi/programmes/from_our_own_correspondent/4250709.stm.

60. Brian Handwerk, "Kayaking to Timbuktu, Writer Sees Slave Trade, More," National Geographic News, December 5, 2002, http://news.nationalgeographic.com/news/2002/12/1206_021205_salakkayak.html.

61. Kevin Bales, *Ending Slavery: How We Free Today's Slaves* (University of California Press, 2007), pp. 12–15. See also Amanda Kloer, "Slaves 450% Cheaper Today than in 1850," Change.org, February 16, 2010, http://human-trafficking.change.org/blog/view/slaves_450_cheaper_today_than_in_1850.

62. Simon Aban Deng, "Simon Deng, Former Sudanese Slave, Human Rights Activist," International Humanist and Ethical Union, June 21, 2005, http://www.iheu.org/node/1539.

63. "Author of Saudi Curriculums Advocates Slavery," Saudi Information Agency, November 7, 2003, http://www.arabianews.org/english/article.cfm?qid=132&sid=2.

64. "Trafficking in Persons Report 2011: Saudi Arabia," U.S. State Department, June 27, 2011, http://www.state.gov/g/tip/rls/tiprpt/2011/164233.htm.

65. Brian Whitaker, "Riot by Migrant Workers Halts Construction of Dubai Skyscraper," *Guardian* (London), March 22, 2006, http://www.guardian.co.uk/world/2006/mar/23/brianwhitaker.mainsection.

66. "'Sex Slave' Trial Starts in US," *Khaleej Times* (Dubai), June 15, 2006, http://www.khaleejtimes.com/DisplayArticle.asp?xfile=data/theuae/2006/June/theuae_June455.xml&section=theuae; "Saudi Gets Long Sentence," *Rocky Mountain News*, September 1, 2006.

67. Bjorn Maeckelbergh, "Sjeik houdt slaven in luxehotel," *De Standaard* (Brussels), July 2, 2008, http://www.standaard.be/Artikel/Detail. aspx?artikelId=4Q1TQ8J5#.

68. Andrew Hough, "Saudi 'Prince' Charged with Murdering His 'Aide' at London Landmark Hotel," *Telegraph* (London), February 18, 2010, http://www.telegraph.co.uk/news/uknews/crime/7266876/Saudi-Prince-charged-with-murdering-his-aide-at-London-Landmark-hotel.html.

69. Sam Jones, "Saudi Prince Guilty of Servant's Murder," *Guardian* (London), October 19, 2010, http://www.guardian.co.uk/uk/2010/oct/19/saudi-prince-servant-murder-guilty.

70. Neil Kirby, "The Five-star World of Sex, Lies and Bribes," *Sunday Times* (London), February 28, 2010, http://www.timesonline.co.uk/tol/news/uk/article7043779.ece.

71. Koran 33:50.

72. Koran 23:5–6, 33:50, 70:29–30.

73. Hadith Sahih Bukhari 3:47:765.

74. Koran 2:177, 24:33, 90:13.

75. Silas, "Slavery in Islam," Answering Islam.org, http://www.answering-islam.org/Silas/slavery.htm.

CHAPTER 7

1. Daniel Pratt Mannix IV, ed., *The Old Navy: A Compilation of the Diary of Rear Admiral D.P. Mannix III* (MacMillan, 1983), p. 164.

2. Napoléon Bonaparte, "Déclaration du général Bonaparte au peuple égyptien," Alexandria, Egypt, Messidor 13, 6 (July 1, 1798), available on Wikisource la bibliothèque libre, http://fr.wikisource.org/wiki/Déclaration_du_général_Bonaparte_au_peuple_égyptien.

3. Speech given at the Town Hall in Lahore, British India, April 13, 1939. Abul Ala Maududi, "Jihad in Islam," Muhammadanism.org, March 27, 2006, pp. 25–26, www.muhammadanism.org/Terrorism/jihah_in_islam/jihad_in_islam.pdf.

4. Mahathir Mohamad, Prime Minister of Malaysia, in his opening address at the Tenth Summit of the OIC in Putrajaya, Malaysia, on October 16, 2003. Quoted in Patrick Sookhdeo, *Global Jihad: The Future in the Face of Militant Islam* (Isaac Publishing, 2007), pp. 18–19.

5. Aldous Huxley, "Letter to Norman Douglas," June 26, 1925. In Grover Smith, ed., *The Letters of Aldous Huxley* (Harper & Row, 1970), pp. 250–51.

6.   Winston Churchill, *The River War*, vol. 2 (Longmans, Green & Co., 1899), p. 250.

7.   "About OIC," Organisation of Islamic Cooperation: Permanent Observer Mission to the United Nations in New York, http://www.oicun.org/2/23/.

8.   Hui Min Neo, "UN Rights Body Narrowly Passes Islamophobia Resolution," Agence France-Presse, March 26, 2010, available on ABS-CBN News.com, http://www.abs-cbnnews.com/world/03/25/10/un-rights-body-narrowly-passes-islamophobia-resolution.

9.   "Human Rights Council Resolution A/HRC/10/L. Combating Defamation of Religions," quoted in full in "Proposal at U.N. to Criminalize 'Defamation of Islam,'" UN Watch, Briefing, Issue 187, UN Watch March 11, 2009, http://www.unwatch.org/site/apps/nlnet/content2.aspx?c=bdKKIS NqEmG&b=1285603&ct=6831061.

10. "Cairo Declaration on Human Rights in Islam," accepted and proclaimed in Cairo, Egypt, on August 5, 1990, available at University of Minnesota Human Rights Library, http://www1.umn.edu/humanrts/instree/cairodeclaration.html.

11. John F. Kennedy, "President John F. Kennedy On the Cuban Missile Crisis," October 22, 1962, http://www.historyplace.com/speeches/jfk-cuban.htm.

12. André Malraux, "Conversation sur l'Islam avec André Malraux," *Armées*, Paris, France, June 3, 1956, available on armees.com, http://www.armees.com/1956-Conversation-sur-l-Islam-avec-Andre-Malraux,7638.html.

13. Ibid.

14. Ali Sina, "Statement on Norway Massacre," Faithfreedom International, July 28, 2011, http://www.faithfreedom.org/articles/op-ed/statement-on-norway-massacre/.

15. Alexis de Tocqueville, "Letter to Arthur de Gobineau," October 22, 1843, in Olivier Zunz and Alan S. Kahan, eds., *The Tocqueville Reader: A Life in Letters and Politics* (Blackwell, 2002), p. 229.

16. Alexis de Tocqueville, *Democracy in America*, vol. 1, ed. J. P. Mayer, trans. George Lawrence, (Doubleday, 1969,original in French, 1840), p. 455.

17. "'Mit Schleier werden Sie nicht bedient!'" *Hamburger Morgenpost* (Hamburg), Germany, March 6, 2010, http://archiv.mopo.de/archiv/2010/20100306/hamburg/panorama/mit_schleier_werden_sie_nicht_bedient.html.

18. Ibid.

19. Von Ernst Schneiders, "Bürgermeisterin: Geert Wilders ist in Monschau unerwünscht," *Aachener Zeitung* (Aachen), March 15, 2010, http://www.

az-web.de/lokales/eifel-detail-az/1239513?_link=&skip=&_g= Buerger-meisterin-Geert-Wilders-ist-in-Monschau-unerwuenscht.html.

20. Winston S. Churchill, *The Second World War*, vol. 1, *The Gathering Storm*, (Mariner Books, 1986, first published by Houghton Mifflin Company, 1948), p. 50.

21. "Kamer: verbod Mein Kampf handhaven," NOS (Hilversum), September 12, 2007, http://nos.nl/artikel/64383-kamer-verbod-mein-kampf-handhaven.html.

22. "Hitler Book Bestseller in Turkey: Adolf Hitler's Autobiography, Mein Kampf, Has Become a Bestseller in Turkey—Sparking Fears of Growing Ant-Semitic Feelings in the Country," BBC News (London), March 18, 2005, http://news.bbc.co.uk/2/hi/europe/4361733.stm.

23. Sean O'Neill and John Steele, "Mein Kampf for Sale, in Arabic," *Daily Telegraph* (London), March 19, 2002, http://www.telegraph.co.uk/news/uknews/1388161/Mein-Kampf-for-sale-in-Arabic.html, and Chris McClure, "Reading 'Mein Kampf' in Cairo: Why Does Arab Press Demonize Israel as Being a 'Second Nazi State'?" *Jerusalem Post* (Jerusalem), October 13, 2007, http://www.jpost.com/Opinion/Op-EdContributors/Article.aspx?id=78209.

24. Koran 20:113.

25. Alexander Stille, "Scholars Are Quietly Offering New Theories of the Koran," *New York Times*, March 2, 2002, http://www.nytimes.com/2002/03/02/arts/scholars-are-quietly-offering-new-theories-of-the-koran.html?pagewanted=all&src=pm.

26. Ellen Knickmeyer, "Saudi Tweets Spark Outrage, Death Threats," *Wall Street Journal*, February 9, 2012, http://online.wsj.com/article/SB100014240529702033158045772111311772266506.html?mod=googlenews_wsj; Ellen Knickmeyer, "Saudi Tweeter Is Arrested in Malaysia," *Wall Street Journal*, February 10, 2012, http://online.wsj.com/article/SB10001424052970204642604577213553613859184.html?KEYWORDS=Saudi+Tweeter+Is+Detained+in+Malaysia; Ellen Knickmeyer and Summer Said, "Malaysia Deports Writer Wanted by Saudi Arabia," *Wall Street Journal*, February 13, 2012, http://online.wsj.com/article/SB10001424052970204795304577218492524993410.html.

27. Koran 44:54, 52:20, 55:72, 56:22.

28. Stefan Theil, "Challenging the Qur'an: A German Scholar Contends That The Islamic Text Has Been Mistranscribed And Promises Raisins, Not Virgins," *Newsweek*, July 27, 2003, http://www.newsweek.com/id/57962.

29. Sheikh Rashid Ahmed, Pakistani Minister of Information, quoted in "What Does the Quran Really Say? Pakistan Bans Article with New Translation on Heaven's Promises," Associated Press, February 11, 2009, available at CBSnews.com, http://www.cbsnews.com/stories/2003/07/25/world/main565035.shtml.

30. Robert Spencer, *The Truth about Muhammad: Founder of the World's Most Intolerant Religion* (Regnery, 2006), p. 31.

CHAPTER 8

1. John K. Cooley, "Meanwhile: Hitler Also Plotted to Bomb New York," *New York Times*, October 24, 2003, http://www.nytimes.com/2003/10/24/opinion/24iht-edcooley_ed3_.html; Dieter Wulf, "Hitler's 'Amerikabomber:' The Idea of Flying Planes into Skyscrapers Didn't Originate with al-Qaeda," *Atlantic*, May 2004, http://www.theatlantic.com/doc/200405/wulf.

2. Albert Speer, *Spandauer Tagebücher* (Ullstein, 1975), p. 126.

3. James Bovard, "FBI Blunders and the First World Trade Center Bombing," *Freedom Daily* (August 2004), the Future of Freedom Foundation, November 10, 2004, http://www.fff.org/freedom/fd0408c.asp.

4. Richard Miniter, *Losing Bin Laden: How Bill Clinton's Failures Unleashed Global Terror* (Regnery, 2003), p. 37.

5. Selwyn Raab, "Jury Selection Seen as Crucial to Verdict," *New York Times*, December 23, 1991, http://www.nytimes.com/1991/12/23/nyregion/jury-selection-seen-as-crucial-to-verdict.html?sec=&spon=&pagewanted=all; Ronald Sullivan, "Judge Gives Maximum Term in Kahane Case," *New York Times*, January 30, 1992, http://www.nytimes.com/1992/01/30/nyregion/judge-gives-maximum-term-in-kahane-case.html.

6. Alison Mitchell, "The Twin Towers; Officials Say Another Major Suspect Emerges," *New York Times*, March 9, 1993, http://www.nytimes.com/1993/03/09/nyregion/the-twin-towers-officials-say-another-major-suspect-emerges.html?pagewanted=1.

7. Margaret Thatcher, *Statecraft: Strategies for a Changing World* (Harper-Collins, 2002), p. xxv.

8. Václav Havel, "The Power of the Powerless," 1978, in Václav Havel et al., *The Power of the Powerless: Citizens against the State in Central-Eastern Europe*, ed. John Keane (M.E. Sharpe, 1985), pp. 23–96.

9. Aleksandr I. Solzhenitsyn, "A World Split Apart," 1978, in Ronald Berman, ed., *Solzhenitsyn at Harvard: The Address, Twelve Early Responses, and Six Later Reflections* (Ethics & Public Policy Center, 1980), p. 3.

10. Ferenc Gyurcsány, quoted in Mark Mardell, "Europe Diary: Political Lies: BBC Europe Editor Mark Mardell on the Hungarian Prime Minister's Admission of Lying, the Motives of the Protesters Hoping to Bring Him down, and the Difficulty of Selling Painful Reforms to Voters," BBC News (London), September 21, 2006, http://news.bbc.co.uk/2/hi/europe/5364372.stm.

11. Vladimir Bukovsky, "The Power of Memory and Acknowledgement," *Cato's Letter* 2, no. 1 (Winter 2010), the Cato Institute, http://www.cato.org/pubs/catosletter/catosletterv8n1.pdf.

12. Ibid.

13. Attributed to John F. Kennedy by his biographer Theodore Sorensen in a 1968 television interview. Quoted in William Safire, *Safire's Political Dictionary* (Oxford University Press, 2008), p. 583.

14. "Giuliani Rejects $10 Million from Saudi Prince," CNN.com, October 12, 2001, http://archives.cnn.com/2001/US/10/11/rec.giuliani.prince/.

15. Ibid.

16. Saudi-American Forum Interview of Ambassador Chas W. Freeman, "A Relationship in Transition—And Then 9/11," Middle East Policy Council, September 4, 2003, http://www.mepc.org/articles-commentary/commentary/relationship-transition-and-then-9/11.

17. Ibid.

18. "Toplines – Mosque – July 19–20, 2010: National Survey of 1,000 Adults Conducted July 19–20, 2010," Rasmussen Reports, July, 2010, http://www.rasmussenreports.com/public_content/business/econ_survey_questions/july_2010/toplines_mosque_july_19_20_2010; Celeste Katz, "CNN Poll: Nearly 70% of Americans Oppose NYC Mosque Plan," NYDailyNews.com, August 11, 2010, http://www.nydailynews.com/blogs/dailypolitics/2010/08/poll-nearly-70-of-americans-op.html; "Mosque-building and Its Discontents: The Islamic Cultural Center that Is Sorta Near Ground Zero," *Economist* (London), August 19, 2010, http://www.economist.com/blogs/democracyinamerica/2010/08/islamic_cultural_centre_sorta_near_ground_zero.

19. Noel Sheppard, "Ground Zero Mosque Imam's Controversial Post-9/11 60 Minutes Interview," NewsBusters, August 19, 2010, http://newsbusters.org/blogs/noel-sheppard/2010/08/19/ground-zero-mosque-imams-controversial-60-minutes-interview.

20. Frank Walker, "West Must Act to End Jihad: Imam," *Sun-Herald* (Sydney), March 21, 2004, available on the *Sydney Morning Herald* website, http://www.smh.com.au/articles/2004/03/21/1079789939987.html.

21. The Editors, "Not at Ground Zero," *National Review*, August 4, 2010, http://www.nationalreview.com/articles/243608/not-ground-zero-editors.

22. Geert Wilders, "No Mosque Here" speech in New York City, September 11, 2010, text available on the Geert Wilders Weblog, http://www.geertwilders.nl/index.php?option=com_content&task=view&id=1712.

23. Jamie Glazov, "Our Culture, What's Left Of It: Interview with Theodore Dalrymple," *Front Page Magazine*, August 31, 2005, http://archive.frontpagemag.com/readArticle.aspx?ARTID=7445.

24. Karl Popper, *The Open Society and Its Enemies*, vol. 1, *The Spell of Plato*, (Routledge, 2003, original publication date of 1945), p. 293.

25. Andrew Cline, "Poverty Does not Cause Terrorism: The Canard That 'Crushing' Poverty Does Cause It Just Won't Die," *American Spectator*, January 7, 2010, http://spectator.org/archives/2010/01/07/poverty-does-not-cause-terrori.

26. "Profile: Umar Farouk Abdulmutallab," BBC News (London), UK, October 12, 2011, http://www.bbc.co.uk/news/world-us-canada-11545509.

27. "Exploding Misconceptions: Alleviating Poverty May not Reduce Terrorism but Could Make It Less Effective," *Economist*, December 16, 2010, http://www.economist.com/node/17730424.

28. "Muslim-Western Tensions Persist: Common Concerns about Islamic Extremism," Pew Global Attitudes Project, Pew Research Center, July 21, 2011, http://www.pewglobal.org/2011/07/21/muslim-western-tensions-persist/.

29. Woodrow Wilson, speech at Des Moines, Iowa, February 1, 1916, quoted in Charles Seymour, *Woodrow Wilson and the World War*, (BiblioBazaar, 2008), p 57.

30. Richard Nixon, *Seize the Moment: America's Challenge in a One-Superpower World* (Simon & Schuster, 1992), p. 195.

31. Ibid., p. 198.

32. Ibid., p. 199.

33. Ibid., p. 231.

34. Ibid., p. 200.

35. Ibid., p. 230.

36. Ibid.

37. Ibid., p. 231.

38. Ibid., pp. 202–205.

39. Ibid., pp. 217–30.

CHAPTER 9

1. M. Gijsberts, W. Huijnk, and J. Dagevos, "Jaarrapport integratie 2011," Sociaal en Cultureel Planbureau (The Hague), January 2012, p. 19.

2. "'Geert Wilders kan de boom in:' Marokkaanse jeugd teleurgesteld in oude buurtgenoot," *De Pers* (Amsterdam), March 27, 2008, http://www.depers.nl/binnenland/186537/Geert-Wilders-kan-de-boom-in.html.

3. "Fortuyn: grens dicht voor islamiet," *De Volkskrant* (Amsterdam), February 9, 2002.

4. Pim Fortuyn, "Grenzen dicht," *Elsevier* (Amsterdam), April 25, 1998, in Pim Fortuyn, *A hell of a job: De verzamelde columns* (Speakers Academy, 2002), 433–34.

5. Pim Fortuyn, quoted in Hugo Camps, "Afscheidsinterview: Ik ga vanuit het Catshuis regeren," *Elsevier* (Amsterdam), October 18, 2001, http://www.elsevier.nl/web/Nieuws/Politiek/319719/Afscheidsinterview-Ik-ga-vanuit-het-Catshuis-regeren.htm.

6. Pim Fortuyn, "Koude Oorlog met islam," *Elsevier* (Amsterdam), August 25, 2001, in Pim Fortuyn, *A hell of a job*, p. 774.

7. Pim Fortuyn, in *Rotterdams Dagblad* (Rotterdam), August 29, 2001, in Albert Oosthoek, *Pim Fortuyn en Rotterdam* (Ad. Donker, 2005), p. 25.

8. Pim Fortuyn, in a television interview, Nederlandse Omroepstichting (NOS), Hilversum, the Netherlands, February 3, 2002.

9. "Ondanks alles ben ik katholiek," *Katholiek Nieuwsblad*, 's Hertogenbosch, the Netherlands, February 15, 2002.

10. Marcel van Dam, during a television debate with Pim Fortuyn, *Het Lagerhuis*, Hilversum, the Netherlands, February 15, 1997, available on YouTube, http://www.youtube.com/watch?v=WVSE3VyjhvQ&feature=related.

11. Joop Garssen, Han Nicolaas, and Arno Sprangers, "Demografie van de allochtonen in Nederland," Bevolkingstrends 3e kwartaal 2005, Centraal Bureau voor de Statistiek, The Hague/Heerlen, the Netherlands, 2005, p. 108, http://www.cbs.nl/NR/rdonlyres/CCD504EA-9D41-40C2-AE28-BFB0A51C2045/0/2005k3b15p096art.pdf.

12. "Van der G. vermoordde Fortuyn uit overtuiging,'" *Trouw* (Amsterdam), March 28, 2003, http://www.trouw.nl/tr/nl/4324/nieuws/archief/article/detail/1765315/2003/03/28/Van-der-G-vermoordde-Fortuyn-uit-overtuiging.dhtml.

13. Geert Wilders during the parliamentary debate on the fight against international terrorism, *Tweede Kamer*, The Hague, "Tweede Kamer der

Staten-Generaal," Vergaderjaar 2004–2005, *Tweede Kamer*, The Hague, September 23, 2004, available on the Buro Jansen & Janssen website, http://www.burojansen.nl/documenten/27925nr149.pdf.

14. "Vrachtwagen ramt hek politiebureau," *De Pers* (Amsterdam), August 20, 2009, http://www.depers.nl/binnenland/330480/Hek-politiebureau-geramd.html.

15. "Samenscholingsverbod op Kanaleneiland in Utrecht," Nu.nl (Amsterdam), September 21, 2007, http://www.nu.nl/algemeen/1245280/samen scholingsverbod-op-kanaleneiland-in-utrecht.html.

16. "Ondergedoken in Slotervaart," *De Volkskrant* (Amsterdam), March 23, 2010; "Ondergedoken in Slotervaart (2)," *De Volkskrant* (Amsterdam), March 30, 2010.

17. Email from Peter van Wateren, chief of the police station August Allebé-plein in Amsterdam-Slotervaart, January 12, 2006, 16:55.

18. Remco Gerretsen, quoted in: "Politie mocht niet in uniform naar Amsterdam-West," *Nieuws.nl* (Amsterdam), February 7, 2006, http://binnenland.nieuws.nl/167569.

19. Arnold Karskens, "Kut-Hollander roepen pik ik niet," *De Pers* (Amsterdam), August 8, 2011, http://www.depers.nl/binnenland/587581/Kut-Hollander-pik-ik-niet.html.

20. "Wilders uitgejoeld door Helmondse kinderen," *De Pers* (Amsterdam), August 24, 2011, http://www.depers.nl/binnenland/591217/Wilders-uit-gejoeld-in-Helmond.html.

21. Ministerie van Volkshuisvesting, Ruimtelijke Ordening en Milieubeheer (Ministry of Housing, Spatial Planning and the Environment), "De aandachtswijken," The Hague, the Netherlands, 2007, http://www.vrom.nl/pagina.html?id=31051.

22. Secrétariat général du Comité interministériel des villes (General Secretariat of the Interministerial Committee of Cities), "Atlas des zones urbaines sensibles," Paris, France, December 26, 1996.

23. Rebecca Leung, "The New French Revolution: Population of France Is Almost 10 Percent Muslim," CBS News, December 5, 2007, http://www.cbsnews.com/stories/2004/05/13/60minutes/main617270.shtml.

24. "Police Escorts for Buses Following Banlieue Blazes," ANSAmed (Rome), April 2, 2010, available on The European Union Yahoo! Group, http://groups.yahoo.com/group/TheEU/message/7483?var=0.

25. "Tremblay: Sarkozy reçoit les chauffeurs de bus victimes de l'agression," AFP (Paris), April 2, 2010.

26. "Les transports en première ligne: crapules dans les villes," *Le Figaro* (Paris), November 3, 2006, http://www.lefigaro.fr/magazine/20061103. MAG000000267_la_vie_brisee_d_une_etudiante_sans_histoire.html.

27. Jon Henley, "Disabled Woman Set on Fire as Paris Riots Spread," *Guardian* (London), November 4, 2005, http://www.guardian.co.uk/world/2005/nov/05/france.jonhenley.

28. France 3 statement, November 9, 2005, quoted in "France 3 Refusing to Publicize Car-beque Figures," No Pasaran! blog (Paris), November 9, 2005, http://no-pasaran.blogspot.com/2005/11/france-3-refusing-to-publicize-car.html.

29. "Nuits du 14-Juillet: la Place Beauvau impose le silence sur le nombre de voitures incendiées," *Le Monde* (Paris), July 17, 2009, http://www.lemonde.fr/cgi-bin/ACHATS/acheter.cgi?offre=ARCHIVES&type_item=ART_ARCH_30J&objet_id=1091629&clef=ARC-TRK-D_01.

30. Claire Cozens, "French TV Boss Admits Censoring Riot Coverage," *Guardian* (London), November 10, 2005, http://www.guardian.co.uk/media/2005/nov/10/france.tvnews.

31. Michael Nazir-Ali, "Extremism Flourished as UK Lost Christianity," *Telegraph* (London), UK, January 6, 2008, http://www.telegraph.co.uk/news/uknews/1574695/Extremism-flourished-as-UK-lost-Christianity.html.

32. "Threats to 'No-go Areas' Bishop," BBC News (London), February 2, 2008, http://news.bbc.co.uk/2/hi/uk_news/england/7223788.stm.

33. Shiraz Maher, "Muslim Britain Is Becoming One Big No-go Area," *Sunday Times* (London), January 13, 2008.

34. Michael Evans, "Military Uniforms in Public 'Risk Offending Minorities'," *Times* (London), March 8, 2008.

35. "Muslim Protest at Luton Army Parade Was 'Upsetting', Says Senior Officer," *Telegraph* (London), March 11, 2009, http://www.telegraph.co.uk/news/newstopics/politics/defence/4972211/Muslim-protest-at-Luton-Army-parade-was-upsetting-says-senior-officer.html.

36. Lucy Ballinger and Dan Newling, "Guilty? It's a Badge of Honour Say Muslim Hate Mob (and because We're on Benefits, the State Will Pay Our Costs)," *Daily Mail* (London), January 12, 2010, http://www.dailymail.co.uk/news/article-1242335/Muslims-called-British-soldiers-rapists-cowards-scum-exercising-freedom-speech-court-hears.html.

37. John Cornwell, "Are Muslim Enclaves No-go Areas, Forcing Other People Out?," *Sunday Times* (London), March 16, 2008.

38. "Unter Feinden," *Die Welt* (Berlin), July 28, 2008.

39. "In Problemvierteln fürchtet sich sogar die Polizei," Der Westen (Essen), August 1, 2011, http://www.derwesten.de/nachrichten/politik/In-Problemvierteln-fuerchtet-sich-sogar-die-Polizei-id4926287.html. Translated in Soeren Kern, "European 'No-Go' Zones for Non-Muslims Proliferating: 'Occupation without Tanks or Solders,'" Stonegate Institute, August 22, 2011, http://www.stonegateinstitute.org/2367/european-muslim-no-go-zones.

40. Jan Hertogen, "In België wonen 628.751 moslims (*), 6,0% van de bevolking. In Brussel is dit 25,5%, in Wallonië 4,0%, in Vlaanderen 3,9%," Berichten uit het Gewisse/Non-Profit Data, Brussels, Belgium, September 11, 2008, http://www.npdata.be/BuG/100/.

41. "Brussel gaat actie ondernemen tegen geweld in probleemwijken," *De Volkskrant* (Amsterdam), February 1, 2010, http://www.volkskrant.nl/buitenland/article1344583.ece/Brussel_gaat_actie_ondernemen_tegen_geweld_in_probleemwijken.

42. Patrick Belton, "In the Way of the Prophet: Ideologies and Institutions in Dearborn, Michigan, America's Muslim Capitol," *Next American City*, October 2003, http://americancity.org/magazine/article/in-the-way-of-the-prophet-ideologies-and-institutions-belton/.

43. Keith Naughton, "Arab-America's Store: Wal-Mart Stocks Falafel, Olives and Islamic Greeting Cards to Attract Dearborn's Ethnic Shoppers," *Newsweek*, March 10, 2008, http://www.newsweek.com/id/117835.

44. Sam Yousif, "Chaldean Dearborn Michigan Resident Freedom Stripped," Chaldean.org, June 2009, http://www.chaldean.org/Home/tabid/36/articleType/ArticleView/articleId/485/Default.aspx.

45. J. Patrick Pepper, "Dearborn Ordered to Pay $100,000 in Attorney Fees from Arab Fest Leaflet Case," *Press & Guide*, February 1, 2012, http://www.pressandguide.com/articles/2012/02/01/news/doc4f298de8cc9e9801363624.txt, and Bob Unruh, "City Faces More Penalties for Arresting Christians: Judge Gives Green Light to Trial on Civil-rights Violations," *World Net Daily*, February 8, 2012, http://www.wnd.com/2012/02/city-faces-more-penalties-for-arresting-christians/.

46. Gregg Krupa, "Dutch Officials Visit Dearborn to Learn About Improving Muslim Relations," *Detroit News*, April 9, 2009, available on the Pluralism Project website, http://pluralism.org/news/view/21791.

47. Ibid.

48. Ibid.

49. "Invandrare 'krigar' mot svenskar med rån," *Dagens Nyheter* (Stockholm), March 25, 2006, http://www.dn.se/nyheter/sverige/invandrare-krigar-mot-svenskar-med-ran-1.730573.

50. "Berlin-Based Hate Preacher Expelled: Invoking New Anti-hate Legislation, a Berlin Court Ruled Wednesday that a Well-known Turkish Religious Leader Accused of Preaching Hatred Should Be Extradited to Turkey," Deutsche Welle (Berlin), March 23, 2005, http://www.dw-world.de/dw/article/0,1564,1527935,00.html.

51. Alain Finkielkraut, interview in *Le Figaro* (Paris), November 15, 2005. English translation by Mark K. Jensen, Associate Professor of French at Pacific Lutheran University, Tacoma, WA, "Alain Finkielkraut on the French Riots and on 'the Illegitimacy of Hatred,'" available on the United for Peace of Pierce County website, http://www.ufppc.org/us-a-world-news-mainmenu-35/3637-translation-alain-finkielkraut-on-the-french-riots-and-on-the-illegitimacy-of-hatred.html.

52. Ibid.

53. Wafa Sultan, *A God Who Hates: The Courageous Woman Who Inflamed the Muslim World Speaks Out against the Evils of Islam* (St. Martin's Press, 2009), p. 66.

54. Koran 9:29.

55. Michel Pajon on French radio, eight o'clock evening news, *France Culture* (Paris), November 7, 2005, available on the Ruines circulaires website, http://ruinescirculaires.free.fr/index.php?2005/11/07/118-dqsh fklqs.

56. Jean de Maillard, "Dans les banlieues, le pire reste à venir," Rue89 (Paris), November 28, 2007, http://www.rue89.com/plume-balance/dans-les-banlieues-le-pire-reste-a-venir; English translation by Tiberge on her blog, "A Magistrate's Warning," GalliaWatch, December 4, 2007, http://galliawatch.blogspot.com/2007/12/magistrates-warning.html.

57. "Police Fired on in Paris Suburb," BBC News (London), March 3, 2008, http://news.bbc.co.uk/2/hi/europe/7274804.stm.

58. Maurice de Hond, "De aanslagen in Noorwegen en de houding to.v. de Islamieten in West Europa," Peil.nl (Amsterdam), July 29, 2011.

59. "Nederlander heeft weinig kaas gegeten van historie," *De Volkskrant* (Amsterdam), March 26, 2008, http://www.volkskrant.nl/vk/nl/2686/Binnenland/article/detail/885241/2008/03/26/Nederlander-heeft-weinig-kaas-gegeten-van-historie.dhtml.

60. "France: Minarets, 46% of Population Wants Ban," ANSAmed (Rome), December 3, 2009.

61. "Zes op de tien Belgen voor minarettenverbod," *De Standaard* (Brussels), December 9, 2009, http://www.standaard.be/artikel/detail.aspx?artikelid= HB2JCGTE.

62. "Quebec Bill Would Ban Niqabs to All Receiving Government Services," *National Post* (Toronto), March, 24, 2010.

63. Thomas Jefferson, as quoted by Bill Clinton, "Message on the Observance of Labor Day, 1997," Martha's Vineyard, Massachusetts, August 29, 1997, available on the William J. Clinton Presidential Center website, "Remarks by President on Labor Day," http://archives.clintonpresidentialcenter.org/?u=082997-remarks-by-president-on-labor-day.htm.

64. Giles Tremlett, "Two Arrested after Fight in Cordoba's Former Mosque: Trouble Erupts as Tourists Break Ban on Muslim Prayers in Spanish Cathedral Which Was Once Word's Second Biggest Mosque," *Guardian* (London), April 1, 2010, http://www.guardian.co.uk/world/2010/apr/01/muslim-catholic-mosque-fight.

CHAPTER 10

1. Elie Wiesel, *Night* (Hill & Wang, 2006).

2. "Netherlands Considers Burqa Ban," BBC News (London), December 21, 2005, http://news.bbc.co.uk/2/hi/europe/4549730.stm.

3. Feisal Abdul Rauf, "Sharing the Core of Our Beliefs," Common Ground News Service (CDNews), March 31, 2009, http://www.commonground news.org/article.php?id=25141.

4. Feisal Abdul Rauf, "What Shariah Law Is All About," *Huffington Post*, April 24, 2009, http://www.huffingtonpost.com/imam-feisal-abdul-rauf/what-shariah-law-is-all-a_b_190825.html?view=print.

5. Hadith Sahih Bukhari 8:82:794; Hadith Abu Dawud 38:4357.

6. Sam Solomon and E. Al Maqdisi, *Modern Day Trojan Horse: Al-Hijra: The Islamic Doctrine of Immigration: Accepting Freedom or Imposing Islam?* (Pilcrow Press, 2009), p. 20.

7. Stefano Allievi, *Conflicts over Mosques in Europe: Policy Issues and Trends* (Alliance Publishing Trust, 2009), p. 23, http://www.alliancemagazine.org/books/MOSQUES.pdf.

8. Patrick Sookhdeo, *Global Jihad: The Future in the Face of Militant Islam* (Isaac Publishing, 2007), p. 95.

9. Sam Solomon and E. Almaqdisi, *The Mosque Exposed* (ANMPress, 2006), p. 38.

10. "Turkey's Charismatic Pro-Islamic Leader," BBC News (London), November 4, 2002, http://news.bbc.co.uk/2/hi/europe/2270642.stm.

11. Hadith Sunan Abu-Dawud 14:2473; Hadith Malik's Muwatta 41.41.9.28.

12. Hadith Sahih Bukhari 4:52:42.

13. Oriana Fallaci, *The Force of Reason* (Rizzoli International, 2006), p. 56.

14. Solomon and Maqdisi, *Modern Day Trojan Horse*, p. 31.
15. "Turkish Prime Minister Says 'Assimilation Is a Crime against Humanity,'" *Local* (Berlin), February 11, 2008, http://www.thelocal.de/politics/20080211-10293.html.
16. Tiberge, "Turkey at the Gates," *GalliaWatch*, April 8, 2010, http://galliawatch.blogspot.com/2010/04/turkey-at-gates.html; "'Stop inmenging Turkse overheid in Nederlandse politiek,'" *Elsevier* (Amsterdam), March 18, 2010, http://www.elsevier.nl/web/Nieuws/Politiek/260888/Stop-inmenging-Turkse-overheid-in-Nederlandse-politiek.htm.
17. Recep Tayyib Erdoğan, speaking on Turkish television, quoted in "PM Erdogan: The Term 'Moderate Islam' Is Ugly and Offensive; There Is No Moderate Islam; Islam Is Islam," Memri Turkish Media Blog, August 21, 2007, http://www.thememriblog.org/turkey/blog_personal/en/2595.htm.
18. Fallaci, *The Force of Reason*, p. 305.
19. David Solway, "A Profile in Courage: An Open Letter to Geert Wilders," *FrontPage Magazine*, March 15, 2010, http://frontpagemag.com/2010/03/15/a-profile-in-courage/.
20. Sam Solomon and E. Al Maqdisi, *Modern Day Trojan Horse*, pp. 82–83.
21. Ibid., p. 82.
22. "Queen Grants Muslim Prayer Room: the Queen Has Given Permission for a Room in Windsor Castle to Be Used as an Area for Muslims to Pray," BBC News (London), September 30, 2006, http://news.bbc.co.uk/2/hi/uk_news/england/berkshire/5395298.stm.
23. "France-Lyon-Musulman-Gynécologue," *journal télévisé 20 heures*, France 2 (Paris), August 3, 2008, http://forums.france2.fr/france2/complement_enquete/prison-agression-hopital-sujet_1819_1.htm; "Moslims weigeren vaak mannelijke gynaecoloog," *De Standaard* (Brussels), September 13, 2007; "Steeds meer moslims eisen vrouwelijke arts," *Elsevier* (Amsterdam), July 26, 2007, http://www.elsevier.nl/web/10131859/Nieuws/Nederland/Steeds-meer-moslims-eisen-vrouwelijke-arts.htm; "Klappen voor arts wegens uitsteken van hand," *Algemeen Dagblad* (Rotterdam), March 20, 2004.
24. Hadith Sahih Bukhari 3:50:874.
25. "Veelwijverij wordt netjes geregistreerd," *De Telegraaf* (Amsterdam), September 19, 2008, http://www.telegraaf.nl/binnenland/1961927/__Veelwijverij_netjes_geregistreerd__.html; "Jaarlijks vele polygame huwelijken," *NRC Handelsblad* (Rotterdam), August 9, 2008, http://vorige.nrc.nl/binnenland/article1951380.ece/Jaarlijks_vele_polygame_huwelijken; Esther, "Amsterdam: 173 Polygamous Marriages," Islam in

Europe: the Premier Source for News about the Muslim Community in Europe blog, September 21, 2008, http://islamineurope.blogspot.com/2008/09/amsterdam-173-polygamous-marriages.html.

26. Esther, "Antwerp: 45 Polygamous Marriages," Islam in Europe: the Premier Source for News about the Muslim Community in Europe blog, August 17, 2009, http://islamineurope.blogspot.com/2009/08/antwerp-45-polygamous-marriages.html.

27. "Italy: Polygamous Muslim Marriages 'On the Rise,'" Adnkronos International (AKI) (Rome), April 2, 2008, http://www.adnkronos.com/AKI/English/Religion/?id=1.0.2032301125.

28. "Polygamy to Blame for French Riots: French Minister," AFP (Paris), November 16, 2005, available on the Nine News website, http://news.ninemsn.com.au/article.aspx?id=72354&rss=yes.

29. Genevieve Oger, "France's Polygamy Problem," Deutsche Welle (Berlin), July 31, 2005, http://www.dw-world.de/dw/article/0,,1664241,00.html.

30. Kim Willsher, "Middle-class Muslims Fuel French Halal Boom: Retailers and Restaurants Cash in on Rapidly Expanding and Highly Profitable Market in Halal Food and Drinks," *Guardian* (London), April 5, 2010, http://www.guardian.co.uk/world/2010/apr/05/france-muslims-halal-boom.

31. Ariel David, "Beach for Muslim Women Planned in Italy," Associated Press, August 4, 2006, available on the Breitbart website, http://www.breitbart.com/article.php?id=D8J9N7UG0&show_article=1; Esther, "Finland: Ombudsman Allows Separate Swimming Times for Muslim Women," Islam in Europe: the Premier Source for News about the Muslim Community in Europe blog, June 18, 2009, http://islamineurope.blogspot.com/2009/06/finland-ombudsman-allows-separate.html.

32. Patrick Sawer, "Swimmers Are Told to Wear Burkinis: British Swimming Pools Are Imposing Muslim Dress Codes in a Move Described as Divisive by Labour MPs," *Daily Telegraph* (London), August 15, 2009, http://www.telegraph.co.uk/news/newstopics/politics/6034706/Swimmers-are-told-to-wear-burkinis.html.

33. "Jail Toilets Face Away from Mecca: Facilities in a Prison Are Being Built so Muslim Inmates Do Not Have to Face Mecca While Sitting on the Toilet," BBC News (London), April 20, 2006, http://news.bbc.co.uk/2/hi/uk_news/england/london/4926114.stm; "New Eco-homes in Asian Community: Eco-friendly Homes Specially Designed for the Local Asian Community Have Been Unveiled in Greater Manchester," BBC News (London), July 25, 2006, http://news.bbc.co.uk/2/hi/uk_news/england/manchester/5213588.

stm; "Olympic Park Toilets 'Will Not Face Mecca,'" *Independent* (London), September 24, 2008, http://www.independent.co.uk/news/uk/home-news/olympic-park-toilets-will-not-face-mecca-941030.html.

34. Koran 3:129.

35. Thomas Landen, "Sharia Banking Conquers Europe," Stonegate Institute, March 24, 2009, http://www.stonegateinstitute.org/422/sharia-banking-conquers-europe.

36. "France: Senate Looks at Easing Limits on Muslim Finance," Adnkronos International (AKI) (Rome), December 23, 2008, http://www.adnkronos.com/AKI/English/Business/?id=3.0.2846242034; Sandra Haurant and agencies, "Lloyds Launches Islamic Portfolio," *Guardian* (London), June 14, 2006, http://www.guardian.co.uk/money/2006/jun/14/religion.islam icfinance; Tony Levene, "Why the Lack of Interest?" *Guardian* (London), April 1, 2005, http://www.guardian.co.uk/guardian_jobs_and_money/story/0,,1450300,00.html.

37. Loretta Napoleoni and Claudia Segre, "Dalla finanza islamica proposte e idee per l'Occidente in crisi," *L'Osservatore Romano* (Vatican City), March 4, 2009, http://rassegnastampa.mef.gov.it/mefnazionale/PDF/2009/2009-03-04/2009030412006886.pdf.

38. French Finance Minister Christine Lagarde, in "France: Senate looks at easing limits on Muslim finance," Adnkronos International (AKI) December 23, 2008, http://www.adnkronos.com/AKI/English/Business/?id=3.02846242034.

39. "Finance Minister to Encourage Islamic Banking," NIS News Bulletin, Netherlands Info Services (Rijswijk), July 17, 2007, http://www.nisnews.nl/public/170707_1.htm.

40. John Sandwick, managing director of Swiss asset management firm Encore Management, quoted in "Swiss Risk Losing Islamic Goldmine: Plans by Arab Partners to Set up an Islamic Private Bank in Switzerland Have Highlighted a Largely Unexploited Market of Muslim Wealth Based in Western Countries," Swiss Info (Bern), April 3, 2008, http://www.swissinfo.ch/eng/Swiss_risk_losing_Islamic_goldmine.html?cid=6556370.

41. "Bos wil islamitisch bankieren invoeren," *Elsevier* (Amsterdam), July 16, 2007, http://www.elsevier.nl/web/Nieuws/Politiek/131022/Bos-wil-islamitisch-bankieren-invoeren.htm.

42. Mervyn Hiskett, *Some to Mecca Turn to Pray: Islamic Values in the Modern World* (Claridge Press, 1993), p. 274.

43.   "Europe's Muslims More Moderate: The Great Divide: How Westerners and Muslims View Each Other," Pew Global Attitudes Project, Pew Research Center, June 22, 2006, http://pewglobal.org/reports/display.php?ReportID=253.

44.   John Thorne and Hannah Stuart, "Islam on Campus: A Survey of UK Student Opinions," Centre for Social Cohesion (London), July 2008, http://www.socialcohesion.co.uk/files/1231525079_1.pdf.

45.   "Helft moslims Nederland: begrip voor aanslagen VS," *Nederlands Dagblad* (Barneveld), September 20, 2001, http://www.nd.nl/artikelen/2001/september/20/helft-moslims-nederland-begrip-voor-aanslagen-vs-.

46.   "Jaarrapport Integratie 2010," Centraal Bureau voor de Statistiek (The Hague/Heerlen), November, 2010, p. 170.

47.   Jodie T. Allen, "The French-Muslim Connection: Is France Doing a Better Job of Integration than Its Critics?" Pew Research Center, August 17, 2006, http://pewresearch.org/pubs/50/the-french-muslim-connection.

48.   "Der Kniefall von Neukölln beunruhigt," *B.Z.* (Berlin), August 27, 2009, http://www.bz-berlin.de/aktuell/berlin/der-kniefall-von-neukoelln-beun ruhigt-article564377.html.

49.   David Leppard, "Muslims Boycott Holocaust Remembrance," *Sunday Times* (London), January 23, 2005.

50.   Catherine Hickley, "Berlin's Deutsche Oper Cancels 'Idomeneo' on Security Concerns," Bloomberg, September 25, 2006, http://www.bloomberg.com/apps/news?pid=20601088&sid=a3Wlr6P8hvUk&refer=muse.

51.   Benjamin Disraeli, speech at Guildhall, London, November 9, 1877, quoted in *Times* (London), November 10, 1877. In Elizabeth M. Knowles, ed., *Oxford Dictionary of Quotations* (Oxford University Press, 1999), p. 269.

52.   Margaret Thatcher, "TV Interview for Granada *World in Action* ('Rather Swamped')", January 27, 1978, Margaret Thatcher Foundation, http://www.margaretthatcher.org/speeches/displaydocument.asp?docid=103485.

53.   "Uproar at Minister's Remark about Sharia," Radio Netherlands Worldwide (RNW) (Hilversum), September 13, 2006.

54.   "Sharia Law in UK Is 'Unavoidable': The Archbishop of Canterbury Says the Adoption of Certain Aspects of Sharia Law in the UK 'Seems Unavoidable,'" BBC News (London), February 7, 2008, http://news.bbc.co.uk/2/hi/7232661.stm.

55.   "Sharia Law 'Could Have UK Role': Principles of Sharia Law Could Play a Role in Some Parts of the Legal System, the Lord Chief Justice Has Said,"

BBC News (London), July 4, 2008, http://news.bbc.co.uk/2/hi/uk_news/7488790.stm.

56. "Revealed: UK's First Official Sharia Courts," *Sunday Times* (London), September 4, 2008.

57. Koran 4:11.

58. "French Minister Says Polygamy to Blame for Riots," *Financial Times* (London), November 15, 2005.

59. Sue Reid, "Polygamy UK: This Special Mail Investigation Reveals How Thousands of Men Are Milking the Benefits System to Support Several Wives," *Daily Mail* (London), February 24, 2009, http://www.dailymail. co.uk/news/article-1154789/Polygamy-UK-This-special-Mail-investiga tion-reveals-thousands-men-milking-benefits-support-wives.html.

60. Sookhdeo, *Global Jihad*, p. 56.

61. "Hamburgs Schlimmster Sozialschmarotzer verurteilt," *Bild* (Berlin), June 2, 2008, http://www.bild.de/BILD/hamburg/aktuell/2008/06/02/ham burgs-schlimmster/sozialschmarotzer-verurteilt.html; Siem Eikelenboom, *Jihad in de Polder: De radicale islam in Nederland* (Veen, 2004), pp. 121, 261; Beila Rabinowitz and William A. Mayer, "Radical Imam Tells Muslims in Holland Not to Pay Taxes to Harm Dutch State—Wilders Calls for Deportation: Dutch Imam Salam Urges Followers to 'Harm State' Counseling 'Don't Pay Taxes,'" Militant Islam Monitor, April 2, 2007, http://militantislammonitor.org/article/id/2799; "Burgemeester: imam Salam hoort hier niet thuis," *De Pers* (Amsterdam), March 29, 2007, http://www.depers.nl/binnenland/47879/Vreeman-imam-Salam-hoort-hier-niet.html; "Radical Muslim Preacher Caught on Film Giving Advice on How to 'Hoodwink' the Government over Benefits," *Daily Mail* (London), March 5, 2008, http://www.dailymail.co.uk/news/arti cle-526483/Radical-Muslim-preacher-caught-film-giving-advice-hood wink-Government-benefits.html.

62. "Inside the Sect That Loves Terror," *Sunday Times* (London), August 7, 2005.

63. Muhammad Zawar Khan, "Farvel, Mekka," *Aftenposten* (Oslo), March 4, 2005, http://www.aftenposten.no/meninger/kronikker/article985370. ece.

64. *Sociaaleconomische trends, 2e kwartaal 2011*, Centraal Bureau voor de Statistiek (The Hague/Heerlen, June 15, 2011), p. 52, http://www.cbs.nl/ nl-NL/menu/publicaties/boeken/sociaal-economische-trends/ archief/2011/2011-k2-v4-pub.htm.

65. "Kabinet berekent geen kosten immigrant," *Trouw* (Amsterdam), September 4, 2009, http://www.trouw.nl/nieuws/politiek/article2854403.ece/Kabinet_berekent_geen_kosten_immigrant_.html.

66. "Nyfer: immigratie kost samenleving 7,2 miljard per jaar," *NRC Handelsblad* (Rotterdam), May 19, 2010, http://www.nrc.nl/binnenland/article2547528.ece/Nyfer_immigratie_kost_samenleving_7,2_mid_per_jaar.

67. Allievi, *Conflicts over Mosques in Europe,* p. 23.

68. "Tales from Eurabia: Contrary to Fears on Both Sides of the Atlantic, Integrating Europe's Muslims Can Be Done," *Economist* (London), June 22, 2006, http://www.economist.com/node/7086222.

69. Esther, "Number of Muslims in Europe," Islam in Europe: the Premier Source for News about the Muslim Community in Europe blog, May 10, 2007, http://islamineurope.blogspot.com/2007/05/number-of-muslims-in-europe.html.

70. Allievi, *Conflicts over Mosques in Europe,* p. 23.

71. "Priest Burns Himself to Death over Islam," *Times* (London), November 3, 2006.

72. YouGov survey commissioned by the Mental Health Foundation, "As World Mental Health Day Approaches, Survey Shows Global Issues Leave 1 in 7 British Adults Reluctant to Have Children," Mental Health Foundation (London), October 8, 2007. See also, "World Troubles Affect Parenthood: One in Seven Adults Is Reluctant to Have Children and One in Four Puts off Planning for the Future because of World Troubles, According to Survey," BBC News (London), October 8, 2007, http://news.bbc.co.uk/2/hi/uk_news/7033102.stm.

73. "Middle Classes Leading the Flight as 250,000 Quit London," *Daily Mail* (London), September 26, 2008, http://www.dailymail.co.uk/news/article-1062314/Middle-classes-leading-flight-250-000-quit-London.html#ixzz0UxCPT7I2.

74. George Walden, *Time to Emigrate?: Letters from a Father* (Gibson Square Books, 2006).

75. "Why Britain's Brightest and Best are Emigrating," *Daily Telegraph* (London), February 21, 2008, http://www.telegraph.co.uk/comment/3555250/Why-Britains-brightest-and-best-are-emigrating.html.

76. "Migration: Und tschüs…," *Der Spiegel* (Hamburg), October 30, 2006, http://www.spiegel.de/spiegel/print/d-49378761.html.

77. "Emigration Up, Birth Rate Down: Graying Germany Contemplates Demographic Time Bomb," *Der Spiegel* (Hamburg), May 27, 2010, http://www.spiegel.de/international/germany/0,1518,697085,00.html.

78. Marlise Simons, "More Dutch Plan to Emigrate as Muslim Influx Tips Scales," *New York Times*, February 27, 2005, http://www.nytimes.com/2005/02/27/international/europe/27dutch.html?.

79. J. Klaver, J. Stouten, and I. van der Welle, *Emigratie uit Nederland: Een verkennende studie naar de emigratiemotieven van hoger opgeleiden*, Regioplan Beleidsonderzoek (Amsterdam), December 2010, http://www.rijksoverheid.nl/bestanden/documenten-en-publicaties/kamerstukken/2011/01/26/aanbieding-onderzoeksrapport-emigratiemotieven-van-hoger-opgeleiden-eindrapport-emigratie-uit-nederland/ii2011035701aeindrapportemigratieuitnederlandregioplan.pdf; L. van der Geest and A.J.F. Dietvorst, *Budgettaire effecten van immigratie van niet-westerse allochtonen*, Nyfer: Forum for Economic Research (Utrecht), May 2010, p. 84, http://www.nyfer.nl/documents/rapportPVVdef_001.pdf.

80. Justin Vaïsse, "Eurabian Follies: The Shoddy and Just Plain Wrong Genre That Refuses to Die," *Foreign Policy*, January/February 2010, http://www.foreignpolicy.com/articles/2010/01/04/eurabian_follies.

81. William Underhill, "Why Fears of a Muslim Takeover Are All Wrong," *Newsweek*, July 11, 2009, http://www.newsweek.com/id/206230/.

82. "Tales from Eurabia," *Economist* (London).

83. Benjamin Franklin, "The Way to Wealth" (From "Father Abraham's Speech" forming the preface to *Poor Richard's Almanac* for 1758), in Benjamin Franklin, *Autobiography of Benjamin Franklin*, ed. F. W. Pine (The Echo Library, 2007), p. 138.

84. "2009 Country Reports on Human Rights Practices," U.S. Department of State, March 11, 2010, http://www.state.gov/g/drl/rls/hrrpt/2009/index.htm.

85. "US Embassy Cables: Barack Obama's Briefing on Dutch Politics," *Guardian* (London), December 15, 2010, http://www.guardian.co.uk/world/us-embassy-cables-documents/215223.

CHAPTER 11

1. "PVV-leraar is baan kwijt," *De Telegraaf* (Amsterdam), June 8, 2010, http://www.telegraaf.nl/binnenland/6891198/__PVV-leraar_is_baan_kwijt__.html.

2. Former Amsterdam Police Commissioner Joop van Riessen, in *Pauw & Witteman*, NPS/VARA, Dutch television channel Nederland 1 (Hilversum), October 1, 2007, http://www.youtube.com/watch?v=Jyx8l7LSVIU.

3. Ibid.

4. Bertolt Brecht, *Die Lösung*, in George Tabori, ed., *Brecht on Brecht: An Improvisation* (Samuel French, 1967), p. 17.

5. Bat Ye'or, *Eurabia: The Euro-Àrab Axis* (Fairleigh Dickinson University Press, 2005), p. 54.

6. Case C-127/08, *Blaise Baheten Metock and Others v. Minister for Justice, Equality and Law Reform*, Court of Justice of the European Communities (Luxembourg City), July 25, 2008, http://eur-lex.europa.eu/LexUriServ/LexUriServ.do?uri=CELEX:62008J0127:EN:HTML.

7. Case C-578/08, *Rhimou Chakroun v. Minister van Buitenlandse Zaken*, Court of Justice of the European Communities (Luxembourg City), March 4, 2010, http://eur-lex.europa.eu/LexUriServ/LexUriServ.do?uri=OJ:C:20 10:113:0013:01:EN:HTML.

8. "Rechter: Turken hoeven geen inburgeringscursus te doen," *Elsevier* (Amsterdam), August 13, 2011, http://www.elsevier.nl/web/Nieuws/Nederland/273172/Rechter-Turken-hoeven-geen-inburgeringscursus-te-doen.htm.

9. Andrew Neather, "Don't Listen to the Whingers—London Needs Immigrants," *London Evening Standard* (London), October 23, 2009, http://www.thisislondon.co.uk/standard/article-23760073-dont-listen-to-the-whingers—london-needs-immigrants.do.

10. Ibid.

11. David Cameron, "PM's Speech at Munich Security Conference," Number 10: The official site of the British Prime Minister's Office, February 5, 2011, http://www.number10.gov.uk/news/pms-speech-at-munich-security-con ference/.

12. Ibid.

13. "Multiculturalism Has Failed, Says French President," AFP (Paris), February 10, 2011, http://www.google.com/hostednews/afp/article/ALeqM5jR 1m5BpdMrDES3u4Cso1v3FwQRUg?docId=CNG.6b096ac0cdcfce7a0f 599fbbb1c85c27.911.

14. "Kanzlerin Merkel erklärt Multikulti für gescheitert," *Die Welt* (Berlin), October 16, 2010, http://www.welt.de/politik/deutschland/arti cle10337575/Kanzlerin-Merkel-erklaert-Multikulti-fuer-gescheitert.html.

15. Rede zur Einheitsfeier, "Wulff: Islam gehört zu Deutschland," *Der Tagesspiegel* (Berlin), October 3, 2010, http://www.tagesspiegel.de/politik/wulff-islam-gehoert-zu-deutschland/1948760.html.

16. "Cohn-Bendit: 'Les Suisses doivent revoter'," *Le Temps* (Geneva), December 2, 2009, http://www.letemps.ch/Page/Uuid/f8f4a4ea-dec3-11de-801c-518ea5779929/Cohn-Bendit_Les_Suisses_doivent_revoter.

17. "Resolution 1605 – European Muslim Communities Confronted with Extremism," adopted by the Parliamentary Assembly of the Council or

Europe, Strasbourg, France, April 15, 2008, http://assembly.coe.int/Main.
asp?link=/Documents/AdoptedText/ta08/ERES1605.htm.

18. Catherine Lalumière, speaking at the Council of Europe conference, "What Future for Human Rights and Democracy?" in Paris, September 11, 2009.

19. Sherry Jones, "Censoring 'The Jewel of Medina'," *Washington Post*, August 11, 2008, http://newsweek.washingtonpost.com/postglobal/islamsadvance/2008/08/censoring_islam.html.

20. Patricia Cohen, "Yale Press Bans Images of Muhammad in New Book," *New York Times*, August 12, 2009, http://www.nytimes.com/2009/08/13/books/13book.html.

21. Brooke Goldstein, "The Disproportionate Use of Lawfare," Stonegate Institute, April 5, 2010, http://www.stonegateinstitute.org/1132/the-disproportionate-use-of-lawfare.

22. Ron Chepesiuk, "Libel Tourism," *Global Journalist*, July 1, 2004, http://www.globaljournalist.org/stories/2004/07/01/libel-tourism/.

23. Goldstein, "The Disproportionate Use of Lawfare."

24. Ezra Levant, "Punished First, Acquitted Later," August 6, 2008, http://ezralevant.com/2008/08/punished-first-acquitted-later.html; "Two Years and $100,000 Later: Ezra Levant Complaint Dismissed by Human Rights Commission," LifeSiteNews.com, August 7, 2008, http://www.lifesitenews.com/news/archive/ldn/2008/aug/08080701.

25. Mark Steyn, "Re: Complaint against Steyn Dismissed," National Review Online, October 10, 2008, http://www.nationalreview.com/corner/171811/re-complaint-against-steyn-dismissed/mark-steyn.

26. "How libel tourism became an 'embarrassment' to Britain's reputation," *Daily Telegraph* (London), February 23, 2010, http://www.telegraph.co.uk/news/7301403/How-libel-tourism-became-an-embarrassment-to-Britains-reputation.html.

27. Rachel Ehrenfeld, *Funding Evil: How Terrorism Is Financed and How to Stop It* (Bonus Books, 2003).

28. "US author mounts 'libel tourism' challenge," *Guardian* (London), November 15, 2007, http://www.guardian.co.uk/world/2007/nov/15/books.usa.

29. "Khalid bin Mahfouz, Saudi Banker, Dies at 60," *New York Times*, August 26, 2009, http://www.nytimes.com/2009/08/27/world/middleeast/27mahfouz.html?_r=1.

30. David A. Paterson, "Governor Paterson Signs Legislation Protecting New Yorkers Against Infringement of First Amendment Rights by Foreign Libel

Judgments," press release by the Office of the Governor of New York, May 1, 2008.

31. George Washington, "Address to the Continental Army before the Battle of Long Island," August 27, 1776, in William J. Federer, *America's God and Country: Encyclopedia of Quotations* (Amerisearch, 2000), p. 639.

32. Jim Fitzpatrick, Minister of State for Farming and the Environment, quoted in Steve Doughty, "Extremist Muslims have 'wormed their way into Labour Party' minister warns," *Daily Mail* (London), March 1, 2010, http://www.dailymail.co.uk/news/article-1254374/Islamic-radicals-infiltrate-Labour-Party.html.

33. Jim Fitzpatrick, Minister of State for Farming and the Environment, quoted in Andrew Gilligan, "Islamic radicals 'infiltrate' the Labour Party," *Sunday Telegraph* (London), February 27, 2010, http://www.telegraph.co.uk/news/newstopics/politics/labour/7333420/Islamic-radicals-infiltrate-the-Labour-Party.html.

34. Michael Nazir-Ali, Bishop of Rochester, in a 2005 interview with Melanie Phillips, in Melanie Phillips, *Londonistan* (Encounter Books, 2006), p. 162.

35. Roger Boyes, "Turkish vote may throw Schröder lifeline," *Times* (London), September 15, 2005.

36. "Minder Amsterdamse allochtonen stemmen PvdA," *Het Parool* (Amsterdam), March 3, 2010, http://www.parool.nl/parool/nl/2064/GEMEENTERAADSVERKIEZINGEN-2010/article/detail/282361/2010/03/03/Minder-Amsterdamse-allochtonen-stemmen-PvdA.dhtml.

37. "Voorkeur allochtoon is lastig voor PvdA," *Trouw* (Amsterdam), March 18, 2010, http://www.trouw.nl/nieuws/politiek/article3017948.ece/Voorkeur_allochtoon__is_lastig_voor_PvdA__.html?all=true.

38. "Turkse PvdA'ers plegen coup in Rotterdam-Zuid," *Algemeen Dagblad* (Rotterdam), December 2, 2009.

39. "Polarisatie en radicalisering in Rotterdamse PvdA-afdeling," *Algemeen Dagblad* (Rotterdam), January 30, 2010, http://hoeiboei.blogspot.com/2010/01/polarisatie-en-radicalisering-in.html.

40. Wouter Bos, quoted in "Bos vreest zijn allochtone partijgenoten," *Elsevier* (Amsterdam), March 17, 2006, http://www.elsevier.nl/web/Nieuws/Politiek/70986/Bos-vreest-zijn-allochtone-partijgenoten.htm.

41. "Ophef over D66-stemadvies Turks ministerie," *Elsevier* (Amsterdam), December 8, 2006, http://www.elsevier.nl/web/10103886/Nieusw/

PolitiekDossiers/Verkiezingen-2006/De-Armeense-genocide-kwestie/
Ophef-over-D66-stemadvies-Turks-ministerie.htm.

42. *Radicale dawa in verandering: De opkomst van islamitisch neoradicalisme in Nederland* (Algemene Inlichtingen- en Veiligheidsdienst [AIVD], October 9, 2007), p. 66, https://www.aivd.nl/publish/pages/1291/radicaledawainverandering.pdf.

43. Shiraz Maher, "'The Wrong Type of Muslim': How Islamists Influence the UK Vote," Stonegate Institute, May 6, 2010, http://www.stonegateinstitute.org/1186/the-wrong-type-of-muslim-how-islamists-seek-to-influence-the-uk-vote.

44. BBC 1, *Panorama*, broadcasted July 30, 2006. The transcript recorded from transmission can be found at: "Faith, hate and charity: Transcript," BBC News (London), August 1, 2006, http://news.bbc.co.uk/2/hi/programmes/panorama/5234586.stm.

45. "Muslim Groups Oppose a List of 'Co-Conspirators'," *New York Times*, August 16, 2007, http://www.nytimes.com/2007/08/16/us/16charity.html.

CHAPTER 12

1. The verses explored in Fitna are Koran 8:60, 4:56, 47:4, 4:89, and 8:39. The entire film can be seen on the LiveLeak website at http://www.liveleak.com/view?i=216_1207467783.

2. The clip can be seen here: "Mocro's schoppen kaalkopjes," Dumpert.nl, March 12, 2008, http://www.dumpert.nl/mediabase/45891/7ba9e370/mocro_s_schoppen_kaalkopjes.html.

3. "Naam 'Wilders' leidt tot doodsbedreiging," *Eén Vandaag* (Hilversum), March 11, 2008, http://www.eenvandaag.nl/politiek/33172/naam_wilders_leidt_tot_doodsbedreiging.

4. "Dutch Muslims Condemn MP's Film," BBC News (London), January 24, 2008, http://news.bbc.co.uk/2/hi/europe/7206644.stm.

5. "De hel zal losbarsten: 'Wat jullie nodig hebben is een zware bomaanslag,'" *De Telegraaf* (Amsterdam), January 12, 2008.

6. Gerard Spong, in *Nova College Tour/Den Haag Vandaag*, NPS/VARA, Dutch television channel Nederland 2 (Hilversum), January 23, 2008, see "Spong daagt Wilders voor de rechter," NOVA, January 23, 2008, http://www.novatv.nl/page/detail/uitzendingen/5751; "Advocaat Spong in rechtszaak tegen Wilders," YouTube, http://www.youtube.com/watch?v=nI8BbTU2ALk.

7. "Iran Warns Hague over Anti-Islam Film," Press TV (Tehran), January 21, 2008, http://www.presstv.ir/detail.aspx?id=39616&sectionid=351020101.

8. Stephen Graham, "Pakistan Lifts Restrictions on YouTube," Associated Press, February 26, 2008, available on ABC News, http://abcnews.go.com/ Technology/story?id=4348045&page=1.

9. "Al-Qa'ida roept op Wilders te vermoorden," *Elsevier* (Amsterdam), February 27, 2008, http://www.elsevier.nl/web/Nieuws/Buitenland/ 159844/Al-Qaida-roept-op-Wilders-te-vermoorden.htm.

10. Jaap de Hoop Scheffer, in "Nato Fears over Dutch Islam film," BBC News (London), March 3, 2008, http://news.bbc.co.uk/2/hi/south_asia/7274259. stm; and "Al-Qa'ida roept op Wilders te vermoorden," *Elsevier* (Amsterdam).

11. "Grootmoefti: Bij geweld is Wilders de schuldige," *Elsevier* (Amsterdam), January 15, 2008, http://www.elsevier.nl/web/Nieuws/Nederland/154145/ Grootmoefti-Bij-geweld-is-Wilders-de-schuldige.htm.

12. "Grand Mufti of Syria: a Single Civilisation Unites Us All," Press release, European Parliament External Relations, Strasbourg, France, January 15, 2008, http://www.europarl.europa.eu/sides/getDoc.do?language= EN&type=IM-PRESS&reference=20080111IPR18241.

13. "Wijers neemt Wilders op de hak," NU.nl (Amsterdam), April 17, 2010, http://www.nu.nl/politiek/2228332/wijers-neemt-wilders-hak.html.

14. "'Schade Arabische boycot verhalen op Wilders,'" *Elsevier* (Amsterdam), March 29, 2008, http://www.elsevier.nl/web/10187507/Dossiers/De-Fitnas-van-Wilders/Fitna-the-Movie/Schade-Arabische-boycot-verhalen-op-Wilders.htm; "Bedrijven willen Wilders aansprakelijk stellen," *Algemeen Dagblad* (Rotterdam), March 31, 2008.

15. Doekle Terpstra, in "Verzetsbeweging tegen Wilders," *De Telegraaf* (Amsterdam), December 2, 2007, http://www.telegraaf.nl/binnenland/ 2671490/Verzetsbeweging_tegen_Wilders.html?p=14,1.

16. "Speciale formulieren voor aangifte om Fitna," *Trouw* (Amsterdam), March 28, 2008, http://www.trouw.nl/nieuws/article1804158.ece.

17. "Ter Horst waarschuwt gemeenten voor Koranfilm," *Elsevier* (Amsterdam), January 16, 2008, http://www.elsevier.nl/web/10154338/Dossiers/ De-Fitnas-van-Wilders/Reacties-uit-het-buitenland/Ter-Horst-waarschuwt-gemeenten-voor-Koranfilm.htm?long=true.

18. Henk Hofland, in *Pauw & Witteman*, NPS/VARA, Dutch television channel Nederland 1, Hilversum, the Netherlands, February 29, 2008, available on YouTube, "Henk Hofland wil Wilders dood hebben," http://www. youtube.com/watch?v=CHhwRG3qnT4.

19. "Auto's in brand bij rellen om Fitna," *Algemeen Dagblad* (Rotterdam), March 28, 2008, http://www.ad.nl/ad/nl/1039/Utrecht/article/detail/357943/2008/03/28/Auto-rsquo-s-in-brand-bij-rellen-om-Fitna. dhtml; "Moslimorganisaties opgelucht na bekijken Fitna," NU.nl (Amsterdam), March 28, 2008, http://www.nu.nl/algemeen/1499824/moslimorganisaties-opgelucht-na-bekijken-fitna.html.

20. Press release by Prime Minister Jan Peter Balkenende, "Reactie kabinet op film Wilders," *Ministerie van Algemene Zaken*, The Hague, the Netherlands, March 27, 2008.

21. "No Justification for Hate Speech or Incitement, Says Secretary-General in Strong Condemnation of 'Anti-Islamic' Film," Statement SG/SM/11483 by UN Secretary-General Ban Ki-moon, the United Nations, Secretary-General, March 28, 2008, http://www.un.org/News/Press/docs/2008/sgsm11483.doc.htm.

22. "EU Presidency Statement on the Release of the Film 'Fitna,'" Slovenian Presidency of the EU 2008 (Ljubljana), March 28, 2008, http://www.eu2008.si/en/News_and_Documents/CFSP_Statements/March/0328MZZ_Fitna.html.

23. Patrick Goodenough, "YouTube Warned to Remove Koran Film," CNS News, July 7, 2008, http://cnsnews.com/news/article/youtube-warned-remove-koran-film.

24. "HT Indonesia: Dutch Government Must Be Held Accountable over FITNA," Hizb ut-Tahrir Britain (London), April 8, 2008.

25. M.J.M. Verhagen, "Kamerbrief betreffende mogelijke uitlevering van het lid Wilders aan Jordanië," Rijksoverheid/Ministerie van Buitenlandse Zaken (The Hague), July 4, 2008, http://www.rijksoverheid.nl/documenten-en-publicaties/kamerstukken/2010/06/02/kamerbrief-betreffende-mogelijke-uitlevering-van-het-lid-wilders-aan-jordanie.html.

26. Geert Wilders, "Bevries desnoods de relaties met Jordanië," *De Volkskrant* (Amsterdam), July 2, 2008.

27. "Imam claimt 55.000 euro om Fitna," *NRC Handelsblad* (Rotterdam), July 13, 2008, http://www.nrc.nl/binnenland/article1935332.ece/Imam_claimt_55.000_euro_om_Fitna.

28. Janny Groen and Annieke Kranenberg, "Imam vervloekte Van Gogh vóór moord," *De Volkskrant* (Amsterdam), October 31, 2006, http://www.volkskrant.nl/vk/nl/2686/Binnenland/article/detail/788105/2006/10/31/Imam-vervloekte-Van-Gogh-voor-moord.dhtml.

29. "Imam: Vervloeken kanaliseert woede," *Elsevier* (Amsterdam), October 31, 2006. http://www.elsevier.nl/web/1098174/Nieuws/Nederland/Imam-Verv loeken-kanaliseert-woede.htm; "Horen & Zien: Het verhaal achter de foto," *De Volkskrant* (Amsterdam), October 31, 2006, http://www.volksk rant. com/animatie/fotospecial/specials/fawaz/horenzien_content.html.

30. "Wilders not Prosecuted for 'Fitna' and Statements," Openbaar Ministerie Arrondissementsparket Amsterdam (Amsterdam), June 30, 2008, http:// www.om.nl/algemene_onderdelen/uitgebreid_zoeken/@148332/wilders_ not/.

31. Amsterdam Police Chief Bernard Welten, "Korte inleiding Hoofdcommis-saris Welten bij de politie Iftar," Amsterdam, the Netherlands, September 18, 2008, available on the Amsterdam-Amstelland website, http://www. politie-amsterdam-amstelland.nl/files/downloads/Welten_speech_iftar_18-9-2008.pdf.

32. "Ed van Thijn: 'Respect politicus nodig,'" *Het Parool* (Amsterdam), November 10, 2008, http://www.parool.nl/parool/nl/4/AMSTERDAM/ article/detail/41921/2008/11/10/Ed-van-Thijn-moslimhaat-aan-de-orde-van-de-dag.dhtml.

33. Afshin Ellian, "Rabbae en Van Thijn, blijf weg bij Kristallnacht," *Elsevier* (Amsterdam), November 11, 2008, http://www.elsevier.nl/web/Opinie/ Afshin-Ellian/211314/Rabbae-en-Van-Thijn,-blijf-weg-bij-Kristallnacht. htm; "Beroepsballing Mohammed Rabae; Ik ben een middelaar, maar niet als het om principes gaat," *NRC Handelsblad* (Rotterdam), January 11, 1994, http://www.nrd.n./redactie/W2/Lab/IRTvervolg/rabbae.html.

34. Ronald Reagan, "Address to Members of the British Parliament," Westmin-ster, London, June 8, 1982, available on the Ronald Reagan Presidential Library website, http://www.reagan.utexas.edu/archives/speeches/ 1982/60882a.htm.

35. "Lord Ahmed's Unwelcome Guest," *Times* (London), April 7, 2005.

36. "£80,000 Reward to 'Execute' Rushdie as Knighthood Row Escalates," *London Evening Standard* (London), June 19, 2007, http://www.thisis london.co.uk/news/article-23401048-80000-reward-to-execute-rushdie-as-knighthood-row-escalates.do.

37. Nazir Ahmed, "Wilders' Ban Is in Britain's Best Interests: His Film Encour-ages Violence from Both Extremist Muslims and Far-right Groups: Despite Abuse and Threats, I Stand by My Actions," *Guardian* (London), Febru-ary 13, 2009, http://www.guardian.co.uk/commentisfree/2009/feb/13/ geert-wilders-extremists-liberty-central.

38. William McKinley, comment to his personal secretary, George B. Corte-
     lyou, in Cortelyou's Diary, December 29, 1899, quoted in Jack C. Fisher,
     Stolen Glory: The McKinley Assassination (Alamar Books, 2001),
     p. 107.

39. Maxime Verhagen, quoted in "Far-right Dutch MP Geert Wilders vows
     to defy UK," *Times* (London), February 11, 2009.

40. "Far-right Dutch MP Refused Entry to UK: Immigration Officials Prevent
     Geert Wilders Leaving Heathrow Airport to Attend Showing of His Film
     about 'Fascist' Qu'ran at House of Lords," *Guardian* (London), February
     12, 2009, http://www.guardian.co.uk/world/2009/feb/12/far-right-dutch-
     mp-ban-islam.

41. David Miliband on BBC television, BBC News (London), February 12,
     2009, available on YouTube, "David Miliband on Geert Wilders FITNA,"
     http://www.youtube.com/watch?v=1ZRn2Fb-qV8&feature=player_
     embedded.

42. "Dutch MP Banned from Entering UK: A Dutch MP Who Called the
     Koran a 'Fascist Book' Says He Still Plans to Travel to the UK Despite
     Being Banned on Public Security Grounds," BBC News (London), Febru-
     ary 12, 2009, http://news.bbc.co.uk/2/hi/uk_news/politics/7882953.stm.

43. "Dutch MP Hails UK Visit 'Victory': Controversial Dutch MP Geert
     Wilders Has Hailed His Arrival in the UK as a 'Victory for Freedom of
     Speech,'" BBC News (London), October 16, 2009, http://news.bbc.co.
     uk/2/hi/8308982.stm.

44. Press release by Gerard Batten MEP, "Showing of the Film Fitna Banned
     by Order of the Conference of Presidents," European Parliament, Stras-
     bourg, France, December 17, 2008, available here: "As Expected: Euro-
     pean Parliament Bans Wilders' Movie," *Brussels Journal* (Brussels), http://
     www.brusselsjournal.com/node/3694.

45. "Florida Group Sues Hotel for Cancelling Wilders Event," Investigative
     Project on Terorrism, June 22, 2009, http://www.investigativeproject.
     org/1302/florida-group-sues-hotel-for-cancelling-wilders-event; Ken White-
     hoiuse, "Loews Vanderbilt Kicks out Controversial Brentwood Group,"
     Nashville Post, May 29, 2009, http://nashvillepost.com/news/2009/5/29/
     loews_vanderbilt_kicks_out_controversial_brentwood_group.

46. Article 12 of the Dutch Code of Criminal Procedure.

47. "LJN: BH0496, Gerechtshof Amsterdam," Amsterdam, the Netherlands,
     January 21, 2009, available on the de Rechtspraak website, http://zoeken.
     rechtspraak.nl/detailpage.aspx?ljn=BH0496.

48. Gerard Spong, quoted in "Dutch MP to Be Tried for Views on Islam," *Independent* (London), January 22, 2009, http://www.independent.co.uk/news/world/europe/dutch-mp-to-be-tried-for-views-on-islam-1488654.html.

49. Gerard Spong, quoted in "Anti-Islam MP Geert Wilders Faces Trial over Controversial Film," *Times* (London), January 22, 2009.

50. "LJN: BL1868, Rechtbank Amsterdam," Amsterdam, the Netherlands, February 3, 2010, available on the de Rechtspraak website, http://zoeken.rechtspraak.nl/detailpage.aspx?ljn=BL1868.

51. Ibid.

52. Kustaw Bessems and Merel van Leeuwen, "Raadsheer en getuige bij penibel diner," *De Pers* (Amsterdam), October 21, 2010, http://www.depers.nl/binnenland/518616/Raadsheer-bij-penibel-diner.html.

53. Hans Jansen, "Schalken, raadsheer," Hoeiboei blog (Amsterdam), October 20, 2010, http://hoeiboei.blogspot.com/2010/10/schalken-raadsheer.html.

54. "LJN: BO1532, Rechtbank Amsterdam," Amsterdam, the Netherlands, October 22, 2010, available on the de Rechtspraak website, http://zoeken.rechtspraak.nl/detailpage.aspx?ljn=BO1532.

55. "The Lost Cause against Wilders: The Case against the Dutch Politician Has Backfired in Every Way Imaginable," *Wall Street Journal*, October 26, 2010, http://online.wsj.com/article/SB10001424052702304915104575571683398618948.html.

56. Geert Wilders, "In Defense of 'Hurtful' Speech: A Dutch Court Vindicates a Politician's Right to Air Controversial Views on Islam," *Wall Street Journal*, June 24, 2011, http://online.wsj.com/article/SB10001424052702304569504576403392105899036.html.

57. "Uitspraak van de rechtbank Amsterdam in de zaak Wilders," Amsterdam, the Netherlands, June 23, 2011, available on the de Rechtspraak website, http://www.rechtspraak.nl/Organisatie/Rechtbanken/Amsterdam/Nieuws/Pages/Uitspraak-van-de-rechtbank-AmsterdamindezaakWilders,23juni2011.aspx.

CHAPTER 13

1. Franklin Delano Roosevelt, "The Arsenal of Democracy," Washington, D.C., December 29, 1940, in Brian MacArthur, ed., *The Penguin Book of Twentieth-Century Speeches* (Penguin Books, 1999), p. 197.

2. "Verslag houdende een lijst van vragen en antwoorden begrotingsstaten van het ministerie van BZK voor het jaar 2012 (33000 VII) 2011D53392,"

Tweede Kamer van de Staten-Generaal, The Hague, the Netherlands, November 3, 2011, p. 48.

3. "Parliamentary Support Agreement VVD-PVV-CDA," The Hague, the Netherlands, September 30, 2010, http://www.kabinetsformatie2010.nl/pdf/dsc2b44.pdf?c=getobject&s=obj&objectid=127512.

4. Han Nicolaas, "Steeds meer niet-westerse arbeidsimigranten en studenten naar Nederland," *Bevolkingstrends 3e kwartaal 2010*, Centraal Bureau voor de Statistiek, The Hague/Heerlen, the Netherlands, 2010, p. 14, table 1, http://www.cbs.nl/NR/rdonlyres/09C891FD-9158-4E78-8B20-E95A2ED77920/0/2010k3b15p13art.pdf.

5. "Parliamentary Support Agreement VVD-PVV-CDA."

6. Ibid.

7. Piet Hein Donner, "Integratienota, Integratie, binding, burgerschap," Rijksoverheid (The Hague), June 16, 2011, http://www.rijksoverheid.nl/documenten-en-publicaties/notas/2011/06/16/integratienota.html.

8. Ekmeleddin Ihsanoglu, "Press Release Regarding Islamophobia," 38th session of the OIC Council of Foreign Ministers, Astana, Kazakhstan, June 30, 2011, http://www.oic-oci.org/topic_detail.asp?t_id=5464.

9. Ibid.

10. Uri Rosenthal, "'Regering gaat Wilders niet de mond snoeren,'" press release by the Dutch Ministry of Foreign Affairs, Rijksoverheid (The Hague), July 6, 2011, http://www.rijksoverheid.nl/nieuws/2011/07/06/regering-gaat-wilders-niet-de-mond-snoeren.html.

11. Uri Rosenthal and Ben Knapen, "Brief van de Minister en Staatssecretaris van Buitenlandse Zaken," *Tweede Kamer* der Staten-Generaal, The Hague, August 23, 2011, http://www.ngo-monitor.org/article/dutch_government_response_to_ngo_monitor_report.

12. "Nederland niet naar VN-racismeconferentie," *NRC Handelsblad* (Rotterdam), July 22, 2011, http://www.nrc.nl/nieuws/2011/07/22/nederland-niet-naar-vn-racismeconferentie/.

13. Wajeha al-Huwaider, quoted in Betsy Hiel, "Dahran Women Push the Veil Aside," *Pittsburgh Tribune-Review*, May 13, 2007, http://www.pittsburghlive.com/x/pittsburghtrib/news/middleeastreports/s_507462.html.

14. Wajeha al-Huwaider, quoted in A. Dankowitz, "Saudi Writer and Journalist Wajeha Al-Huwaider Fights for Women's Rights," Middle East Media Research Institute (MEMRI), December 28, 2006, http://www.memri.org/report/en/0/0/0/0/0/0/1805.htm.

15. Ibid.

16. Ibid.

17. Hiel, "Dahran women push the veil aside."

18. "The Saudi Woman Who Took to the Driver's Seat," France 24, May 23, 2011, http://observers.france24.com/content/20110523-saudi-woman-arrested-defying-driving-ban-manal-al-sharif-khobar.

19. "Saudi Women Make Video Protest: Saudi Women's Rights Activists Have Posted on the Web a Video of a Woman at the Wheel of Her Car, in Protest at the Ban on Female Drivers in the Kingdom," BBC News (London), March 11, 2008, http://news.bbc.co.uk/2/hi/middle_east/7159077.stm.

20. Neil MacFarquhar, "Saudi Arrest Woman Leading Right-to-Drive Campaign," *New York Times*, May 23, 2011, http://www.nytimes.com/2011/05/24/world/middleeast/24saudi.html?_r=1, and "Detained Saudi Woman Driver to Be Freed on Bail," AFP (Paris), May 30, 2011, available on the France 24 website, http://www.france24.com/en/20110530-detained-saudi-woman-driver-be-freed-bail.

21. "Detained Saudi woman driver to be freed on bail."

22. "Saudi Arabia Women Test Driving Ban: It Was not a Mass Movement but about 30 or 40 Women across the Country Took the Wheel," *Guardian* (London), June 17, 2011, http://www.guardian.co.uk/world/2011/jun/17/saudi-arabia-women-drivers-protest; "Manal...from Driving Activist to Prison Activist," Emirates 24/7 (Dubai), June 4, 2011, http://www.emirates247.com/news/region/manal-from-driving-activist-to-prison-activist-2011-06-04-1.400974.

23. "Saudi Woman Driver's Lashing 'Overturned by King: Saudi Arabia's King Abdullah Has Overturned a Court Ruling Sentencing a Woman to 10 Lashes for Breaking a Ban on Female Drivers, Reports Say,'" BBC News (London), September 29, 2011, http://www.bbc.co.uk/news/world-middle-east-15102190.

24. Andrew Jackson, as quoted in Ronald Reagan, "Radio Address to the Nation on the Supreme Court Nomination of Robert H. Bork," October 10, 1987, available on the American Presidency Project website, http://www.presidency.ucsb.edu/ws/index.php?pid=33539.

25. Wajeha al-Huwaider, quoted in Dankowitz, "Saudi Writer and Journalist Wajeha Al-Huwaider Fights for Women's Rights."

26. Geert Wilders, "Muslims Debate Asked Mr. Geert Wilders Why He Became Anti-Islam and What Is His Message to the Muslims?" Muslims Debate (London), July 19, 2010, http://www.muslimsdebate.com/search_result.php?news_id=4399.

27. George Orwell, "The Freedom of the Press," the original preface of his novel *Animal Farm*, but it was never used and remained unpublished until 1971. Quoted in John Rodden, ed., *Understanding Animal Farm: A Student Casebook to Issues, Sources, and Historical Documents* (The Greenwood Press, 1999), p. 164.

28. William Ewart Gladstone, *Bulgarian Horrors and the Question of the East* (J. Murray, Sept. 1876), available on Open Library, http://openlibrary. org/b/OL7083313M/Bulgarian_horrors_and_the_question_of_the_east.

29. Geert Wilders in the Dutch Parliament, November 7, 2007, "Handelingen, Tweede Kamer der Staten Generaal," The Hague, the Netherlands, 2007–2008, p. 1392.

30. Theodor Herzl, quoted in Ehud Olmert, "PM Olmert's Speech at the 2006 United Jewish Communities General Assembly," Prime Minister's Office (Jerusalem), Israel, November 14, 2006, http://www.pmo.gov.il/PMOEng/ Archive/Speeches/2006/11/speechujc141106.htm.

31. Winston Churchill, "Never Give In," speech given at Harrow School, Harrow, UK, October 29, 1941, available on the Churchill Centre and Museum at the Churchill War Rooms, London, website, http://www. winstonchurchill.org/learn/speeches/speeches-of-winston-churchill/103-never-give-in.

32. Abraham Lincoln, "Second Annual Message" to Congress, Washington, D.C., December 1, 1862, available on the Miller Center of the University of Virginia website, http://millercenter.org/scripps/archive/speeches/ detail/3737.

Index